ENGLISH PSYCHOLOGY.

ENGLISH PSYCHOLOGY

TRANSLATED FROM THE FRENCH OF

TH. RIBOT

HARTLEY—JAMES MILL—HERBERT SPENCER
A. BAIN—G. H. LEWES—SAMUEL BAILEY
JOHN STUART MILL

NEW YORK:
D. APPLETON AND COMPANY,
549 & 551 BROADWAY.
1874.

CONTENTS.

INTRODUCTION.

CHAP. II.—PSYCHOLOGY.

ENGLISH PSYCHOLOGY.

INTRODUCTION.

1. Past and future Philosophy—2. Two meanings of the word Philosophy—3. Why the Sciences become independent—4. That Philosophy will become Metaphysics; Poetry and Metaphysics—5. Psychology as an independent science—6. Object and method of ordinary Psychology—7. Object and method of experimental Psychology—8. Divisions of Psychology; general, comparative, teratological Psychology,—science of characteristics—9. Object of the work.

I.

To the question, What was philosophy in the beginning? a reply is easy. It was universal science. It would be more difficult to answer an inquiry as to what it is to be in the future; and yet the study of the past, and certain inductions founded upon history, may perhaps enable us to foretell its destiny. At its origin philosophy has for its object the universality of things, the All, and philosophy, like its object, is One; outside it there is no idea of distinct and independent sciences. It resembles those rudimentary organisms in which the physiological distribution of labour has not yet taken place. The slow and continuous labour of life, a natural tendency towards progress, will bring the sciences out of philosophy, as the organs are brought out of the embryo. Let us follow the march of this development in the past; it may cast a light upon the future, and afford us a glimpse of it.

The first branch which became detached from the common tree, and entered upon a separate life, is the science of numbers and of sizes—Mathematics. The Pythagorean school confounded mathematics with philosophy, but two centuries later they became clearly separate. Plato did not admit that a man might be a philosopher without having been a geometrician, but thenceforth geometry did without philosophy. The nature of mathematics explains this. Among all the sciences, not one has less need to disquiet itself concerning facts and experience. If, at their origin, mathematics were empirical, as they probably were, they speedily elevated themselves to the abstract notions which form their bases, and found their true method. In the third century B.C. there existed in Greece an order of precise, rigorous sciences, recognised as such, and perfectly distinct from philosophical researches. We are about to trace the continuation of the first example of this emancipation of the particular sciences.

Many ages had to elapse before a new science was to achieve its autonomy. The ancient philosophy, which reached its greatest height in Plato and Aristotle, still remains the universal science, or nearly so; in it metaphysics follow physics, politics follow morals, studies in physiology were weighed with studies in psychology (*Timæus*, *De Animâ*); it is still the science of all that is; it studies man, nature, and God. Thus it remains in the Middle Ages; outside of philosophy, there is nothing but mathematics and that which relates to them, and the *Arts*, such as medicine and alchemy. But now we find a new science growing up, aided by calculation and experience, which accumulates facts and seeks out laws, which observes instead of reasoning, and which speedily finds itself strong enough to assert its independence. This science is called physics. It was a slow and progressive emanation, whose facts are nearer to us, and better known, so that we can follow them. Galileo, though breaking away from Aristotle, is still a 'philosopher.' He boasted of having devoted 'more years to philosophy than months to mathematics,' and his doctrine is declared 'absurd in philosophy' in the judgment of the Inquisition. Descartes held that philosophy is 'a tree whose root is metaphysics, and whose trunk is physics.' His system of physics, like that of Newton, is explained under the title *Principia Philosophiæ.* Philosophical instruction, which from its nature can only follow workers and inventors from afar, comprised physics until the end of the eighteenth century. The disruption was not rude; it took place because it was inevitable. When the domain of a science is actively utilized, when every corner of it is explored and turned over, when its object and its means are thoroughly understood, then that science has won her right to independence by success.

But thenceforth philosophy could no longer claim as its object everything which exists: man, nature, and God. Physics and the kindred sciences wrest from it nature; shall man and God be left to it?

The science of language is a purely human science, cultivated by philosophers at first rather by chance, but whose importance never escaped their notice. Plato gives a sketch of it in his *Cratylus*. The Epicureans and the Stoics, two schools which had then fallen into decadence, had written largely on this subject. Among moderns, we need only recall the names of Leibnitz, Locke, Condillac, and their disciples. Less than a century ago, the science of language was at that point, when the discovery of Sanscrit enabled it to find its true method and line, and to establish itself as an independent science. Since then, it has collected facts, defined laws, classified languages, determined roots; it is constantly advancing in its almost chemical analysis of words; it has its own vocabulary, its distinct parts, its phonetics, its morphology, etc. It is singularly jealous of its independence. It will have nothing in common with metaphysics, but repels such relation as a crime. Here then is a purely human science detached from the common trunk.

In later times the science of morals has likewise claimed its independence. The task of some of our contemporaries has been to constitute the theory of the rights and duties of man, without asking the aid either of religion or philosophy; to invest morals with the rank of a primary science, arising from itself alone; to release it from the preliminary necessity of a metaphysical doctrine whose mere consequence it should be. This undertaking has found many partisans and many enemies. Without entering into the question of the value of this attempt, let us state the fact that the science of morals fearlessly asserts its independence, and claims a separate domain of its own.

This would be the place in which to show that psychology has the same tendencies; to show that its most recent transformations have set it free from the yoke of metaphysics, and that it also demands its autonomy. But the subject is to be treated at length in a later portion of this work.

Is it necessary to call attention to the fact that physiology is independent of philosophy? The truth is, that their relations never were close.[1] Physiology is, above all, born of experience. It has been science springing from an art, rather than a particular science arising from general science. Medicine, which has existed always and everywhere, has not been able to dispense with the study of the living body. Thus, physiology was, in the first place, a means, before it became a science with a self-contained object. In this it resembles chemistry, born of certain practical inventions and of the mysterious researches of the Middle Ages into the transmutation of metals, which were not altogether discovered from philosophers, as the name 'hermetic philosophy,' so frequently employed to designate those researches, proves. Besides, the popular imagination readily confounds the philosopher with the alchemist, placing him in one of the dark vaults which Rembrandt has painted, surrounded by books, furnaces, and crucibles.

In short, all the special sciences which now exist have been derived from a double source,—from philosophy and from art. These latter, whose origin is the more humble, are not the least sound or fruitful. In comparing the facts accumulated by experience, they have been able to eliminate accidents, to separate that which is fixed and permanent, and to define its laws; that is to say, to arrive at precise knowledge, and 'at that essential character of science which is to foresee.' As for the independence of those sciences which have already come out, or are tending towards coming out from philosophy, we have seen it produced naturally, by unceasing and unwitting work, and the severance results from the very nature of things. An exact and positive science cannot limit itself to vague affirmations, it must prove and verify its assertions, it must weigh the most minute details; a chemist will not hesitate to devote several years to the study of

[1] Nevertheless, Aristotle did much for anatomy and biology; and among the predecessors of Hippocrates his learned translator names the φυσιολόγοι.

a single body and of its compounds; a zoologist would do the same for some humble infusoria visible only under the microscope. It is necessary to specialize one's-self, as the present phrase is, to insure the progress of science. But a result of this endless analysis is that each particular science becomes a world. In fact, greatness is a relative thing. If chemistry be only a small item in the total of human knowledge, it is immense when compared to a simple study of azote and its compounds. How can we be surprised that it amply suffices to the labourers in it, and that they seek for nothing beyond its horizon? It is the same everywhere. Beyond this, even; that interior process which resolves philosophy into particular sciences resolves them again into sub-sciences, physics into thermology, optics, acoustics; biology into physiology, etc. etc. In this labour of decomposition, which has no assignable limits, each step in analysis leads further away from the primitive unity.

II.

Let us now inquire what remains to philosophy after those successive subtractions? What are its pretensions, it limits, its object? If we examine the different senses in which the word philosophy is used in correct language, discussions, or books, we shall be struck by the various acceptations to which it lends itself, and by the confusion which it may produce. A man who describes, analyses, and classifies the phenomena of thought like Mr. Herbert Spencer or Mr. A. Bain is called a philosopher. A man who regulates morals, lays down prescriptions, proposes an ideal of conduct, is equally a philosopher. Do you place logic among the recent discoveries of science, as Mr. Stuart Mill has done, or discourse upon the attributes of God, or search into first causes?—the same title is bestowed upon you. A high philosophical bearing is justly acknowledged as belonging to a theory like that of the unity of physical forces, which establishes their correlations and transformations. Here are different significations, and we may add to them many others. Whence this confusion? It seems to us to originate thus: Two very different things may be meant by philosophy; that which is, and that which tends to be; the first consisting of a rather incoherent assemblage of four or five sciences; the second offering a precise rational signification, having a determinate object, and limits assigned by experience.

In the ordinary sense of the word this is philosophy. It is a study which comes from the human mind and from its various manifestations, which, by the faculty of reasoning, is led up to logic, and, by the faculty of willing and acting conformably to a law, is led up to morals, and from thence mounts up to the first cause of all things, to God; it is completed by some metaphysical researches into the essence of the soul, the nature of certitude, and the fundamental principles of morals. Can this be rightly designated a science having an object? If you ask what is the object of physics, astronomy, chemistry, anthropology, the reply is easy and ready. But has philosophy an object, or objects, or portions of objects? It has one, in the first place, with which no other science occupies itself. That object is God. Must we add to this, Man? Assuredly not man as a whole, for anatomy, physiology, in short the biological sciences, have taken a share in him for themselves. A portion of man then,—his soul? This is also to be contested. History, in its extended sense, the science of language, jurisprudence, even political economy, claim their share of that. It comes to this, then, that the object of philosophy is God, *plus* a certain portion of man,—an object, *plus* a portion of an object. How can it henceforth claim the title of a primary and universal science? How, above all, can it arrive at unity? That would be possible only according to the idealist solution, which holds that God, nature, history, everything, has no reality except in human thought.

This is what philosophy actually is. But what does it tend to become? If we admit, as facts constrain us to admit, that the special sciences detach themselves from it, as time goes on, at uncertain intervals,—if it be granted that this rupture is naturally produced by the accumulation of facts, the incessant progress of analysis, and the necessity of specialization,—if we remark that psychology is already almost independent, that morals desires to become so, and that logic is only a portion of psychology, we foresee the possibility of new sciences, more or less distant, and a further impoverishment of philosophy, at least in appearance.

Its actual incoherence appears to us to be caused by its containing, besides general science, special sciences, which are regarded as an integral part of itself. It resembles those beings which are reproduced by division, or cutting into pieces, and which, at certain moments, present the strange spectacle of three or four individuals still adhering to the common stem.

III.

In order that we may understand what philosophy tends to become by the progress of human knowledge, let us see what is produced in the special sciences when they detach themselves. Let us suppose mathematics cultivated by the philosophers, not as a special science, but as forming a portion of philosophy; this is what would happen. The method of all philosophic minds is to give the precedence to questions of principles over everything else; they will therefore begin by examining axioms, discussing the legitimacy of method, investigating quantity, measuring time and space, at the risk of never believing themselves sufficiently certain to begin. They may even lose themselves in strange systems of numbers, like the Pythagoreans and Plato. Mathematicians go to work differently. They do not trouble themselves to reconcile Newton with Leibnitz, or Locke with Kant, on the nature of time and space; they accept axioms without discussing them, on the guarantee of common sense only, but they go on. The constitution and development of this science depended upon the condition that they should lay aside at the outset a number of unresolved questions, abandoning them to discussion by the philosophers.

It is the same with physics. Before Galileo, physics were merely metaphysics with some roughly explained facts over and above. In Aristotle's works the one is hardly to be distinguished from the other,—they succeed and supplement, and naturally suppose each other. What is matter? What is nature? Does it comprehend *matter* and *form?* What is motion? Is it infinitely divisible? What is power, and what is action? Does the external world exist? What is the worth of our senses? May we trust them? All these questions are put aside by the physicist. He accepts the faith of common sense in the material world, and the senses which reveal it to us; he deals not with the essence, but with the facts and their laws; he controls the testimony of the senses without discussing it. He relegates to philosophy all researches into the ultimate reasons of things; let philosophy solve them, if it can. Even chemistry, which in analysis descends to quite the last elements, does not go beyond the study of secondary causes.

In the science of language, the question dear to philosophy is that of origin. Put forward in the time of Democritus, it has been again debated in our days by the theological school of De Maistre and De Bonald. But when linguistics was definitively constituted a special science, this question of origin was laid aside, and though it appears obscure rather than insoluble, it is banished from the positive study of languages. The linguist accepts the existence of various idioms and dialects as a fact; he classifies them, traces them, and explains their radiations, but the question of origin he regards as hazardous or at least premature.

The study of economical facts is gaining in importance every day; in France especially, notwithstanding the strong prejudices against it. The dissent of the economists does not hinder the science from establishing itself, little by little, and destroying the pretended axioms of common sense by solid reasons. But political economy holds by facts, and though it presupposes philosophical principles, it does not discuss them. Locke, in his Essay on Civil Government, did not separate this science from the other methods of being of social life. Boisguillebert gave it a more distinct position; at length Quesnay and Smith constituted for it an independent domain, and since that time its independence, with respect to metaphysics, has increased daily.

It would be easy to multiply proofs by mentioning other sciences; for instance, to show that biology deals only with manifestations of life, but resolutely sets aside all theories on its *nature* and *origin*;—it places them outside scientific knowledge—that biology regards vitalism, animism, organism, etc., merely as ingenious, unverified systems.

It appears still more unfortunate for philosophy, that from the moment at which any science shakes itself free from metaphysical researches, it immediately begins to make progress. This is exemplified by mathematics, with Archimedes and Euclid; astronomy, with Kepler and Copernicus; physics, with Galileo, Huyghens, and Newton; chemistry, with Lavoisier; biology, with Bichat and contemporaries; the science of language with Bopp and Max Müller. And yet this is not in reality surprising; there are very plain reasons for it: in the first place, because the genius which was expended in solving the insoluble and finding the undiscoverable is now devoted only to purely scientific researches; and in the second, because the aim of science is changed; theories are now subordinated to facts, and not facts to theories; systems pass away, but experiences remain.

Thus then, everywhere and always, particular sciences which have a special object are only constituted by leaving a balance of unsolved questions aside at their outset. Exactly speaking, they have no commencement; they come out by chance, as they can; no one knows from whence they come, nor whither they go; but on the other hand, every one knows what they are. To those who judge them as philosophers, their point of departure is ruinous, ill established, not discussed; but if philosophy condemns, experience absolves them. And even logic does the same, by proving that thus they ought to proceed. Now we can understand under what conditions the particular sciences still adherent to philosophy will be able to render themselves independent of it. They must start from some postulate, from certain rational or experimental truths; they must not stop at questions of principles, and they must leave discussions to philosophy. Morals, for instance, will not seek beyond that which is good in itself. Psychology will not ask what the soul is; it will interdict all excursions into the region of primary causes. This is the absolute condition of their existence as exact sciences capable of progress. Those who have reproached these attempts at emancipation with an absence of foundation, who have said to morals and to psychology: 'It is anti-philosophical to endeavour to do without preliminary metaphysics; your commencement is arbitrary; your data are affirmed, not discussed; you are not fixed upon principles'—how have they failed to see that this was a logical necessity, and that debates on principles prevent arrival at consequences? How have they failed to see that their reproaches might as well be directed to geometry, to physics, to chemistry, in short, to all the actually constituted sciences? Will they oppose the gratuitous difficulty that that which is possible for the study of nature is not possible for that of man; that we may do without first principles in investigating matter and its properties, but that we cannot dispense with them when we are concerned with mind and its manifestations? Not only would this assertion be devoid of facts, but it would be in contradiction to the facts. For, among the number of the sciences which are called *moral*,—that is to say, whose objects are the manifestations of human thought and will, do we not place the science of languages, law, political economy, which interdict as much as possible, and every day more strongly, all metaphysical discussions?

IV.

We can now perceive what philosophy tends to become, and what a transformation the continuous coalition of the sciences must inevitably oblige it to undergo. Universal in its origin, philosophy will in the future be still universal, but in another manner. Formerly, it contained everything—principles and consequences, causes and facts, general truths and results. It now presents the strange spectacle of a science, universal on certain sides, particular on others. At a later date, it will contain only the general speculations of the human mind upon the first principles and the last reasons of all things. *It will be metaphysics and nothing more.* That which will thus occupy the philosophers, and constitute their own domain, will be that unknown upon which every science establishes itself, and which it then abandons to their disputes. In that there will still be an eternal source of discussion and research; and, as they will extend over the whole field of human knowledge, of all sciences which exist, or which shall come into being, philosophy will remain universal. Nor is this all. The progress of particular sciences leads them necessarily to wider and wider generalizations, supported upon facts indeed, but which frequently outrun them—such are the hypotheses which explain so many phenomena, summarize so many laws, have resisted so many verifications, that they are almost demonstrated truths. In these will be other materials for future philosophy. The law of universal attraction, and that of the correlation of forces, enable us to foresee what the sciences may discover by the accumulation of facts, by calculation, and exact methods. Let us suppose some analogous discovery in chemistry. Let us admit that some of its mysteries are stolen from life, and that biology finds its Newton. Let us hope for some generalization in the phenomena of thought, which shall associate them with those of life; that history will, in part at least, yield up its secret to us. Let us add all the great views which we cannot forestal, all that the sciences yet unborn shall reveal to us; can we then believe that method will be wanting to philosophical minds, that is to say, to minds engaged upon the general whole? Let it not be said either that there is a contradiction in maintaining that the progress of the sciences brings them back to philosophy, after its having been stated that it detaches them from it. All science is contradicted by the double action of analysis and synthesis. It arrives at precise, active, verified knowledge, only by constantly descending towards the infinitely little; it distinguishes, separates, divides, seeks out exceptions and differences. But a heap of well-established facts is not a science; the relations remain to be appreciated, the resemblances to be grouped, the laws to be reached by induction, the whole to be sought out. There must, therefore, be two orders of problems in philosophy, identical at bottom: those from which sciences spring, and those which are their result. Philosophy will be always sounding this double ignorance. The entire collection of human knowledge resembles a great river flowing full between its banks, under a sky glowing with light, but whose source and mouth are unknown, which springs and dies in the clouds. Bold spirits have never been able either to solve this mystery or to forget it. There are always some sufficiently intrepid to throw themselves resolutely into this inaccessible region, whence they return blinded, giddy, and relating such strange things that the world holds them to be hallucinations.

Is philosophy, thus understood, to remain a science? How can it so remain, if everything which is scientifically to be known is taken away from it, if, wherever there are facts to be observed, laws to be sought into, rotations to be calculated, some particular science constitutes a domain of its own, and leaves to philosophy such questions only as it cannot solve? How can there be a science where there is no measure or verification possible? Metaphysics is a collection of truths outside and above all demonstration, because they are the foundation of all demonstration; it is negatively determined by the collective action of all the sciences, which eliminates everything that outruns them. Besides this, metaphysics is subjective, and science ought to be objective. That which is demonstrated, established, formulated in laws, is invariably acquired independently of time and place. Mathematical truths are the same for the Hindu and the Greek, the Italian and the Englishman. Science does not reflect the genius of a race, it is the work of an impersonal spirit. There is no such thing as French physics as opposed to English physics; that which was true for Galileo is true for Ampère and Faraday. This must be so, since the affirmations of science are capable of verification, since science fashions the human mind after nature, instead of fashioning nature according to the arbitrary conceptions of the human mind. In metaphysics the contrary is the case; the work is personal, it is impressed with the character of an individual, or at least of a race. It is local and ephemeral, for the individual communicates his fragility to his work.

It has been ingeniously said 'that metaphysicians are poets who have missed their vocation.'[1] The more one thinks of it, the more just the saying appears. When philosophy shall have become that which it ought to be, when nothing will remain to it but the general, the abstract, the ideal, then it will be seen clearly by every one to be the work of art rather than of science; to be, to some, tiresome ill-written poetry, while to others it is elevated, powerful, truly divine.

Why should we not already face this truth, which is only paradoxical to those who stop at appearances? If you are not one of those dull minds which cannot conceive anything above the

[1] M. Vacherot, *La Métaphysique et la Science*, vol. i. p. 5. He disputes this opinion.

most vulgar reality, if you are searching for something under facts and above them, you enter into an ideal world. The poet conceives it to be in the image of ours, but more beautiful, more harmonious; life in it is wider and has more flavour; he contemplates living forms, visible, palpable, concrete, more real to him than reality itself. To the metaphysician it is quite different. It is a region of abstract truths, of laws and formulas, accessible only to pure spirit, the mysterious domain of the impossible and the invisible, where the principles of all things reign, like the mothers of the second *Faust*, 'who are enthroned in the infinite, eternally solitary, their heads encircled with the images of life active, but without life.' Both are creators in their several ways; one because he understands the handling of colours, words, the picturesque forms which give life and drapery to ideas; the other because he believes that he has seized the hidden springs which make the world move, the fruitful formulas which translate the laws of the universe, and whence the flow of phenomena issue as from an inexhaustible spring. Hence those philosophical constructions which resemble great poems. Hence it is that, in general, metaphysics and the high order of poetry meet and mingle, as in the *Paradise* of Dante. Each reflects the genius of a people. In India, the *Bhagavad-gita* is the episode of an epopee. The reserved and, at bottom, little subversive Cartesianism, in which, as Ritter says (*Histoire de la Philosophie Moderne*, vol. i.)—'the thought of the limitation of our knowledge evidently dominates,' resembles the sober and measured poetry of the seventeenth century. Hegel's Logic borders on Faust. Who was more of a poet than Plato and Plotinus? We should go through the whole history of metaphysics, in order to show how closely it resembles poetry. They shared between them the ardent minds of the Renaissance, of which Giordano Bruno is the most complete type. When Hegel maintains (*Gesch. d. Phil.*, p. 194, vol. iii.) 'that the mystics only knew how to philosophize,' does he not say that the higher metaphysics reaches the more it resembles an effusion or a reverie? They who, like Aristotle, seem to have nothing of the poet about them, arrive at astonishing conceptions—that of a world which, in its ultimate depths aspires to good, is drawn by love, moved by a 'metaphysical Newtonism.'

A great German poet, Heinrich Heine, has said of the driest of metaphysicians: 'The reading of Spinoza lays hold of us like the aspect of great nature in its living calm; it is a forest of thoughts, as lofty as the sky, whose crowned crests undulate harmoniously, while their indestructible stems plunge their roots into the eternal earth. In his writings one feels a breath which moves one in an indefinable way; it is as though one were breathing the air of the future.' Metaphysicians are poets, whose aim is the reconstruction of the synthesis of the world.

Are these great cosmogonic epopees to disappear? Will the repeated experience of their insufficiency condemn them hopelessly? Is philosophy to continue to give us poetry for science, to drape its fictions in undecipherable formulas, and to announce to the world for the hundredth time that it has found the key to its enigma?

Why not? There are many in these days who think that the human mind ought to renounce those researches, to put them aside like the toys of childhood. This seems neither desirable nor possible. If positivism limited itself to stating that metaphysics could not be seriously regarded as a science, because it affirms but is unable to verify or demonstrate, no contradiction could be offered without shutting our eyes to evidence. When positivism applies itself to the elimination of all metaphysics from experimental sciences, it also does a service, since it follows the rules of a good method, separating the knowable from the unknowable; preventing us from sacrificing everything to hypothesis; from bending facts to theories; from *letting go the substance for the shadow.* But to condemn all researches into ultimate reasons as a vain and dangerous illusion,—to consider all time lost which was consecrated to them,—to desire to cure the human mind of them, as if of a chronic infirmity, is in reality to lessen the human mind. The importance of studies is not measured by their success. To seek without hope is neither senseless nor vulgar,—one may discern without finding. The true nobility of human intelligence consists less in the results which it obtains, than in the end which it proposes to itself, and in the efforts by which it essays to attain that aim. Experience is much, but it is not all. And, besides, who shall prove to us that facts are of more value than ideas, discoveries than researches? Philosophy must ever remain an eternal attempt upon the unknown. It will never find the last word of all things; and that is well, because it may be said, without any paradox, that if metaphysics were to give all it promises, it would be better to force it to keep silence. Let us suppose all our questions concerning God, nature, and ourselves, finally answered, —what would remain for human intelligence to do? This solution would be its death. All inquiring and active minds will be of Lessing's opinion on this point:—'There is more pleasure in coursing the hare than in catching it.' Philosophy will keep up its activity by its magical and deceiving mirage. Were it never to render any other service to human intelligence than that of keeping it always on the alert, of elevating it above a narrow dogmatism, by showing it that mysterious *beyond*, which surrounds and presses upon it in every science, philosophy would do enough for it.

V.

Now let us approach the proper object of this study—psychology; the preceding remarks are merely prefatory. Our purpose is to show that psychology may be constituted an independent science, to investigate the conditions of such constitution, and to see whether that independence is not an accomplished fact among several contemporaries. At first sight, I know, this proposition may appear unacceptable. Is not psychology the basis of philosophy, and the object of its most constant if not most ancient study? How can they be separated? There is an equivoque in this which must be removed. Psychology, like every science, like physics, chemistry, or physiology, contains ultimate, transcendental questions,—questions of principles, of causes, of substances. What is the soul? whence does it come? whither is it going? These are purely philosophical discussions. But there is more than that in psychology. There are facts of a special nature, difficult to observe, still more difficult to classify, but which do not the less constitute the most solid and the most indisputable portion of the science.

It is the pure and simple study of these facts which can constitute an independent science. I observe that, since Wolf, a distinction is commonly made between an experimental psychology which occupies itself with phenomena only, and a rational psychology which occupies itself with substance only. But as, according to Wolf and those who follow him, these two studies are the complementary parts of one same whole, to our mind this experimental psychology alone constitutes all psychology; the remainder belongs to philosophy, or metaphysics, and is, consequently, outside of the science.

Having laid this down, we propose, in the following pages, to examine the current conception of psychology, particularly in France, and to see to what results it leads. We shall then investigate purely experimental psychology, in what it consists and how it proceeds; and finally, we shall endeavour to sketch its divisions.

VI.

Let us turn to the most accredited treatises on psychology for a definition of that science. 'Psychology,' says Jouffroy,[1] 'is the science of the intelligent principle, of the man, of the *me*.' 'Psychology is that part of philosophy whose object is the knowledge of the soul and of its faculties, studied by the single means of consciousness.'—(*Dict. des Sciences Phil.*, Art. *Psychol.*)

The first criticism to be made upon these definitions is, that they confound two very different things, psychological phenomena and their substratum; or, as Kant would say, phenomena and noumena. Without going into the question whether we actually have a knowledge of things in ourselves, we must at least grant that it is very vague, since there is no common accord on this subject, and that it is not scientific, since it cannot be verified. I am not ignorant that of late years it has been repeated, after Maine de Biran and Jouffroy, that 'the soul knows itself, lays hold on itself, immediately.' But not only have these psychologists passed twenty or thirty years in study before they discovered this *immediate knowledge* (which is sufficiently surprising),—their *discovery* does not seem to advance us much; because, when we

[1] *Mélanges Philosoph.*, p. 191. He even endeavours to establish that psychology is the science of the whole man, physiology occupying itself with the animal only.

have long and scrupulously sought what this intimate essence thus revealed is, we succeed only in finding such vague expressions as 'absolute activity,' 'pure spirit outside of time and space,' whence we may conclude that still the clearest part of our knowledge consists in phenomena. The fault of the current definition, then, is that it confounds two essentially distinct things, psychological facts with ontological speculations. Hence it happens that the study of facts, which is fruitful, is so often abandoned for the construction of theories, which is sterile and slow,—useful observation forsaken for the rash and ruinous process of hypothesis.

Nor is this all. We are told that psychology is the science of the *human* soul. That is a very narrow and incomplete idea of it. Is biology ever defined as the science of *human* life? Has physiology ever believed, even in its infancy, that its only object was man? Have they not considered, on the contrary, that everything which has organized and manifested life belongs to them, —the infusoria, as well as man? Now, unless we admit the Cartesian opinion of animal machines—which has no longer, to my knowledge, an adherent,—we must acknowledge that animals have their sensations, their sentiments, their desires, their pleasures, their pains, their character, just like ourselves; that there is a collection of psychological facts which one has no right to subtract from the science. Who has studied those facts? The naturalists, and not the psychologists. If we were to go further, we might show that ordinary psychology, in restricting itself to man, has not even included the whole of mankind; that it has taken no heed of the inferior races (black and yellow), that it has contented itself with affirming that the human faculties are identical in nature and various only in degree, as if the difference of degree might not sometimes be such as to be equivalent to a difference of nature; that in man it has taken the faculties already constituted, and rarely occupied itself with their mode of development; so that, finally, psychology, instead of being the science of psychical phenomena, has simply made man, adult, civilized, and white, its object.

We have seen how psychology understands its object, let us now see how it understands its method. This consists entirely

2

in reflection, or interior observation. Assuredly, no one believes more firmly than we do in the necessity of this mode of observation; it is the point of departure, the indispensable condition of all psychology, and those who have denied it, like Broussais and Aug. Comte, have so completely gone against evidence, and given the game to their adversaries, that their most faithful disciples have not gone so far with them. It is certain that the anatomist and the physiologist might pass centuries in studying the brain and the nerves, without ever suspecting what a pleasure or a pain is, if they have not felt both.

No testimony is so valuable on this point as that of consciousness, and we are always brought back to that saying of an anatomist,—'In the presence of the fibres of the brain, we are like hackney coachmen, who know the streets and the houses, but know nothing of what takes place inside them.' It is also certain that the objections made to this method of observation have been very well discussed. But is it true that interior observation is the *unique* method of psychology? that it reveals everything, that it suffices for everything? Taken in its rigorous meaning, this doctrine would lead to the impossibility of the science. For, if my reflection apprises me of that which passes in me, it is absolutely incapable of enabling me to penetrate into the mind of another. A more complicated process is necessary for that. We are talking; a man present at our conversation joins in it with an absent manner, says a few words with evident effort, and forces a smile; I *conclude* from all this that he is a prey to some hidden trouble. I may soon divine its causes if I have a penetrating mind, and if I am acquainted with this man and his antecedents. But this psychological discovery is a very complex operation, of which the following are the stages: perception of signs and gestures, interpretation of those signs, induction from effects to causes, inference, reasoning by analogy. It has nothing in common with interior observation except that aptitude for knowing others better which comes from knowing one's-self better. Thus, one of two things is the case: either psychology is limited to interior observations, and these being completely individual, it has no longer any scientific character; or else it is extended to other men, it searches out laws, it practises induction, it reasons, and then it is susceptible of progress; but its method is to a great extent objective. Interior observation alone is not sufficient for the weakest psychology.

Another defect of the ordinary method is, that it has led, as might have been foreseen, to abstraction. It has led philosophers to study the phenomena of mind rather as logicians than as psychologists, rather as reasoners than as observers. One of its chief consequences has been the current doctrine of faculties.

It may be said, in many respects to be useful, to be necessary. Psychology has facts to classify, like physics or botany; it separates those which are different, it unites those which are like, and thus it forms groups; to each group it assigns a name, which, like the terms heat, light, magnetism, designates the *unknown causes* of known phenomena. But the almost inevitable danger of this method is to personify causes, to erect them into distinct and independent entities; we forget that these are only abstracts, convenient formulas for the explanation of the science, which have no value unless they are referred back to the concretes whence they have been taken, that therein consists all their value, all their reality. The history of ancient physics, embarrassed by substantial forms and occult causes, shows us how the clearest minds yield to the temptation to realize abstractions. Hence, in psychology, we have a first result, which consists in the substitution of a verbal study, that of faculties, for a real study, that of phenomena. Discussions on free-will might well be of that nature, the problem being perhaps inextricable only because it is ill stated. Thus the time which might be devoted to observation is lost in idle disputes, and in place of impartial observers, parties are formed, who push their hypotheses to extremes, and who are perpetually contending for chimeras, because phantoms can neither be killed nor imprisoned. A third result is to dissimulate the unity of composition of psychological phenomena. Mental life has its degrees, and, so to speak, its stages; they are only separated by vague limits made out by the doctrine of faculties to be fixed and absolute. Ad. Garnier says very justly that in order to attribute facts to diverse causes, it is necessary that the facts should be not only different, but independent of phenomena, not only very different from, but even opposed to, each other, as the ascent of gases to the fall of bodies; yet capable of having an identical cause. But we look in vain for this character of independence in psychological phenomena; we find them confounded, mixed up together, and reciprocally supposing each other. One of the philosophers of whom we propose to speak in this volume, Mr. Samuel Bailey, has acutely criticised the mixed phraseology which is inherent in the method by which faculties are erected into entities, distinct from man himself:—'The faculties have been represented acting like independent agents, giving birth to ideas, passing them on to each other mutually, and transacting their business among themselves. In this kind of phraseology the mind often appears like a sort of field, in which perception, reason, memory, imagination, will, conscience, the passions, produce their operations, like so many powers, either allied or hostile. Sometimes one of these faculties has the supremacy and the others are subordinate; one usurps the authority and the other yields, one explains and the others listen, one deceives and the other is deceived. Meantime the mind, or the intelligent being himself, is completely lost to view in the midst of these transactions, in which he does not appear to have any part. At other times we are shown these faculties treating with their proprietor or master, lending him their services, acting under his control, or his direction, furnishing him with evidence, instructing him, enlightening him by their revelations, as if he himself were detached and apart from the faculties which it is said he possesses, commands, and hearkens to.' The same remarks may be made upon the senses; *the organs* of the senses are no doubt distinct from the mind, but the senses themselves are not so. When a man sees or hears, it is he, it is the conscious being, who sees or hears. To say that the senses see and hear is to make entities of them, whereas in reality there are simply certain mental affections produced.

Hobbes, Locke, Leibnitz, Hume, have more than once criticised this inexact language without however succeeding in avoiding it themselves. Bailey quotes numerous examples, among which Kant would be the most flagrant, if M. Cousin had not written. According to German philosophy, the major of a syllogism refers to the understanding, the minor to the judgment, the conclusion to reason. 'Thus,' says Bailey, 'the intelligent being, like a constitutional monarch, governs regularly by means of his ministers; the Understanding being the Secretary of State for the Home Department, the Faculty of Judging being the Chief Justice of the Common Pleas, and the Reason the First Lord of the Treasury.'

Is it always possible to avoid these expressions? No. 'And,' continues Bailey, 'I have no more objection to make to the employment of the term "faculties" on ordinary occasions than to the habit which one of my friends has of measuring distances with sufficient exactness by the number of his own strides. But the methodical "investigation" of the facts of consciousness demands as much exactness and precision as any researches into physics or mathematics; and the method of "faculties" resembles that no more closely than my friend's calculation resembles a carefully drawn up trigonometrical plan.'[1]

It would be no more reasonable to abandon the use of such terms as will, reason, memory, etc., than to cease to use the words much, little, some. But what would we think of a statistician who, instead of saying that in such and such a country each marriage produces on an average four children, and that three-fifths of the population know how to read and write, should content himself with announcing that these marriages produce *some* children, and that the people who can read and write are *numerous*. The quantitative determination is the important matter. A criticism of 'imaginary operations,' almost entirely at the expense of M. Cousin, leads the author to conclude, that 'the predominance of those imaginary facts in metaphysical (psychological) works shows that humanity in point of mental philosophy has arrived at the period at which, in physics, people talked of the transmutation of metals, the elixir of life, the abhorrence of a vacuum by nature, and other similar things.'[2]

---

1 Bailey's *Letters on the Philosophy of the Human Mind*, vol. i. Letter 3.

2 *Ibid.* Letter 5.

VII.

Psychology, understood in its ordinary sense, is then a study more occupied with abstractions than with facts, founded upon a subjective method, and full of metaphysical discussions. Let us now see what psychology might be, conceived of as an independent science.

We have seen that in every order of knowledge, when the number of facts and accumulated observations is tolerably large, there comes, by the very nature of things, a tendency to anatomy, and that the new science, leaving to metaphysics the care of discussing the first principles, constitutes itself on its own basis, sufficiently solid for its purpose, though often utterly insecure to those who examine it in the light of philosophy.

In a word, the conditions of independence are simply the constant study of facts and separation from metaphysics.

Are there enough materials yet accumulated to constitute an experimental psychology? They are so numerous that no one has yet been found to classify them, to set them in order, and to reduce them to a system. The progress of physical and natural sciences, of linguistics, and of history, has reached unexpected facts, suggested novel appreciations, at least to those who have no taste for a stagnant and scholastic psychology, studies on the mechanism of the sensations, on the conditions of memory, on the effects of the imagination and the association of ideas, on dreams, somnambulism, ecstasy, hallucination, madness, and idiocy, researches hitherto unknown into the relation between the physical and the moral, a new conception of moral (psychological) nature, of humanity, resulting from a profounder study of history and of races, languages serving, as it were, for a petrified psychology.

An effort has been made of late to subject psychological acts to the precise control of measure. That is, in two words, what we find in thousands of books, memoirs, observations, or experiences; an immense mass of facts which still awaits its Kepler or its Newton. Let us now bring these experimental data into connexion with the little which antiquity has left us on this subject (Aristotle: *Treatise on the Soul*, *Sensation*, *Memory*, *Sleep*, etc.). Then let us bring the ontological psychology of our time into connexion with the metaphysics of Plato and Aristotle. Where is the progress?

Does psychology tend to separate itself from metaphysics? Instead of deciding this question, I prefer to place certain facts before the reader. In the seventeenth century, the science of the soul was called metaphysics. There is no other word in Descartes, Malebranche, and Leibnitz. Locke and Condillac employ the same language. Nevertheless, the word psychology, invented by the obscure Goclenius, was used by Wolf as the title of a work. The Encyclopædists, while continuing to use the term metaphysics, limited its sense. 'Locke,' says d'Alembert in the preliminary discourses of the Encyclopædia, 'reduces metaphysics to what it ought to be, the experimental physics of the soul.' The Scotch employ it with reserve, and prefer the expression 'philosophy of the human mind.' In short, the word psychology is coming into current use, and is common in France, Germany, and England. If it be further observed that in the two last-named countries psychology is cultivated as an independent science, and expurgated of metaphysics by writers who not only do not make any explicit profession of positivism, but are even in complete disagreement with that doctrine on several points, I think it will be granted that this anatomy is more than a mere tendency, that is in many respects an accomplished fact.[1]

The psychology in question here will then be purely experimental; it will have no other object than phenomena, their laws, and their immediate causes; it will concern itself neither with the soul nor its essence, for this question, being above experience and

[1] Lewes's *Hist. of Philosophy*, vol. ii. p. 225; Ribot, note, p. 29. 'Several writers have remarked the enormous predominance of psychological inquiries from Spinoza to Fichte; but the reason of this turn in the direction of philosophy has not, I think, been recognised. The fact is patent, the connexion of the predominance of psychology with the necessary decrease of ontology required explanation; the more so as psychology occupied but little attention in the ancient and mediæval schools. I believe that the importance acquired by psychology, especially in its treatment of the origin and scope of human faculty, was the natural result of the same objective tendency which had given prominence to the inductive method.'

beyond verification, belongs to metaphysics. If it seem paradoxical that psychology, which is the science of the soul, does not occupy itself with the soul, let it be remarked that biology and physics do not any longer occupy themselves with life and matter; that while they did so they made no progress; and that psychology has only been enriched by the facts of experience, for its metaphysics has not perhaps made one step since Aristotle. Shall this psychology be spiritualist or materialist? We reply that such a question has no meaning, and might as well be asked in regard to experimental physics. Spiritualism and materialism supply a solution of the question of substance, which is reserved to metaphysics. It is possible that the psychologist may, in the pursuit of his studies, incline to one of the two solutions, or to another, as the physiologist may incline to mechanism or animism, but these are personal speculations which he does not confound with science. Psychology will have its metaphysics like the other sciences, while remaining entirely distinct from it. This no doubt makes it incomplete, but that is the cost of progress. If psychology desires to be both psychology and metaphysics at the same time, it will be neither. In this it will resemble the other sciences which all eliminate questions of origin and of end, referring them to metaphysics. Philosophy exists that they may be discussed.

The method to be employed is at the same time *subjective* and *objective.* Discussions between those who will admit nothing but interior observation like Jouffroy, and those who recognise nothing but exterior observation like Broussais, resemble indecisive battles, after which both the combatants claim the victory. The former triumphantly produce their analysis and defy their adversaries to divine, without the aid of reflection, what it is to feel, to desire, to wish, to abstract. The latter reply that the dialogue of the *ego* with the *ego* cannot last long, and that they prefer to cultivate the fertile soil of experience. On both sides, the question is only half understood. Each of these systems has need of the other. In the ensuing essay on Mr. Herbert Spencer we shall see how they complete each other reciprocally, the subjective method proceeding by analysis, and the objective method by synthesis; the interior method being the most necessary, since without it we do not even know of what we are talking the exterior method being the most fruitful, since the field of its investigation is almost unlimited.

But in what does this objective method consist? In studying psychological facts from the outside, not from the inside; in the internal facts which translate them, not in the consciousness which gives them birth. The natural expression of the passions, the variety of languages, and the events of history are so many facts which permit us to trace the mental causes that have produced them: the morbid derangement of the organism which produces intellectual disorders; anomalies, monsters in the psychological order, are to us as experiences prepared by nature, and all the more precious as the experimentation is more rare. Study of the instincts, passions, and habits of the different animals supplies us with facts whose interpretation (often difficult) enables us by induction, deduction, or analogy, to reconstruct a mode of psychological existence. In short, the objective method instead of being personal, like the simple method of reflection, lends to facts an impersonal character; it bends before them; it moulds its thrones upon the reality. Among other advantages, I propose to mention only two: it introduces the idea of progress into psychology, it renders a compared psychology possible.

The idea of progress, of evolution, or of development, which of late has become preponderant in all the sciences which have a living object, has been suggested by the double study of natural sciences and of history. The scholastic ideas of the immutability of the forms of life, and the uniformity of the epochs of history have given place to a contrary conception. The doctrine of Heraclitus has been revived and confirmed by the experiences of twenty centuries; all melts, all changes, all moves, all becomes. Physiology, linguistics, religious, literary, political and artistic history bear testimony in favour of development. This idea, without which only an erroneous conception of life and history can be obtained, has remained inexplicably absent from ordinary psychology. And, nevertheless, it is not possible that the effects should differ incessantly, and the cause remain motionless. History being the result of two factors,—human activity and nature,—in which it displays itself, the source of change must needs be in either one or the other, and, as it is not in nature,[1] it must be sought for in the human soul, and in its dynamic tendencies. If it be pretended that the psychologist ought to set aside all these accidental variations in order to arrive at the final and absolute condition of mental activity, then a concrete study must be turned into an abstract study, an entity substituted for a reality; as if a zoologist should take the ideal type of animality as the basis of his researches. Psychological phenomena are treated as pure mechanics treats bodies, motions, and forces. Spinoza is imitated without acknowledgment. 'I will analyse the actions and the appetites of men as if it were a question of lines, planes, and solids.'—(*Ethics* 3.) [2]

Whence comes this result, if not from the exclusive employment of the subjective method, which cannot lay hold of development in psychological facts? The same method renders every attempt at comparative psychology impossible, because, if there are no other processes to follow than that of reflection, the psychical phenomena of the various races of animals cannot be studied. It is true that the method of interior observation being strictly personal, as soon as the results of it are applied to others, it is violated; the process becomes objective, and the most decisive step is taken. But other prejudices which need not be examined here oppose themselves to the extension of this study to animals. Hence resulted an enormous lacune in the science. The physiologist who should have experimented upon vertebrates only, would refuse to recognise in other animals those functions which are proper to the animal, because they are more simple and more obscure in them. But modern naturalists have traced the fundamental functions in even the lowest mollusca and zoophytes. The acts are less numerous, less complicated, but the function exists for all that. Thus, while in almost all animals the chemical

1 Nature also contributes; but at second-hand, by *stimulus*. On this point see Herder, and Buckle, *Civilisation of England*.

2 It is certain that the elimination of what is variable and accidental is necessary to constitute the science, and to determine the general conditions, but then the statical study must be completed by the dynamical, as will appear hereafter.

process takes place in the interior of the stomach, sometimes, as in the case of the hydra, the creatures seem to be entirely transformed into stomach; while in the case of others, the act is performed outside, between the numerous appendices which serve at once for mouth and arms. All naturalists are agreed that no study has been so fruitful for them as that of anatomy and of comparative physiology; that the knowledge of the rudimentary organs enables them better than anything else to understand the organs and the functions. Nothing like this has been attempted, or at least accepted, in ordinary psychology; the idea of a comparative method is hardly beginning to dawn. If it gains some adherents, the result will show what it is worth and what it gives. But even if this superior psychology should add nothing to our knowledge of man, it will remain none the less indispensable to it, since it is clear that psychology must embrace *all* the psychological phenomena.

Thus understood it will lose the abstract character which frequently makes it resemble logic, to which, indeed, it is proper to proceed *in abstracto;* to take the fully constituted, adult mind, and to study its mechanism, it cannot and ought not to attach itself except to the invariable groundwork;[1] while psychology studies the phenomena and the faculties in their origin, their development, and their transformation. Psychology must also keep clear of morals, because it is one thing to prove that which is, and another to prescribe that which ought to be, to abide by facts or to seek an ideal. The psychologist differs from the moralist, as the botanist differs from the gardener. For the one there are no vegetables either good or bad, they are all equally an object of study; for the other there are noxious or parasite plants, which must be extirpated and burnt; his rapid justice is concerned rather to condemn than

[1] See Cournot's *Fundamental Ideas*, vol. i. p. 213, *et seq.* The author distinguishes two orders of sciences: those which relate to the ideas of order and of form, and those which study the functions of life, and make perpetual use of the idea of force. The former serve as a basis for the latter. Thus logic is opposed to psychology, etc. The obscurity of the idea of force accounts for the inferiority of these latter sciences.

to know. Moral preoccupations have done harm to psychology more frequently than we think, by preventing it being seen as it is.

VIII.

Psychology, as understood in its widest sense, embracing all the phenomena of mind in all animals, and considering them, not only under their adult form, but in the successive phases of their development, offers an almost boundless field for research. Hence it is striking to observe how summary all the hitherto most accredited treatises upon Psychology are. If we subtract historical digressions, what, in many instances, remains? We shall be still more impressed by this brevity if we compare psychological books with those of naturalists, which are laden with details. Whence arises this difference, if not from the method employed? The latter collect facts with indefatigable patience, noting exceptions and differences, the former consisting only of a vague sketch, and some abstract formulas. And yet, has not that principle which thinks, feels, acts, and wills, in animated beings, almost infinite varieties, which are to be revealed only by the most minute investigation? Can we believe that a human soul may be described more briefly than a plant?

As the inevitable result of progress in every science is to produce division and subdivision of labour in it, we may safely predict that an extended and truly complete psychology will sever itself into many branches, and form sub-sciences, which shall become the objects of special study. It would be rash to indicate those divisions beforehand, but perhaps we may foresee some of them. Mr. John Stuart Mill, in the weighty pages which he has devoted to method in psychology, after having pointed out that the object of this science is 'the uniformities of successions,' bids us remark that we can conceive an intermediate case between the perfect science and its extreme imperfection. Such is the theory of the tides; when we consider the general causes of this phenomenon only, it can be predicted with certainty, but local or accidental circumstances (such as the configuration of the coasts or the direction of the wind) modify it, so as to render the result of the general calculation inexact. 'The science of the tides is not yet an exact science, not because of a radical impossibility relating to nature, but because it is very difficult to establish desired uniformities with precision. The science of human nature is of the same kind.'

Mr. Stuart Mill divides psychological studies into two great classes: of the one part, those which are *experimental*, of the other part, those which are *deductive*.

Experimental psychology, founded upon observation, establishes the facts from which it draws its laws, and 'constitutes the universal or abstract part of the philosophy of human nature.'

Deductive psychology, which constitutes ethology, or the science of character, supposes the preceding. It examines into how the general laws of psychological facts produce such variety of national or individual character, by their meetings, their combinations, their crossings.

If, following these indications, we endeavour to trace the divisions of a truly scientific psychology, this is what we shall find it ought to contain.

Firstly, we may comprehend in the term *General Psychology* the study of the phenomena of consciousness, sensations, thoughts, emotions, relations, etc., considered under their most general aspects. This study, which ought to serve as a point of departure and a basis for all the others, is the only one which has hitherto been cultivated by the psychologists. It is, besides, clear that general psychology ought to profit by all the discoveries due to its subordinate parts. It would complete itself, firstly by *Comparative Psychology*, whose object and importance we have already endeavoured to show, and afterwards by a study of anomalies or monstrosities, which might be called *Psychological Teratology*. It is unnecessary to delay here in order to demonstrate the usefulness of the study of deviations towards the complete understanding of phenomena, but the indifference of psychology on this point is truly remarkable. With the exception of Diderot's *Lettre sur les Aveugles*, which does not fulfil its promises, the pages of Dugald Stewart upon James Mitchell (*Elements of the Philosophy of the Human Mind*, vol. iii.), and some scattered observations, psychology has completely shut its eyes to exceptions and anomalies.[1]

It is the physiologists who have drawn the conclusions to which it led from the curious history of Laura Bridgeman, conclusions totally contrary to the doctrine of transformed sensations, and which, founded upon the facts, had not the vague character of the ordinary arguments. A deaf man, a blind man, a man originally deprived of any sense, is he not a ready-made subject for observation, one to whom one of the strictest processes of method, the differential, may be applied? Have studies upon madness, though still very incomplete, been altogether sterile hitherto?

If we now pass from *abstract* to *concrete* psychology, if, quitting analysis for synthesis, we deal no longer with general but with derived laws; if we try to determine how these laws by crossing each other determine psychological varieties, we shall meet with a new science, that of *character*, or, as Mr. Mill calls it, Ethology. We can understand how ordinary psychology, which has little taste for facts, and an habitual tendency towards abstraction, has neglected this study. Phrenology and Cranioscopics, which have been suffered to sleep, understood its importance better. The science of characters constituted a practical or applied psychology, whose utility in education, in the con-

---

1 The philosopher of whom we have already spoken in reference to the faculties, proposes to classify as follows all studies whose object is man, which he designates under the name of *Anthropology*:—

I. Researches relative to man as an individual.

1. Relative to Organism: Physiology and Anatomy.
2. Relative to mental operations and affections: Psychology.
3. Relative to the connexion between the phenomena of organism with the phenomena of consciousness (comprising Cranioscopics and Physiognomy).
4. Relative to the individual character.

II. Researches relative to humanity: its origin, races, progress, and civilisation.

III. Researches relative to the connexion between humanity and superior beings, or theology.

SAMUEL BAILEY, *Letters on the Philosophy of the Human Mind*, vol. ii. Letter 20.

duct of life, and even in politics, is evident. No doubt this *science* will always partake considerably of the nature of *art;* but will it not be sufficiently exact to render its employment legitimate? The naturalists have discovered certain organic correlations, on which they rely for the reconstruction of an animal from a few fragments. They know that there is a relation between the foot and the jaw, that the tooth of a carnivorous animal indicates a bony structure, consequently a skeleton, a cerebro-spinal axis, etc., etc. Might not psychological conditions be equally arrived at? Let us suppose that by an accumulation of sure and varied experiments, we were enabled to establish for instance, that a certain manner of feeling supposes a certain variety of imagination, which, in its turn, supposes a certain mode of judging and reasoning, which again supposes a certain method of willing and acting, and that this determination should be as precise as possible; surely by the aid of a single fact it might be possible to reconstitute a character, since the problem would reduce itself to the following: Given a number of the series, to find the entire series.

It will be granted that this hypothesis is in no way chimerical, if we will only remark that penetrating minds effect such a reconstruction instinctively, by a swift and sure intuition, though there is nothing scientific in it; that there exists a particular art which is called the knowledge of men. The question is, whether this *Art* may not become a *Science;* that is to say, whether, instead of being arbitrary, it may not be formulated into laws applicable to a great number of cases, and verified in the great majority. When this shall have been successfully done, Ethology will be constituted.

It seems that Ethology might be divided into an ethology of of *individuals*, an ethology of *peoples*, and an ethology of *races*.

Individual ethology, the most important and the most concrete of the three, would seek after the psychological differences resulting from difference of sex and temperament. It would determine the psychological characters which distinguish those various forms of mind which we designate under the names of poet, geometrician, industrial, warrior, etc. etc., thus limiting its study to that of a certain number of types. Among psychologists

I know only Dugald Stewart who has attempted this task (Appendix to his *Philosophy of the Human Mind*, vol. iii.), in incomplete and vague essays, whose diffuseness is not their least defect.

The ethology of peoples and races would derive its materials from linguistics and history. It is easy to see that ethology is not in any way confounded with history. There is as much difference between defining the character of a people and relating its history, as there is between drawing a man's likeness and writing his biography. The history of a people and the biography of a man are not only composed of that which comes from them, but also of the action of exterior circumstances upon them. Ethology eliminates this latter element, and takes no account of it, except in so far as it serves to elucidate the character. Ethology would not propose to itself simply a statical study of characters, it would endeavour to determine the phases which they undergo, and to follow them throughout their evolution.

Such, keeping in view phenomena only, and without speaking of the metaphysics of psychology, is the framework of one division of that science. But so long as it shall not be subdivided, it will be impossible for it to embrace the whole of its domain; it will not get beyond the brevity and meagreness of the ordinary treatises.[1] And yet, when we consider the immense variety of facts and questions contained in it, the task seems inexhaustible; infinite perspectives spread themselves before the seeker, and we find that there is so much to do that we venture to say nothing has been done.

It seems to me that the best we can hope for psychology is that it may be entering upon that period of apparent disorder and real fecundity, in which every question is studied separately, and excavated to its utmost depths. A good collection of monographs and memoirs upon special points would be perhaps the best service which could now be rendered to psychological

1 The only work, within our knowledge, in France, in which the insufficiency of ordinary psychology and its neglect of many important questions are treated, is in Vacherot's *Essais de Philosophie Critique*, p. 152 *et seq.*

studies. No doubt all this is not a science, but without all this there is no science. Such a method would possess not only the advantage of substituting better tendencies for those which actually exist, the study of facts for hypothetical generalizations, it would also offer a task within the reach of all. In this work of detail each might share according to his measure and his strength. Many who could not be architects might cut stones skilfully enough. A hundred workers might perhaps wear themselves out over one obscure point. What matter, if a result be obtained? The science will accept their work, and forget their names. It will assume its true character—impersonality. *Multi pertransibunt, sed augebitur scientia.*

IX.

We have only a few more words to say, relative to the aim of this work. Since the time of Hobbes and Locke, England has been the country which has done the most for psychology. In our own time two currents of doctrines have been produced there: on one side the *a priori* school, represented by Sir W. Hamilton, Dr. Whewell, Mr. Mansel, Mr. Ferrier,[1] etc.; on the other, the *a posteriori* school (*Association-Psychology*), which numbers among its adherents James Mill, John Stuart Mill, Messrs. Bailey, Herbert Spencer, Bain, Lewes, and several others.[2] A complete

[1] Professor Ferrier, of the University of St. Andrews, has published *Institutes of Metaphysics* in thirty-three propositions: 'one of the most remarkable books of our time,' says Mr. Lewes (a positivist), 'but which resembles a solitary obelisk in a vast bare plain.' It is remarkable that Professor Ferrier distinguishes experimental psychology very clearly from psychology metamorphosed into metaphysics. 'In case,' he says, 'it may be thought that psychology has not been sufficiently spared in this work, let it it be remarked that it is only in so much as psychology ventures to treat the fundamental question of knowledge, and to introduce itself into the region of *prima philosophia*, that it has been criticised and its insufficiency shown. In its own sphere, *i.e.* the study of mental operations, such as memory, the association of ideas, etc., the labours of psychology ought not to be disdained in any respect.'—*Institutes of Metaphysics*, p. 116.

[2] Sir H. Holland, *Chapters on Mental Physiology;* Dr. Noble, *Medical Psychology;* Brodie, *Psychological Enquiries;* Dunn, *Physiological Psychology*, etc.; Morell, *An Introduction to Mental Philosophy;* Maudsley, *Pathology and Physiology of Mind;* Murphy, *Habit and Intelligence*, etc. etc.

study of English contemporary psychology would necessarily comprehend both these schools. At present we shall only endeavour to make known the second. As it is unknown, or very nearly unknown, in France, and as it seems to hold the first rank, in virtue of the celebrity of the names which represent it, of its harmony with the general tendencies of the age, and the most recent discoveries of the natural and physical sciences, and of the originality of its researches and results, we believe that it must be useful to make known its doctrines, and that this work of *pure exposition* cannot be displeasing either to those who accept or to those who repel them.

HARTLEY.

In considering English contemporaneous psychology, the theories of Hartley have only a retrospective interest. Thus we give him in this instance the place of a precursor merely, for all that is to be found in his work is either left behind or forgotten. Nevertheless, it seems that he has not been done sufficient justice. On the appearance of his *Observations on Man, his Frame, his Duty, and his Expectations* (1748), the book had but moderate success. Hartley had preceded its publication, sixteen years previously, by that of a brief Latin treatise, entitled *Conjecturæ quædam de Sensu, Motu, et Idearum Generatione.* This little work has been republished by Dr. Parr in his *Metaphysical Facts by English Philosophers of the Eighteenth Century* (1837). But the public, Hartley's contemporaries, seem to have been indifferent to this new manner of conceiving the mechanism of mind. On the other hand, the *Association-Psychology*, whose theory we propose to explain, is so superior to Hartley, that it is easy to see why that philosopher has almost fallen into oblivion. Nevertheless, as it is a fact that the original idea of associational-psychology is in Hartley, it will be interesting to explain it briefly in this place, were it only to enable us to measure the way which has been made since the *Observations on Man.*

Hartley is a plain, lucid, methodical writer,—perhaps he is a little too methodical. He proceeds by geometrical method, by propositions, corollaries, and scholia. He divides, subdivides, and distinguishes in a manner worthy of a scholastic. Without losing ourselves in all these subdivisions, let us examine some general points.

The whole of Hartley's system may be resolved into two principal theories :—

1. The *theory of vibrations*, by which he explains all nervous

phenomena, and consequently the relations of the physical and the moral.

2. The *theory of association*, by which he explains all the mechanism of mind, and all psychological phenomena without exception.

The first is borrowed from Newton's *Optics* and *Principia Philosophiæ*. The second, from Locke's doctrine of the association of ideas, contained in the *Essay on the Human Understanding*. The following is the explanation of what both consist in.

I.

In order to understand what is new and original in the physiological portion of Hartley's* work, we must recall the current universally received ideas of his epoch.

The physicists of the two last centuries habitually resorted, for the explanation of phenomena whose nature was imperfectly known to them, to the intervention of special electric fluids, so defined as to explain those phenomena. Thus they imagined two electric fluids, the one positive, the other negative, and they represented heat, light, and magnetism as other imponderable fluids. They even tried to explain nervous action by the intervention of a new fluid, circulating in the nerves, as if in tubes, and which would be thus conducted from the nervous extremities to the brain.

This doctrine had obtained great credit when Hartley, struck with the important part which the discoveries of Newton attributed to *vibrations* in optics, and particularly in vision, conceived the idea that an analogous phenomenon must be produced in the cerebro-spinal system. He drew attention to the fact that since a luminous ray, falling upon the eye, determines vibrations in the retina, these vibrations must be propagated by the fibres of the optic nerves, until they reach the brain, in order to produce the sensation of vision, and that they may last for a long time; the same being the case, not only in the sense of sight, strictly speaking, but in the entire nervous system, so that that portion of our organism is in a state of continuous vibration.

But how are these vibrations effected, and in what do they

consist? 'They are motions backwards and forwards of the small particles, of the same kind as the oscillation of the pendulum, and the trembling of particles of sounding bodies. They are excited, propagated, and kept up, partly by ether, partly by uniformity and continuity of the brain, spinal marrow, and nerves.'

We perceive that Hartley makes his explanation depend on the hypothesis of the ether, as established by Newton. 'Let us suppose the existence of the ether, with its properties, to be destitute of all direct evidence, still, if it serve to explain and account for a great variety of phenomena, it will have an indirect evidence in its favour by those means.' We must then conceive the nervous system as penetrated with this elastic compressible substance, apt to receive vibrations. 'It will therefore follow that the nerves are rather solid *capillamenta* according to Newton, than small *tubuli* according to Boerhaave.' Hartley attaches the phenomena of light, heat, sound, attraction, and electricity to his hypothesis of vibrations, very ingeniously.

Thus, the impression of any object upon our organism, disturbance of the nerves, vibrations, transmission of those vibrations to the brain, permanence of vibrations after the sensible object has disappeared, is a summary of the physiological hypothesis of Hartley.

We shall not stop to show how insufficient such physiology is. We will only remind our readers that, at that time, the anatomy of the brain and of the nervous system hardly existed. Thus Hartley believes that it is the white substance of the encephalus which presides over the psychological functions, whereas we now know that the *grey* substance is much the more important of the two. Nevertheless, we cannot deny that he is right upon a number of points. His hypothesis of vibrations, independently of all theories upon ether and its nature, agrees with the tendencies of modern physics and physiology, which incline to refer everything to movements. Recent researches have shown that there is no nervous fluid, or nervous circulation, such as Hartley's contemporaries believed in, but that impression travels in the nerves in an intermittent manner, like the electric current in a conducting wire. Certain physiologists of our time conceive the mechanism of thought as a communication of vibrations having their seat in the grey substance of the brain.[1] The initial movement can transmit itself from one cell to another in every possible direction; hence the variety of associations. Thus, then, without pronouncing upon the value of Hartley's hypothesis, we may say that the scientific theories which have been professed for a century are far from being unfavourable to him.

II.

Now let us approach the psychological study, with which we are more directly concerned.

We have seen that the impression of exterior objects causes vibrations, by means of the ether, which produce *sensation.* Now, 'sensory vibrations, by being often repeated, beget in the medullary substance of the brain a disposition to diminutive vibrations, which may also be called vibratiuncles, or miniature vibrations, corresponding to themselves respectively.' These vibratiuncles, which are vestiges of the primitive vibration, may be called 'simple ideas of sensation.' The vibratiuncles then produce *Ideas.*

Hitherto we have explained only the simple elements of thought; we must now enter upon its conditions and complex operations. Here comes in the law of Association.

'Any associations, A, B, C, etc., by being associated with one another a sufficient number of times, get such a power over the corresponding ideas, A, B, C, etc., that any one of the sensations A, when impressed alone, shall be able to excite in the mind B, C, etc., the ideas of the rest.' (Prop. X.)

'Any vibrations, A, B, C, etc., by being associated together a sufficient number of times, get such a power over *a*, *b*, *c*, etc., the corresponding miniature vibrations, that any of the vibrations A, when impressed alone, shall be able to excite *b*, *c*, etc., the miniature of the rest. (Prop. XI.)

Thus, then, it is by means of association that simple ideas merge into complex ideas, and concur in their composition.

[1] Luys, *Recherches sur le Système nerveux, cérébro-spinal*, Paris, 1865.

After having explained man as a *thinking* and *feeling* being, he remains to be explained as an *active* being,—that is to say, capable of movement. Here also everything reverts to vibrations, vibratiuncles, and association.

In the first place, 'That propensity to alienate construction and relaxation which is observed in almost all the muscles of the body, admits of a solution from the doctrine of vibrations;' the 'motory vibrations,' which contract the muscles, account for *automatic* movements.

If we admit that the motory vibrations leave vibratiuncles after them, exactly as sensory vibrations do, we may, by the aid of these motory vibrations explain *voluntary* and *semi-voluntary* movements. They are rendered possible by an association of the primitive motory vibrations. Hence the whole doctrine of association may be confirmed in the following theorem:—

'If any sensation A, idea B, or muscular motion C, be associated for a sufficient number of times with any other sensation D, idea E, or muscular motion F, it will at last excite *d*, the idea belonging to the sensation D, the very idea E, or the very muscular motion F.' (Prop. xx.)

We can now arrive at a collective view of the entire doctrine, and see how all is explained by two things only, vibrations and association.

To simple vibration corresponds sensation.
To associated vibrations complex sensations.
To the vibratiuncle, the simple idea.
To associated vibratiuncles, complex ideas.
To the motory vibrations automatic movement.
To motory vibratiuncles, voluntary and semi-voluntary movements.

Such are the general laws which, according to Hartley, regulate and explain all the mechanism of the human mind. It only remains for us now to say how he explains the various faculties, *senses*, *memory*, *imagination*, *understanding*, *affections*, and *will*, by attaching them to the law of association.

1. There is no occasion for us to linger over his analyses of the senses. He distinguishes the general sense or *feeling*, which

is nothing but touch, from the four special senses, and applies himself to explain all by vibrations and associations.

2. Memory is that faculty by which traces of sensations and ideas come, or are recalled, in the same order and proportion, accurately or nearly as they were once presented. The relations between memory and the association of ideas are so evident, so universally recognised, that it is useless to dwell upon them.

3. It is the same with regard to the imagination. 'When ideas and trains of ideas occur, or are called up in a vivid manner, and without regard to the order of former actual impressions and perceptions, this is said to be done by the power of fancy.' Odd and extravagant associations explain reverie, dreaming, mental alienation, and all their cognate phenomena.

4. 'The understanding is that faculty by which we contemplate mere sensations and ideas, pursue truth, and assent to or dissent from propositions.' This faculty, in all its essentials, reduces itself to judgment, and, as Hartley says, to proposition, and leads itself back to an association of ideas.

Propositions (affirmative and negative) are of two kinds, rational and practical.

The former are those who have for their object mathematical truths: now, in this case, what is the process followed when I say $2 \times 2 = 4$, or $12 \times 12 = 144$? My rational assent to the proposition may be defined as a readiness to affirm it to be true, proceeding from a close association of the ideas suggested by the proposition, with the idea or internal feeling belonging to the word truth.

The latter are those which have for their object natural bodies. Hartley's thought may be differently expressed, by saying that the objects of the one are abstracts, and the objects of the other are concretes. The former consist in associating a sensation or a group of sensations given by experience to another sensation, or group of sensations, equally given by experience. For instance: gold is ductile, or soluble in *aqua regia*. As we see, then, the fundamental operations by which we find scientific or vulgar truths, are brought back by final analysis to associations, to the fusion of simple elements.

5. Hartley afterwards shows how the passions, *i.e.* the moral

life of man, have their point of departure also in an association of ideas. They set out from two fundamental phenomena—pleasure and pain. But complex sentiments proceed from these simple conditions, by fusion and association.

The passions result from certain sentiments, certain emotions which have been once or several times united to ideas or to circumstances which have the power to reawaken them by the very principle of association.

Let us take fear, for example. We may observe any day that a child is not afraid of a thing except from the moment that that thing has been made to him the real or apparent cause of suffering or punishment. He is not afraid of fire until he has been burned; or of a dog, until the dog has bitten him. In the same way, the passion of love is born of the association of agreeable circumstances with the idea of the object which produces this love.

Our passions may also be all reduced to the sentiments of fear or of affection, varying according to the relation which subsists between their objects and ourselves. In its origin, every passion is always interested, that is to say, it is engendered by an association of ideas founded on pain and on pleasure. But, in consequence of our associations, our passions, in becoming more complex, assume a disinterested character. It is thus that the child loves his mother or his nurse. The idea of that passion associates itself with the various pleasures which she has caused him, which he has experienced in her presence.

Hartley classifies our passions in rather an arbitrary way, which is also a little confused, under the following titles:—

The pleasure and pain of imagination, of ambition, of self-interest, of sympathy, of theopathy, of moral sense.

When he discusses the instincts, he is weak. He shows, however, that they lead back to association. Their point of departure is automatic; the muscles have at first been contracted involuntarily, then this involuntary action has associated itself with the cerebral disturbance which has accompanied it; in other words, the idea unites itself to motion, and motion follows it immediately and mechanically.

6. A mechanism so strict as Hartley's leaves no place for

free-will, and he is too rigid a logician to permit it to enter by an inconsequence. Thus, in the ordinary sense of the word, he absolutely rejects it.

Free-will, he says, may be understood in one of the two following senses :—1. A power of doing either the action *A*, or its contrary *a*, while the previous circumstances remain the same. 2. A power of beginning motion. Both one and the other of these two senses are perfectly incompatible with the hypothesis of the mechanism of the mind.

'But, if by free-will be meant anything different from these two definitions of it, it may not perhaps be inconsistent with the mechanism of the mind here laid down. Thus, if free-will be defined as the power of doing what a person desires or wills to do, of deliberating, suspending, choosing, or of resisting the motives of sensuality, ambition, resentment, free-will, within certain limitations, is not only consistent with the doctrine of mechanism, but even flows from it; since it appears from the foregoing theory, that voluntary and semi-voluntary powers of calling up ideas, of exciting and restraining affections, and of performing and suspending actions, arise from the mechanism of our nature. This may be called free-will in the popular and practical sense, in contradistinction to that which is opposed to mechanism, and which may be called free-will in a philosophical sense.'

Hartley even maintains that the hypothesis of free-will, reducing itself to the admission of effects without causes, ruins thereby the principle of causality, and consequently, the existence 'of the First Cause.' This constitutes the second portion of his book, into which we shall not follow him.

We do not wish to dwell here upon a philosopher who is interesting, only because he was the first of a school which has gone far beyond him.

His merit consists in two principles. He has clearly perceived that all the operations of the mind are reducible on final analysis to the law of association. He has said this very plainly, and he has tried to demonstrate it. Before him, nothing comparable was to be found in Locke, or even in Hobbes. He has perceived that the question of the relations between the physical and the moral seem to lead back to this question :—how is a nervous vibration united to a sentiment? This was much in his age, at an epoch in which the importance of the nervous system was too often misunderstood, when questions of this kind were put under the form of a strange or unintelligible hypothesis. Thus, he has perceived the fundamental law of psychology, and the fundamental fact of the relations of the physical and the moral.

On the other hand, he has the defects of his time, a somewhat superficial clearness, a talent for simplifying things which leads him to suppress difficulties. We are astonished to see how simple the complicated mechanism of the human soul becomes in his hands. All this comes from a defect of method. Hartley, though a physician, had the tendencies of a geometrician rather than a naturalist. Not with impunity did he borrow his principles from Newton. All his parade of demonstrations, of scholia, and of corollaries, shows that he is much more occupied in setting forth his theory in fine logical order, than in illustrating it by facts. After his day, the method of the natural sciences remained to be applied to psychology; but, though he did not do this, he prepared the way for its being done.

MR. JAMES MILL.

'The sceptre of psychology,' says Mr. Stuart Mill, 'has decidedly returned to England.' We might go further, and maintain that it has never departed thence. No doubt, psychological studies are now cultivated in England by first-class men, who, by the solidity of their method, and, which is more rare, by the precision of their results, have caused the science to enter upon a new epoch; but this is rather a redoubling than a renewal of its brilliancy. Since the time of Locke, and even before it, the empirical study of the facts of consciousness has always been in favour among the English; no people have done so much for psychology considered apart from metaphysics. If, indeed, we look at the three or four peoples of modern Europe who only have had a philosophical development, with the exception of Germany, apt at everything, though loving metaphysics above all,[1] we shall see that in Italy experimental psychology is poor, almost *nil*, because that light, imaginative race, whose life is all outside, have an instinctive repugnance to it; that in France it soon turns to logic, because we have too little taste for patient observation, for exceptions, for accumulated facts, and that we are too fond of compartments, divisions, and subdivisions, order, symmetry, brief and decisive formulas. In England it is natural; it is the simple result of that disposition to the interior life, to that falling back upon one's-self, whence come poetry and romance of the order which we call *intimes*. The

[1] Among the contemporary German works in which psychology is more or less considered as 'a natural science,' we may quote Wundt, *Vorlesungen über die Menschen und Thierseele*; Waitz, *Lehrbuch der Psychologie als Naturwissenschaft*; Fechner, *Elemente der Psychophysik*; Lotze, *Medicinische Psychologie*, and the psychologists of the school of Herbart, Drobisch, Wolkmann, etc. etc.

English contemporary school is therefore the continuation of an uninterrupted tradition; allied, through Brown, to the Scotch school, linked through James Mill with Hartley and Hume, and holding especially by the latter.

As we are now occupied with contemporaries, we shall not go further back than the nineteenth century. As our object is the experimental school, we shall lay aside some illustrious names, such as Hamilton, Mansel, Ferrier, etc., those of metaphysicians or logicians rather than of psychologists.

James Mill, the first on our list, would seem to be excluded by the date of his death (1836). But some of our contemporaries acknowledge him as a precursor. A new edition of his *Analysis of the Phenomena of the Human Mind* has appeared lately, enriched with full critical notes by Mr. John Stuart Mill, his son, and Mr. Bain, completed in all which concerns linguistics by a philologist, Mr. Andrew Findlater, and in all that concerns erudition by Mr. Grote. The date of this book makes it curious. It is too new, and yet not new enough to obtain a great success. It is a transitional work which is not well understood until *after*. Clear, lucid, methodical, well put together, the book errs from want of width and insufficiency of development. Now, opinion does not understand, and above all does not accept a doctrine except by dint of hearing it repeated. Contemporary labours, directed in the same sense, but less concise, and more familiar with the sciences, seem to have lent to his a retrospective value.

The *Analysis* proceeds much more from Hartley than from the Scotch School. No declamation, no recourse to eloquence; it says, with Hobbes, '*philosophia vera, orationis non modo fucum, sed etiam omnia fere ornamenta ex professo rejicit.*' No appeal to prejudices or to common sense; no explanation by faculties which are invented to solve difficulties. He particularly dreads 'the mystic,' and 'the mysterious.' His explanation of the phenomena of mind is very simple, too simple indeed, for we find in it the logician rather than the psychologist. He reduces everything to sensations, ideas, and the associations of ideas. In the psychical world there is only one fact, *sensation*, only one law, *association*.

What is his method? He does not tell us that; but he almost

always proceeds subjectively. In this respect he belongs to the eighteenth century. We do not find in his works any trace of a comparative psychology. He also belongs to this century by his tendency to consider phenomena only in adult minds, and among a civilized people. Carrying the practical spirit of his nation into psychological studies, he thinks, with reason, that education would be more enlightened and more systematic if psychology were more advanced; and that a good analysis of the phenomena of mind ought to serve as the basis of three practical treatises,—one Logical, to lead us to the true, one Moral, to regulate our actions, one Emotional, to develop the individual and the species.

Mr. James Mill, who was at least as well known an historian and economist as philosopher, has left a *History of British India*, which is considered a powerful and fine work,[1] and *Principles of Political Economy*, inspired by Smith and Ricardo, which competent judges regard as a solid book, a little difficult because it is so excessively concise, 'too abstract, perhaps, to be of popular utility.'

Some details borrowed from the recent Preface to his works will make the reader acquainted with the man :—

'Though, like all who value their time for higher purposes, he went little into what is called society, he helped, encouraged, and not seldom prompted, many of the men who were most useful in their generation. From his obscure privacy he was during many years of his life the soul of what is now called the advanced Liberal party; and such was the effect of his conversation, and of the force of his character, on those who were within reach of its influence, that many then young, who have since made themselves honoured in the world by a valuable career, look back to their intercourse with him as having had a considerable share of deciding their course through life. . . . As a converser Mr. Mill had few equals; as an argumentative converser, in modern

[1] Mr. John Stuart Mill says in his Preface, that by his labours as Administrator of the East India Company, James Mill did much good, and prepared the way for much more, to the millions for whose good or ill government England is responsible.

times, probably none. All his mental resources seemed to be at his command at any moment.'[1]

At the outset of his philosophic life, Hartley's doctrine took strong hold of his mind. He applied himself to its completion and extension; he is, as Mr. Stuart Mill says, the second founder of the psychology of association.

'I am far from thinking that the more recondite specimens of analysis are always successful, or that the author has not left something to be corrected as well as much to be completed by his successors. The completion has been especially the work of two distinguished thinkers in the present generation, Professor Bain and Mr. Herbert Spencer, in the writings of both of whom Association-Psychology has reached a still higher development. . . . What there is in the work that seems to need correction, arises chiefly from two causes. First, the imperfection of physiological science at the time at which it was written. . . . Secondly, a certain impatience of detail. The bent of his mind was towards that, in which also his greatest strength lay, in seizing the larger features of a subject—the commanding laws which govern and connect many phenomena. . . . From this cause (as it appears to me) he has occasionally gone further in the pursuit of simplification, and in the reduction of the more recondite mental phenomena to the more elementary, than I am able to follow him.'[2]

We think that the majority of our readers will agree with Mr. Mill when they shall have perused the following analysis.

CHAPTER I.

SENSATIONS AND IDEAS.

Sensations and ideas.—1. The association of ideas—2. Language—3. Memory, imagination, classification, abstraction—4. Belief.

EVERY one who has read Hume's *Essays* will remember that this philosopher explains all by three things,—impression, idea,

---

[1] *Preface* to the Works of James Mill, by John Stuart Mill, vol. i. p. xv.

[2] P. xv. vol. i., *Preface* by John Stuart Mill.

and the union of ideas. The primitive phenomenon is impression, or, as it is commonly called, sensation; idea is a feebler copy of this; then ideas associate themselves, unite, and there result complex or aggregate phenomena. Mr. James Mill admits only *sensations*, *ideas*, and *associations of ideas*.[1]

He classes our sensations under eight heads,—Smell, Hearing, Sight, Taste, Touch, Sensations of disorganization in some portion of the body, Muscular sensations, Sensations of the alimentary canal. As we shall see hereafter, contemporary psychologists generally reduce the last three groups to two,—muscular sensations, organic sensations; the former relating to the muscles, and which reveal tension or effort, the latter relating to the good or bad condition of the organs. But it is important to remark, that our author has seen more clearly than the Scotch school,[2] which, adhering to the traditional five senses only, could not achieve more than a curtailed analysis of the sensations. Thence came the impossibility of any scientific explanation of exterior perception; for had not this school neglected the analysis of the muscular sense, which reveals to us resistance; that is to say, the fundamental sensation of exteriority? Thus James Mill is right when he says, 'there is no element of consciousness which demands more attention than this, though until of late it has been deplorably neglected.'

It is a peculiarity of our constitution that when our sensations cease through the absence of their objects, something remains. After having seen the sun, if I shut my eyes I no longer see it, but I can think of it. That which thus survives sensation I call 'a copy, an image of the sensation, sometimes a representation or a trace of the sensation.' This copy is *the idea.*[3]

The general faculty of having sensations is called sensation: the general faculty of having ideas is called by the author *Ideation.* As the idea is the copy of the sensation, and as

---

[1] See *Essays* 2 and 3.

[2] That of Reid, Dugald Stewart, and their contemporaries.

[3] *Analysis*, etc., vol. i. ch. ii. p. 52.

there are eight groups of sensations, there are eight groups of ideas of which it is easy to find examples.[1]

We know the simple sensations and those secondary sensations, which are their images. These are the two primitive states of consciousness. From thence all those combinations whose varieties are innumerable result; they are produced by the *association of ideas.*

All the philosophers of whom we treat regard the phenomenon of association as one of the most general laws of psychology, and even as the fundamental fact to which they endeavour to bring back everything in our mental life. This doctrine, known in England by the generic name of Association-Psychology, is only in its beginning in James Mill's works, but supported by the preceding studies of Hume and Hartley, it is presented in a clear and decided form, as we shall presently see.

Association is so general a fact that our whole life consists in a succession of sentiments (*train of feelings*). Can an order be discovered in this? Let us remark, in the first place, that association is produced as well between *sensations*, as between *ideas.*

Association between the sensations ought to take place conformably to the order established between the objects of nature; that is to say, according to a *synchronic order* or according to a *successive order.* Synchronic order, or that of simultaneous existence, is order in space; successive order, or that of anterior and posterior existence, is order in time. The taste of an apple, its resistance in my mouth; the solidity of the earth which carries me, etc., this is synchronic association. I see a bombshell thrown, I follow it with my eyes, I see it fall, and cause destruction, this is successive association.

As our ideas are derived, not from the objects themselves, but

1 Mr. Stuart Mill calls attention in Note 24 to the fact that the idea, being the copy of the sensation, it may be asked whether there is not also a copy of the copy, an idea of the idea. My idea of Pericles, or of an existing person whom I have never seen, corresponds to a real existing object, or one which has been existent in the world of sensation. Nevertheless, as my idea is derived not from the object, but from the words of another person, my idea is not a copy of the original, but a copy of the copy of another; it is the idea of an idea.

from our sensations, we may expect from analogy that their order shall be derived from that of the sensations, and this most frequently occurs. '*Our ideas are born or exist in the order in which the sensations, of which they are the copies, have existed.*' Such is the general law of the association of ideas.[1]

When sensations are produced simultaneously, ideas are also awakened simultaneously; when sensations have been successive, ideas spring up in succession. The causes of association seem to be two in number: the vivacity of the associated sentiments, and the frequency of the association.

Association takes place not only between simple, but between complex ideas, which melt together so as to form an idea which appears simple. Such are our ideas of most familiar objects; the idea of a wall is a complex idea resulting from the already complex ideas of bricks and lime.

Hume, as we know, had said that our ideas associate themselves on three principles: contiguity in time and space, resemblance, and causality. The author, who admits the first principle only, contiguity in space (synchronic order), and contiguity in time (successive order), endeavours to bring the two others into this one, an attempt at simplification which, in the judgment of Mr. John Stuart Mill, 'is perhaps the least happy in the whole work' (Note 35).

II.

Before approaching imagination and memory, which, it would seem, ought immediately to follow, we shall find a study of words, parts of speech, the act of *naming*, which appears to us the most antiquated portion of the book.

It is remarkable that English contemporary psychologists, who have profited so largely by the recent progress of physiology, have borrowed nothing from linguistics. It may be main-

[1] Vol. i. ch. iii.

[2] In the tribunals, says the author, it is observed that ocular and auricular witnesses always follow the chronological order in their narratives; that is to say, the order of their sensations, whereas those who invent seldom observe that order.

tained that that science is as yet neither sufficiently mature nor sufficiently well co-ordinated; but it is incontestable that it has much to reveal to us concerning the constitution, and above all the development, of the human soul. It will become one of the elements of that objective and inductive method which tends to prevail in psychology. Maupertuis, in his *Réflexions philosophiques sur l'origine des Langues,* speaks of the utility of studying the languages of the savages, 'which are conceived on a plan of ideas so different from our own.' It has been done, and we can readily believe that comparative philology will reveal things to us, of much more intimate and delicate bearing upon the mechanism of the soul and its variations, than physiology.

From the time of Aristotle, who said, 'We do not think without images, and words are images,' until the almost contemporary group of the ideologists, the sensualist school has always understood the importance of language. James Mill is of their school on this point; his general Grammar resembles that of Condillac or of Destutt de Tracy. His authorities are Horne Tooke and Harris. A long exposition of doctrines which have been left far behind since the author's time, would be useless here. A few words will suffice.

After having spoken of the simple states of consciousness, we must pass, he says, to the complex states. But all these imply, in some manner, the 'process of naming.' We must, therefore, first see in what this 'artifice' consists. It consists of 'inventing' signs or marks which we impose upon sensations and ideas. 'Substantive' names are marks of ideas or of sensations; adjective names are marks placed upon substantive names, or marks upon marks, in order to limit the signification of the substantive, and instead of marking one great class, to mark a subdivision of that class. Example: a 'great' man. The verb is also a mark upon a mark.

Three different sorts of marks render *predication* or *affirmation* possible. 'I have the name of the individual, *John,* and the name of the class, *man.* I can place in juxtaposition my two names, *John, man.* But it is not sufficient to effect the communication which I desire to make, that the word 'man' is a mark of the idea of which 'John' is a mark, and a mark of other ideas with those; that is, those of which James, Thomas, etc., are the marks. In order to execute my design completely, I invent a mark, which, placed between my marks John and man, fixes the idea that I wish to express, and I say, "John is a man." In every language the verb which denotes existence, has been employed to respond to the design of adding the copula in the affirmation.'

The method of the author, which is that of the eighteenth century, is unacceptable on several points, and is now generally rejected. It has the primary defect of explaining natural things artificially, of believing in too much regularity in the march of the human mind, of not allowing a sufficient place to its spontaneity. It has no feeling for that which is primitive, for that far distant epoch when the senses and the imagination predominated, and when the mind seized only upon living and concrete things.[1] It treats language after the fashion of logic, and not of psychology. A second defect is, that these explanations are at most applicable only to the family of Aryan languages. We cannot see how the theory of 'marks of marks' can be applied to the agglutinative or monosyllabic languages.

Thus Mr. A. Findlater makes important reservations in the name of comparative philology (Note 53). This theory of affirmations, he says, is in conformity with the phenomena of the family of languages known as Indo-European. Logicians, in fact, in treating this subject, have never taken into consideration any other languages than Greek, Latin, and the modern literary languages of Europe. It may then be presumed that this theory would not apply to languages of a totally different structure. The mental process must, no doubt, be the same in all, but the means are new and without precedent. If the naturalists had wished to construct a type of animal organism without having ever seen anything but vertebræ, their theory would certainly have failed in its generalization. In the same way, the current theory of affirmation, considered by the light of a more and more profound knowledge of the organism of speech, seems to attach

[1] On this point see Renan, *De l'origine du Langage*; Max Müller, *Science of Language*, vol. ii. chiefly.

an exaggerated importance to a power of affirmation presumed to be inherent in verbs, and particularly in the verbs of existence. It is now a well-known fact, that in the monosyllabic languages spoken by a third of the human kind, there is no distinction between the parts of speech. The substantive verb is wanting in many languages. Among the Malays, the Javanese, and in the peninsula of Malacca, pronouns or indeclinable particles take the place of the verb *to be.* The affirmative faculty belongs so little exclusively to the verb, that the pronouns and the articles very often express affirmation, as may be proved by numerous examples, especially from the agglutinative languages. As for the other verbs, comparative grammar finds no trace of a substantive verb forming part of their structure.

It is now an accepted doctrine of philology that the root of a verb is of the nature of an abstract name, *and that it becomes a verb simply by the addition of a pronominal affix.*[1] And Mr. Findlater concludes, that if this analysis of the verb is correct, affirmation of existence did not find expression in the early periods of language : *the real copula, joining the subject with the predicate, was the proposition contained in the oblique case of the pronominal affix.*

III.

After this excursion into the domain of philology, let us return to purely psychological analysis, with imagination and memory.

Consciousness is the name of our feelings taken one by one, imagination is the name of a succession of sentiments or ideas. 'The phenomena classed under this head, are explained by modern philosophers upon the principles of association.' Dugald

[1] Findlater, according to Garnett, gives an example of a declension, a conjugation of a verb in Wotiak, by means of pronominal affixes :—

Pi-i,	*son of me.*	Bera-i,	*word of me.*	(*I speak*)
Pi-ed,	*son of thee.*	Bera-d,	*word of thee.*	
Pi-ez,	*son of him.*	Bera-z,	*word of him.*	
Pi-mi,	*son of us.*	Bera-my,	*word of us.*	
Pi-dy,	*son of you.*	Bera-dy,	*word of you.*	
Pi-zy,	*son of them.*	Bera-zy,	*word of them.*	

Stewart has given a technical sense to the word Imagination, without deriving any advantage from it: he restricts it to the case in which the mind creates, forms new combinations.

Imagination, then, consists in a succession of ideas, but great is the diversity of these successions. They are different in the shopkeeper, occupied with purchase and sale, from those of the lawyer, occupied with judges, clients, and witnesses; they mean one thing in the soldier, another in the metaphysician. The author ingeniously brings out the character by which the associations of ideas of the poet differ from all others while appearing to resemble them.

'The ideas of the poet are ideas of all that is most lovely and striking in the visible appearances of nature, and of all that is most interesting in the actions and affections of human beings. . . . There is also nothing surprising in this, that, being trains of pleasurable ideas, they should have attracted a peculiar degree of attention, and in an early age, when poetry was the only literature, should have been thought worthy of a more particular naming than the trains of any other class. . . . In the case of the lawyer, the train leads to a decision favourable to the side which he advocates. The train has nothing pleasurable in itself. The pleasure is all derived from the end. The same is the case with the merchant. His trains are directed to a particular end. And it is the end alone which gives value to the train. The end of the metaphysical and the end of the mathematical inquirer, is the discovery of truth; their trains are directed to that object; and are, or are not, a source of pleasure, as that end is or is not attained. But the case is perfectly different with the poet. His train is its own end. It is all delightful, or the purpose is frustrated.' [1]

Memory, according to the opinion of all who have studied it, is a complex faculty.[2] Into what has it been resolved? According to the author, it contains only ideas and associations of ideas.[3]

In the first place, it is certain that ideas constitute its fundamental portion; for we do not recall anything to ourselves except

[1] Mill's *Analysis*, vol. i. p. 242. [2] Chap. vii. [3] Chap. x.

by an idea, and in order that there may be memory, it is necessary that there should be an idea.

But how is the idea, which forms a portion of the imagination, produced? By association. It is easy to prove it. We have been acquainted with a person of whom we have not thought for a long time; a letter from her, a remark which she liked to make, and which is repeated in our hearing, these are circumstances associated with the idea of the person, and which recall her to our memory. In the same way, when we try to remember something, we run through different series of ideas, with the hope that one or the other will suggest to us the idea which we seek.

So far, then, there is no difficulty. In memory there are ideas, and these ideas are bound together by association. And yet, the memory is not the same thing as the imagination. There is in memory all that there is in imagination, with something more. What is this additional element? Let us remark, in the first place, that there are two cases in memory, the case in which we recall sensations, and the case in which we recall ideas. I remember to have seen George III. deliver a speech on the opening of Parliament: memory of sensations. I remember to have read the report of the sitting in which Napoleon I. opened the French Chambers for the first time: memory of ideas.

In both one and the other case, the recognition of the remembrance as belonging to the past, is a very complex idea, which consists of three principal elements:—1. A state of actual consciousness, which we call the remembering *ego;* 2. A state of consciousness, which we call the perceptive or conceptive *ego;* 3. The successive states of consciousness, which fill up the interval between those two points. Thus, as we follow the author, we thread rapidly in our thought the series of the states of consciousness, intermediary between the moment of the remembrance and the moment at which the event took place, and it is by this rapid movement that a fact appears to us as past, and consequently that memory differs from imagination. Everything then reduces itself to an association of ideas, since there is only the idea of the present *ego* (the *ego* which remembers), the idea of the past *ego* (the word which one remembers), and the idea of a series of states of consciousness which fill up the interval.

This explanation of memory is simple and ingenious; unfortunately it is not without difficulties. The difference between imagination and memory will probably continue to embarrass philosophers for a long time to come, says Mr. Stuart Mill (Note 94), without inquiring whether, as the author has it, we really repeat in our thoughts, though briefly, the whole intermediate series. To explain memory by the *ego*, strongly resembles explaining a thing by that thing itself. For what notion can we have of the *ego* without memory? 'The fact of remembering, that is to say, of having an idea combined with the belief that the corresponding sensation has been actually felt *by me*, this seems to be the elementary fact of *the ego*, the origin and the basis of that idea.'

We will now pass on to the operations which abstract and general notions give us; classification and abstraction.

Classification is the process of the mind by which we gather together the objects of our senses and of our ideas into certain aggregates called classes.[1] But, in what consists this process, by which, forming individuals into classes, separating such and such from others, 'we consider them under a certain idea of unity as being something in themselves'? It has been regarded as a 'mysterious' thing, it has been 'explained mysteriously,' expounded into a 'mystic jargon,' and has caused ages of warfare between the realists and the nominalists. Mr. James Mill explains it solely by means of the word, and of the association of ideas; as follows:—

'The word *man*, we shall say, is first applied to an individual; it is first associated with the idea of that individual, and acquires the power of calling up the idea of him; it is next applied to another individual, and acquires the power of calling up the idea of him; so of another and another, till it has become associated with an indefinite number, and has acquired the power of calling up an indefinite number of those ideas indifferently. What happens? It does call up an indefinite number of the ideas of individuals, as often as it occurs; and calling them up in close connexion, it forms them into a species of com-

[1] Chap. viii.

plex idea. . . . It thus appears that the word *man* is not a word having a very simple idea, as was the opinion of the Realists, nor a word having no idea at all, as was that of the Nominalists; but a word calling up an indefinite number of ideas, by the irresistible laws of association, and forming them into one very complex and indistinct, but not, therefore, unintelligible idea.'[1]

It is with the object of naming, and naming with a greater facility, that we form classes; and it is resemblance which, when we have applied a name to an individual, leads us to apply it to another and another, until the whole forms an aggregate, bound together by the common relation of the aggregate to one single and same name. The great peculiarity of this theory, as Mr. Grote remarks with regret, is that it does not employ, or even name abstraction. It sees in classification only a common name, associated with an indefinite and indistinct aggregate of concrete similar individuals. This is a novelty. But the former philosophers, 'who thought that abstraction is included in classification, were, in my opinion, right,' adds Mr. Grote, 'if we consider classification as a great operation. An aggregate of concretes is neither sufficient to constitute a class in the scientific sense, nor useful in the march of reasoning. We require, besides, *a particular manner of* considering the aggregate (a phrase which Mr. James Mill calls mysterious, but which it would be difficult to exchange for more intelligible terms); one or several elements of a complex idea must be separated from the rest, which has received the name of Abstraction.'

This latter process, regarded by the author as subsidiary, is defined by him, and by every one else, as the act or separating a portion of that which is contained in a complex idea, in order to make of it an object to be considered in itself.[2] Reduced almost entirely to a process of *notation* by means of words, abstraction does not seem to us to be treated in proportion to its importance. Association-psychology is in general more engaged with the means by which the mind adds its ideas and

[1] Mill's *Analysis*, vol. i. pp. 264, 265.

[2] Vol. i. chap. ix. p. 294.

forms them into couples and into masses, than with the processes of decomposition which it applies to them. Nevertheless the mind employs not only addition but subtraction. If it composes it also decomposes; if it unites the similar, it divides the dissimilar. How? No clear answer on this point.

IV.

We shall now see how the author of the *Analysis* employs association of ideas to explain various states of consciousness, which he comprises under the common name of belief.[1]

It is difficult to treat separately of memory, belief, and judgment; for a portion of memory is contained in the term belief, as is a portion of judgment. The different cases of belief may be classed under these heads: belief in events or in real existences; belief in testimony; belief in the truth of propositions.

1. Belief in real events or existences, may have for their object the *past*, the *present*, the *future*.

(1.) Let us begin with the belief which has a present fact for its object.

Here is a first case: that in which the fact is actually and immediately present to my senses. I believe that this is a rose. This belief implies, in the first place, belief in my sensations, and to believe in my sensations is purely and simply another mode of saying that I have sensations. But to believe in external objects, is not simply to believe in my present sensations. It is that, and something more. It is that something more which is the object of our search. In seeing a rose I have the sensation

---

[1] We collect in the following table the various forms of belief, classified and explained by the author:—

Beliefs having for their object:			
	1. Real facts.	Actual.	Present to the senses: Ex. There is a rose.
			Not present to the senses: Ex. St. Paul's Church exists.
		Past.	Ex. I have seen a certain theatre burning.
		Future.	Ex. It will be daylight to-morrow.
	2. Testimony.	Ex. The great fire of London.	
	3. The truth of propositions.	Identical: Ex. Man is a reasonable animal.	
		Non-identical: Ex. Man is an animal.	

of colour, but I have, besides, that of its distance, and its figure or form. Those ideas, which are due to touch, are associated with that of colour. Others, such as scent, taste, and resistance, may associate themselves with these. My idea of a rose is thus formed by the fusion of several ideas, among which one or two are predominant (colour and figure). Now I consider my sensations as an *effect*, and I believe in something, which is their *cause*, and it is to that cause, and not to the effect, that the name of objects is appropriated. 'To each of the sensations which we have of a particular object, we join in our imagination a cause; to these various causes we join a cause common to all, and we mark it with the name of *substratum*.'[1] In short, we experience *clusters* of sensations; these sensations awaken the idea of antecedents (qualities) which awaken the idea of an antecedent common to all qualities (the substratum) and the substratum with its qualities we call *the object*.[2] Thus then in our belief in external objects there are two things: first, a cluster of ideas melted into a whole by association; and then the idea of an antecedent (cause) of this whole.

This belief then implies a theory of cause, which the author states very simply. Let a fact be *B* and an antecedent *A*: if their association is given as inseparable, and the order of their associations as constant, we shall say that *A* is the cause of *B*.

Here is a second case: that in which the fact is not actually present to my senses. I believe that St. Paul's, which I have seen this morning, still exists, which is equivalent to saying that if I, or one of my fellows, were placed in a certain part of London, we should have the sensation of St. Paul's Cathedral. This belief implies the remembrance whose nature has been examined under the title of memory, and then an extension of past facts into the future, which we shall study presently.

(2.) The belief which has for its object a past fact attaches itself to memory. When I say that I recall the burning of Drury Lane Theatre, my saying that I *recall* that incident, and that I believe it, is exactly the same thing; these are two indiscernible conditions of consciousness.

---

[1] Vol. i. p. 351.

[2] Vol. ii. p. 100.

(3.) The belief which has future facts for its object is the groundwork of that process of the mind which is called induction. The author thinks that it also may be resolved into a simple association. 'The anticipation of the future by means of the past, far from being a phenomenon *sui generis*, is included in one of the most general laws of the human mind.'. When, therefore, Dugald Stewart and others exalt it into an object of admiration, into a prodigy, into a thing which is not included in any general law, and that they tell us it can only be referred to an instinct; which is equivalent to saying to nothing at all—the term instinct merely signifying, in every case, our ignorance,—they only show their powerlessness to bring the phenomena of mind under the great comprehensive law of association. They seem to have had a most inexplicable and most anti-philosophical aversion to admit this law in its wide meaning; as if the simplicity, by virtue of which a certain law is included in a higher law, and so on, even to a small number in which all appear to be included, ought not to be found in the world of mind, as it is found in the world of matter.[1]

Whatever may be thought of the following explanation, it must at least be acknowledged that the author has seen very clearly that a theory of induction is in fact a theory of cause.

We cannot, he says, have an idea of the future, because, strictly speaking, the future is a non-entity, and we cannot have an idea of nothing. When we speak of the future, we speak in reality of the past. I believe that the sun will rise to-morrow, that there will be vehicles in the streets of London, that the tide will be full at London Bridge, etc.; these are ideas of the past. 'Our idea of the future and our idea of the past is the same thing, with this difference, that in the one case there is anticipation, and in the other there is retrospection.' What is this anticipation?

The fundamental law of association consists in this, that when two things have been frequently found together, one recalls the other. Among these habitual conjunctions, there is none which interests us more than that of the antecedent and the consequent.

But among the numerous antecedents and consequents which

[1] Vol. i. pp. 376, 377.

form the matter of our experience, some present them in a constant, others in a variable order. Thus, I have seen a crow flying from the east to the west, as well as from the west to the east. On the contrary, a stone thrown into the air will not go from low to high as well as from high to low; it follows an immoveable direction. Thence an association of ideas whose order is also invariable. Thus the idea of every fact awakens the idea of constant antecedent (which produces it) and the idea of constant consequents (which it produces). This great law of our nature shows us immediately in what manner an idea of the future is produced. Night has always been followed by morning. The idea of night is followed by that of morning; the idea of morning by that of the incidents of the morning (the vehicles in the streets of London) and of the entire day. Then there is the idea of to-morrow, to which another to-morrow succeeds, and an indefinite number of those 'to-morrows' compose the complex idea of the future.

But, it may be said, that is the *idea* of to-morrow, and not belief in to-morrow; tell us, what is that belief? I reply, that not only you have the idea of to-morrow, but you have it in an inseparable manner. Now it is to this case of indissoluble association of ideas, and to nothing else, that you apply the name of belief.

2. There is no occasion for us to linger over belief in testimony. It also belongs to association. In short, I refer all the words (written or spoken) of my fellows to the facts and ideas which they represent: this is an association. Now, our belief in facts is founded upon our own experience, and this form of belief has already been explained.[1]

3. A third class of beliefs is that in the truth of propositions, 'in other words, in verbal truths.' The process by which this belief is produced is called *judgment*. Proposition is the form of

[1] This explanation of belief in testimony does not seem satisfactory. 'The belief in testimony is derived from the primary credulity of the mind, in certain instances left intact under the wear and tear of adverse experience Hardly any fact of the human mind is better attested than the primitive disposition to receive all testimony with unflinching credence. It never occurs to the child to question any statement made to it, until some positive force on the side of scepticism has been developed.'—Bain's *Notes to Analysis*, p. 386.

affirmation. 'Affirmation essentially consists in applying two marks to the same thing. Example: Man is a reasonable animal.'

'Or else names of which one has less and the other more extension, are applied to the same thing. Example: Man is an animal.'

In the first case, the equivalence of the two words is acknowledged by association: *man* and *reasonable animal* are two words for one same condition of consciousness; they are associated as marks with a same group of ideas.

In the second case, the association is more complex; that is all the difference. Man is the name of a cluster of ideas suggested by association (see on this subject, *classification*); animal is also the name of a cluster which includes the first cluster and others besides.

Thus, sensations, ideas, associations of ideas; the whole varied, complicated, aggregated, crossed, grouped in a thousand ways,—this is the whole mechanism of the human mind.

CHAPTER II.

ABSTRACT TERMS.

General terms.—1. Of general terms—2. Space, time, movement, the infinite.

I.

'SOME words which require a special explanation,' is the title of a long chapter in the *Analysis*,[1] devoted to the obscure and disputed questions of time, space, motion, etc. 'Under this modest title,' says Mr. John Stuart Mill, 'this chapter presents us with a series of discussions on some of the most profound and intricate questions in the whole of metaphysics. The title would give a very incomplete idea of the difficulty and importance of the speculations which it contains. It is almost as if a treatise upon chemistry had been given, as an explanation of the words air, water, potass, sulphuric acid, etc.'

---

[1] Chap. xiv. pp. 1 to 176, vol. ii.

It is really a study of the origin and the mode of the formation of the most general ideas, which we find under this title. The transition period to which the work belongs makes itself particularly evident in this portion of it: the author is still wavering between the too verbal method of the eighteenth century, and the more concrete analysis, which shall be that of his successors. We find in it, in the condition of sketches, and of foreseen solutions, a number of explanations which have been given in a clearer and more complete manner by contemporaries.

One of its principal merits, in our opinion, is that it endeavours to show that certain abstract terms appear to be inexplicable, only because they are too distant from their concretes. Perhaps it has never been sufficiently borne in mind that abstraction has its degrees, as number has its powers: red is an abstract, *colour* is more abstract, *attribute* is still more abstract. This growth in abstraction, very easy to prove in this instance, is not always so. But if philosophy should arrive at noting the ascending degrees of abstraction with sufficient exactness, as arithmetic determines the growing powers of a number; if it should succeed, as far as the nature of things permits, in doing for quality that which has been done for quantity; if it should succeed in resolving the highest abstractions in inferior abstractions, and these into concretes, it seems to us that many vain questions and factitious difficulties would disappear. Here and there some such attempts are made by our author, but they are very incomplete. Now, so long as precise verification shall be wanting, sensualism will in vain claim for itself simplicity, truthful-seeming, and above all, that most scientific characteristic, the elimination of everything supernatural; the question will always remain an open one between its adversaries and itself.

II.

Under the name *Relative Terms*, the author treats of the various ideas of relation. Their essential character is to exist only by couples or pairs, such as *high* and *low*, *like* and *unlike*, *antecedent* and *consequent*. These couples are suggested to us by association.

Under the name *Primitive Terms*, he treats of the ideas which are generally called negative.

As it is almost impossible to analyse exactly an analysis, we shall not try to follow the author in his examination of the ideas of resemblance and difference, antecedent and consequent, position in space, order in time, quantity, quality, etc. We shall find the substance of all this when we have to deal with the other philosophers. Thus Mill seems to have partly seen that which Bain and Spencer will hereafter show us more clearly, that the fact of primitive consciousness consists, in the first place, in the perception of a difference, and then in the perception of a resemblance.

Let us restrict ourselves to the important ideas of space, infinite, time, and motion.

Space.—Let us remark, firstly, that concrete terms are connotative, abstract terms are non-connotative; that is to say, that concrete terms, in expressing one or several qualities which is their *notation*, or principal signification, connote the object to which these qualities belong. Thus the concrete 'red' always connotes something which is red, such as a rose. Now, how is the abstract formed? It is formed of the concrete, and it notes precisely that which is noted by the concrete, *but rejecting the connotation.* Thus, in *red*, take away the connotation and you have *redness;* in *hot*, take away the connotation and you have *heat.* Red signifies something red, redness signifies redness without something. There is the same difference between the concrete extended and the abstract extension. What the concrete extended is with its connotation, the abstract extension is without that connotation. We have then to explain in what this connotation consists. When we say *extended*, signifying something of extent, we mean one or other of these three things,—a line, a surface, a volume. We owe these ideas to different sensations, among which we must count in the first place those due to touch and to muscular action. The sensation or sensations which we mark by the word resistant, seem to be the only ones connoted by the word extended. Thus the essential connotation of the concrete 'extended' is resistant, and nothing else. It is true that those who enjoy the faculty of seeing, cannot conceive of a thing as extended without conceiving of it as coloured; they unite the visual qualities to the tactile qualities, which even become predominant by association. But for the man who is born blind there exists only the sensation of the tactile qualities, that is to say, resistance.

Now, we can understand what extension is in all its cases. Linear extension is the idea of a line without the connotation; that is to say, without the idea of resistance. Extension in superficies is the idea of a surface without the connotation (resistance). Extension in volume, is the idea of a volume without the connotation (resistance). But a volume without resistance, what is it? The place for a volume. And this place, what is it? A portion of *space*, or, more exactly, space itself without limit.

Infinite.—The idea of infinite is comprised in that of space. 'When the word infinite is not employed metaphorically, as when we speak of the infinite perfections of God (in which case it is not a name of an idea, but a name for a lack of ideas), it is applied only to number, extension, and duration.'

We augment numbers by adding one to one, one to two, etc.; and by giving a name to each aggregate. It is the association of ideas that constitutes this process. Number is limited, consequently not infinite. Number is the negation of the infinite, as black is the negation of white. The word infinite, in this case, is only a mark for that condition of consciousness in which the idea of one more is intimately associated with every number that presents itself. In short, the abstract term is the particular idea without the connotation.

We also apply this word to extension by the same process. A strict irresistible association of ideas makes us conceive of the continuous increase of a line, of a surface, of a volume. 'That which we call the idea of an infinite extension, and which some call *the necessary* idea, simply signifies that the idea of an additional portion is necessarily awakened; that is to say, by indissoluble association, and that we cannot prevent it.'

The idea of infinite, which has been called a simple idea, is in reality an extremely complex idea. But the association which is its foundation is so close that it appears to us a unit.

Time.—Space is a comprehensive word, comprising all positions, or the totality of the synchronical order. Time is a comprehensive word, comprising all successions or the totality of the successive order.

The idea of time is an idea of successions; it consists in that, and nothing more. Let us now recall how a concrete may be changed into an abstract, by taking away the connotation, and let us apply this doctrine to the case of successions. When a man recalls the peculiarities of a battle in which he commanded, a succession of sensations or ideas cross his mind. In this succession, as in every other, there are always ideas, past, present, and future. Take away the connotation of 'something present,' 'something past,' and of 'something future,' and you have past, present, and future. But these three things are *time.* It is an abstract term, covering the signification of three distinct abstracts.

Motion.—The word 'motion' is abstract of 'moving.' What we have to look for, are the sensations by virtue of which we call a body 'moving,' motion being simply moving without the connotation. In the idea of a moving body we find the following elements: the idea of a line (for a body always moves according to a line, right or otherwise), and the idea of succession. All these ideas are complex, some of them are very complex. United in one idea (motion), they compose one of the most complex of our ideas.

It is important to observe that, though it is most frequently the eye which informs us of motion, it is not from the sensations of sight that the idea of motion is derived. It is only by an association of ideas that we imagine that we *see* motion. This idea comes to us, like that of extent, *from the muscular and tactile sensations.* A man born blind has the idea of motion just as we have it. Our ideas of extension and of motion are derived, without any doubt, from the action of our own body.

I touch something, and I have the sensation of resistance, the idea of resistance being that which is fundamental in every aggregate to which we give the name of object. In this case there are two things: the object touched, the finger which touches. Here is another case: I lent an action to my finger in touching the object. This action implies certain sensations; I combine them with the object and with my finger, and thus I have two ideas: the object extended, the finger moved. Our idea of a moving body consists of a series of successive sensations ; a sum in which the present condition is united, thanks to memory, with all the anterior conditions. And when we have familiarized ourselves with the application of the term *moved*, as a connotative term to various objects, it is easy, in the various cases, to suppress the connotation, and thus we have the abstract—motion.[1]

CHAPTER III.

THE FEELINGS AND THE WILL.

Feeling and Will.—1. The insufficiency of English Psychology on this point—2. Feelings—3. Free Will—Mr. John Stuart Mill.

THE doctrines of the English experimental school on the psychology of the feelings, the emotions, the affective phenomena in general, do not seem to be so precise or so complete as upon the question of sensations and ideas. By some it is not handled at all, by others, for instance Mr. Herbert Spencer and Mr. John Stuart Mill, it has been as yet barely touched. Two only have attempted to treat it profoundly—our author and Mr. Bain. The work of the latter, probably the fullest and deepest which has yet appeared on this subject, seems to us nevertheless the weakest portion of his labours.[2]

Whence arises this inferiority? Must we believe that among philosophers there exists a certain tendency to neglect the affective phenomena and to study the psychology of the mind more than that of the heart? May we not think that it is rather the complexity, the heterogeneousness of these phenomena which renders their analysis so difficult? Judgment, reasoning, abstract conception, association of ideas, are facts naturally simple and above

---

Mr. John Stuart Mill points out that this explanation is to be found in other words, but identical in meaning, in the works of Messrs. Bain and Herbert Spencer.

See chap. iii., Mr. Bain.

all *homogeneous.* But a passion, a feeling, an emotion, most frequently comprehends very various elements; firstly, physiological phenomena, variable according to organization, temperament, sex, etc., but which nevertheless play a preponderating part, and afterwards a condition of pleasure or pain, which is, properly speaking, the affective element; finally, an idea, a notion; for the sensible phenomenon cannot be absolutely separated and detached from all knowledge; a pain envelops the idea of that which causes it, an emotion implies the knowledge of its object. The ideal of psychology would evidently be to be able to explain all sentiments by a double method of synthesis and analysis; to be able to trace back a complex emotion to one more simple, and thus to arrive gradually at an irreducible fact; or, on the contrary, to start from the simplest affective phenomena, and to show how, by addition, aggregates of more and more complex emotions are found, and thus theoretically to reconstitute the reality. But we are very far from that ideal. The fundamental irreducible emotions are not yet even determined. Mr. Bain gives nine. We shall see hereafter what this classification is, and what may be thought of it. Mr. Herbert Spencer, who has been especially occupied with the question of method, takes the point of view of comparative psychology. He wishes to have the most general emotions determined; in the first place, those which are common to all animals; secondly, those which are common to us and to the inferior races; then those which are proper to us, and the order of their evolution. Our author, exclusively occupied with the human point of view, has chiefly sought to show how the complex emotions come by association from the simple emotions. The method then remains the same, and the doctrine of association is also at the bottom of the study of the feelings. The mode of exposition is clear, lucid, simple,—perhaps simple to excess, which is very near inexactness;—for, though clearness and simplicity are eminently philosophical sentiments, when we see that an author replies to a complex question by a precise formula, and pretends to embrace all phenomena, and to clear up all obscurities, it is well to be on our guard against some errors.

An exposition of the physiological conditions of the sentiments and the emotions is wanting in this work. We also look in vain for a study of the appetites and the instincts, and the chapter on the Will suffers accordingly. In our opinion these deficiencies are partly explained by the epoch at which the book appeared. Later psychologists have largely supplemented it.

II.

The phenomena of thought, says the author, have long been divided into two classes: intellectual faculties, and active faculties. In the first, sensations and ideas are considered as simply existing; in the second, they are considered as exciting to action.

We have seen that those of the first class may be formed into more or less complex groups, and that they succeed each other, following certain laws. Those of the second class are equally capable of being formed into groups, and of succeeding each other, following certain laws. So far, then, there is an agreement between the two classes of phenomena. It remains for us now to seek the differences proper to the last.[1]

All our sensations are agreeable, disagreeable, or indifferent. We desire to prolong the first; to put an end to the second; as to the third, we do not seek either to prolong or to abridge them. The author limits himself to saying that the indifferent sensations are probably the most numerous, without studying them.

Pleasure and pain,—these are the two primitive facts. But the facts are *causes*, and these causes are of two sorts: proximate and distant. The bitter medicine which I swallow is the *immediate* or proximate cause of my sensation of disgust: the sentence of the judge is the *distant* cause of the execution of a criminal.

This is not all. We have seen that all sensations may be preserved and reproduced by the mind, and that these mental reproductions of sensations are called ideas. So every sensation of pleasure or of pain may be reproduced by the mind, and thus ideas of pleasure and pain be formed.

An idea of pleasure or of pain is a very clear condition of

[1] Vol. ii. chap. xvi.

consciousness, familiar to us all. But the idea of a pleasure is not a pleasure, and the idea of a pain is not a pain. The idea of burning one's hand does not cause pain, the idea of eating sugar does not cause pleasure. The idea of a pleasure is called *desire*, the idea of a pain is called *aversion*. Agreeable or disagreeable sensations, and the ideas of those sensations, are not only actual. They may be related to the past by memory, to the future by anticipation. We know the mechanism of memory. As for 'the anticipation of the future, it consists in the same series of associations, with this difference, that in the memory the association of states of consciousness which converts the idea into memory goes from the consequent to the antecedent, that is to say, backwards; whereas, in the case of anticipation, association goes from the antecedent to the consequent, that is to say, forwards.'

When an agreeable sensation is conceived of as future, but without one's being certain of it, this state of consciousness is called *hope;* if one is certain of it, it is called *joy*. When a disagreeable sensation is conceived of as future, but uncertain, that state of consciousness is called *fear;* if it is certain, it is called *sorrow*. An agreeable sensation, or the idea of that sensation, joined to the idea of the cause which produces it, engenders *affection* or love for that cause. A disagreeable sensation, joined to the idea of its cause, engenders *antipathy* or hatred for that cause.[2]

The causes of our pleasures and of our pains are, as we have already seen, proximate or remote. According to the author, the immediate causes are much the less interesting. This apparent paradox is the necessary result of one of the most general of the laws of our nature; those immediate causes never having a very extensive field of operations, the idea of them is associated with only a limited number of pleasures or pains. Compare,

[1] Vol. ii. chap. xx.

[2] Love is nothing but joy accompanied by the idea of an exterior cause. Hate is nothing but sadness accompanied by the idea of an exterior cause. Spinoza, *Ethics*, iii. prop. 13. Compare the Third Book of the *Ethics* with Mill's *Analysis*, props. 13, 14, 16, 17, 18, 19, and Appendix to Book III.

for example, an immediate cause of pleasure, food, with a remote cause, money, and you will see that the latter plays a preponderating part, because it is an instrument calculated to procure for us almost every pleasure. 'When the idea of one object is associated with a hundred times more pleasure than another idea, it is generally a hundred times more pleasant.' Thus the author confines himself almost entirely to these remote causes, which he ranges under three heads :—

1. Riches, power, dignity, and their contraries.
2. Our fellows : relatives, friends, fellow-citizens, etc.
3. Objects which are known as beautiful and sublime.

These remote causes of our pleasures and our pains may be called egoistical causes, social causes, and æsthetic causes. Let us examine them.

One remarkable thing is, first of all, to be noticed : the three above-named great causes of our pleasure agree in this, that they are all the means of procuring for us the services of our fellow-creatures, and themselves contribute to our pleasures in hardly any other way. It is obvious from this remark, that the services of our fellow-creatures are the great cause of all our pleasures ; since wealth, power, and dignity, which appear to most people to sum up the means of human happiness, are nothing more than means of procuring those services. This is a fact of the highest importance, both in morals and in philosophy.[1]

1. The author easily shows that wealth is a means of procuring the services of others, by remunerating them ; that power is a means of bending them to submission through hope or fear ; that dignities procure for us their respect, not only in outward appearance, but as manifested by their actions.[2]

It is, in the first place, however, to be observed, that wealth, power, and dignity afford, perhaps, the most remarkable of all examples of that extraordinary case of association where the means to an end, means valuable to us solely on account of this end, not only engross more of our attention than the end itself, but actually supplant it in our affections.

[1] Mill's *Analysis*, vol. ii. p. 207. [2] *Ibid.* p. 215.

How few men seem to be at all concerned about their fellow-creatures! How completely are the lives of most men absorbed in the pursuit of wealth and ambition! With how many men does the love of family, of country, of mankind, appear completely impotent when opposed to their love of wealth, or of power! This is an effect of misguided association, which requires the greatest attention in education and morals.

2. Wealth, power, and dignity being the source of such powerful affections to our fellow-men, it would be surprising if our fellows themselves were not a source of affections to us. They are a cause of various pleasures, whether individually or in groups. Friendship, Kindness, Family, Country, Party, Humanity, such are the six somewhat confused titles under which the author classes them. The object of his analysis is to show that our strongest sentiments are aggregates, and that hence is their strength; that they are formed by juxtaposition, or, as it is better expressed, by the fusion of the simple sentiments; that affection being the result of a pleasure, a profound affection results from a great sum of pleasures experienced. In order to understand this doctrine more clearly, suppose an unknown person to render you a small service,—he causes you a pleasure, and the idea of this pleasure makes the unknown person an object of affection to you—an affection as slight as the pleasure caused. But if you come to know this man better, so that his mind, his heart, his society, his confidence, all become to you the cause of so many pleasures, and that these are repeated during many years, a strong affection will be produced, the result of a crowd of sentiments of affection, which are themselves the result of a crowd of sentiments of pleasure. Everything is thus explained in final analysis by association.

Let us now see how the author accounts for one of our most general sentiments, the love of parents for children.[1]

In the first place, it is well known that the pleasures and pains of others affect us; that is to say, associate themselves with the ideas of our own pleasures and pains. This phenomenon has

[1] Vol. ii. ch. xxi. section 2.

been correctly called *sympathy*. Now, a child can, like every other person, excite this sentiment in us.

Moreover, a man regards his child as a cause, much more certain than any other, of pleasures and of pains. To him his child is an object of great interest; in other words, a succession of interesting ideas,—ideas of pleasure or of pain,—associate themselves with him. The vivacity and simplicity of a child's expressions, of his ways and attitudes, give him a special power of awakening our sympathy. As the child is, besides, in a state of entire dependence on his parents, who must incessantly watch over his safety, the idea of him is therefore constantly associated with those of pleasures and of pains, in addition to which it awakens an idea of power which is always agreeable. Another source of pleasant association is the following: It is a fact of daily experience, that we come to love a person to whom we have frequently done good. This is not only true in the case of our fellows, but also in that of animals. By the mere fact that they have been the object of repeated acts of kindness on our part, they become an object of affection to us. The idea of those individuals, united to that of the pleasures which we experience, form a composite idea, an affection.

Every time a man is placed in the circumstances which produce these associations, he feels the paternal affection even when parentage does not exist; as in the case of a husband, who, being ignorant of the infidelity of his wife, loves the child of another man as though he were his own son.

In very rich and in very poor families, circumstances are but little favourable to those associations from which the affection of parents results.

In the case of extreme (not moderate) poverty, the circumstances which lead to the association of the idea of the child are either wanting, or are neutralized by the necessity for ceaseless toil, for being but little occupied with him, etc.

In the case of extreme opulence, parents are engrossed by the pleasures and obligations of society, etc. As they attend but little to his education, they can associate but few pains or pleasures with his idea. Thence comes an imperfect affection.

3. Objects called beautiful or sublime, and their contraries,

are a third source of pleasures or pains to us. These æsthetic emotions [1] are also referable to an association. Regarded as a whole, feeling for the sublime and for the beautiful appears perfectly simple.[2] It is by taking their stand on these appearances, many, even eminent, philosophers have argued that a particular sense was necessary to explain their existence. This apparent simplicity is only an example of that mode of association which unites several ideas so closely that they appear to be no longer several ideas but one alone.

A sound, a colour, any object is called beautiful or sublime, according to the ideas which it awakens in us by association. Thus the sounds which associate themselves with ideas of power, majesty, and profound melancholy, are generally sublime; such as the roar of a tempest, the fall of a cataract, the tones of the organ. Sounds of another kind produce the feeling of the beautiful,—a water-fall, the murmurs of a stream, the bells of a flock of sheep.[3]

---

[1] It is the custom of English philosophers to comprehend in their study of the affective phenomena that of the pleasures and pains which are caused us by the beautiful and the ugly, by good and evil. They thus include Æsthetics and Morals among their psychological ground-work. The feeling of the Beautiful and that of the Good admits of manifestations as varied and important as those of the Fine Arts, Manners, Legislation, etc., and we cannot be astonished at the importance accorded to them. But should not the same be granted to the religious sentiment? Our author does not mention it. Mr. Bain, generally so thorough in his treatment, disposes of it in two pages (*Emotions and Will*, ch. vi.) The Germans study this point. See Wundt, vol. ii. p. 218 to 311.

[2] Vol. ii. chap. xxi. p. 250.

[3] The author, who relies here upon Alison's theories, does not say in what the associations consist which awaken the feeling of the Beautiful. The examples given seem rather to refer to the *Agreeable*. Mr. John Stuart Mill (Note 48) directs us to Mr. Ruskin on this point, saying that he supplies unconscious evidence in favour of the theory of association. According to Mr. Ruskin, 'we call all those objects beautiful and sublime which express these ideas :—Infinite, Unity, Repose, Symmetry, Purity, Measure, Adaptation to an end.' Is not this saying that the things which excite the emotion of the Sublime and Beautiful, are those which are naturally associated with certain ideas profoundly rooted in us?' The above list is neither exact nor complete; but that does not affect the correctness of the doctrine.

White pleases us, because it recalls day and light; black displeases us, because it reminds us of darkness. These associations vary according to different countries, and are not absolute. In China, white is the colour of mourning, and consequently is far from being considered beautiful. In Spain, black is liked, because it is the colour of the garments worn by the grandees.[1]

A more true and weighty remark than the preceding is, that those who do not associate any agreeable idea with sounds or colours have no feeling for the beautiful. 'Children wait long before they evince any sensibility to the beauty of sound. And the majority of men are totally indifferent to a great number of sounds which we call beautiful. To the peasant the curfew marks simply the hour of evening, the sheep-bells are merely a sign that there is a flock in the vicinity, the noise of a cascade only announces a fall of water. Give him the associations which cultivated imaginations join to these sounds, and he will infallibly feel their beauty.'[2]

III.

When the idea of an action emanating from us (cause) associates itself with the idea of a pleasure (effect), a particular state of mind is produced, characterized by tendency to action, and which is properly called *motive.* A motive is the idea of a pleasure which may be attained; a particular motive is the idea of a particular pleasure which may be attained (*Fragment on Mackintosh*, Note 49). Motive, according to the author, means aim, end, term.

Not only pleasures and pains, but also the *causes* of pleasures and of pains, become motives of action. These causes, associating themselves in our mind with the pleasures and pains which they produce, become, in the first place, agreeable or disagreeable in themselves; afterwards, associating themselves with such of our actions as may put them into execution, they become very strong motives. Thus it is that wealth, power, dignities, our fellows, the

1 Might it not just as well be said that black is the colour of the garments of the grandees, because Spaniards like black?

2 Vol. ii. p 240.

beautiful and sublime objects which, as we have seen, have become *affections* through association, become also *motives.*

We can now explain the phenomena classed under the titles moral sense, and moral faculties or affections. Although many of the psychologists with whom we are engaged have a marked tendency towards sketching a treatise on morals, we shall be very brief on this point, for though psychology touches upon Morals, it is not Morals.[1]

The actions from which men derive advantage, have all been classed under four titles,—Prudence, Fortitude, Justice, Beneficence.

In the present state of education, the praise and blame of most men are very erroneously bestowed, with great precipitation, commonly in excess upon small occasions, with little regard to its justice; blame being very often inflicted where applause is due, and applause lavished where blame ought to be bestowed. When education is good, no point of morality will be reckoned of more importance than the distribution of praise and blame; no act will be considered more immoral than the misapplication of them.[2]

Motives lead us to the Will.

The work on the Will, though very insufficient in many respects, is valuable, especially on account of the questions which it indicates, and the method which it inaugurates. When we compare two Analyses of the Will, one written by Mr. Mill, the other by Mr. Bain, with an interval of thirty years between them; when we see how far the last surpasses the first in the amount of facts observed, in precision, in descriptive exactitude, we are forced to conceive a good opinion of the experimental method in psychology,—of a method which, taking up the task where the forerunners had laid it down, profits by acquired results, by the progress of years, by discoveries, ever adding to them, and thus causes the science to grow, instead of constantly beginning over again.

One of the principal merits of the author of the Analysis

[1] Mill's *Analysis*, vol. ii. p. 280, line 15.
[2] Vol. ii. p. 300, line 16.

is that he saw the necessity for studying the development of voluntary power.[1] He understood the falseness of the idea of a Will being, so to speak, armed at all points, whose first act would be to command imperiously, and to be instantly obeyed. He had endeavoured, though imperfectly, to show the first efforts and the first conquests of the Will. He may be reproached with errors in his choice of examples, with confusion between voluntary acts and acts which are purely reflex, into which a more advanced physiologist would not have fallen; but the fundamental fact remains, that he perceived the method.

The author, though not absolutely silent on the subject of free-will, barely touches it, and does not use the word at all. No doubt, 'an Analysis of the phenomena of the human mind,' ought to limit itself to facts; but liberty, whether one regards it as real or illusory, is also a question of fact, and it is not possible to relegate it to the domain of Metaphysics.

In the only passage in which he touches the question (ch. xxiv. p. 328), the author says that a false conception of the idea of cause has obscured the 'controversy' on that state of the mind which we call will. Will was invariably and with reason regarded as the cause of action; unfortunately an element which has been found to be entirely imaginary, was also always regarded as making a portion of the idea of that cause. In the sequence of events called cause and effect, a third thing was imagined, called force or power, which was not the cause, but emanated from it. A recent philosopher[2] has shown incontestably that cause and power are one; and thus everything is reduced to inquiring into 'What is the state of mind which immediately precedes an act?'

We will not analyse this chapter on the Will, as it is our chief aim to make *results* known, and we shall find them more fully stated by Mr. Bain.

[1] We find the study carried out by Mr. Bain.

[2] The philosopher to whom the author alludes, without naming him, is Thomas Brown, in his *Inquiry into the Relation of Cause and Effect.*

MR. JOHN STUART MILL.

MR. JOHN STUART MILL is well known in France. His reputation as an economist; his works on politics and social questions; his various translations; an analysis of his Logic, which the author M. Taine in his *Etude sur Stuart Mill* pronounces 'masterly;' the attacks of his numerous adversaries;—all these have contributed to spread abroad his fame. No name has been more frequently quoted among us in contemporary polemics. Unfortunately for philosophy, many of those who have spoken of him, seem to have known him only vaguely and at second-hand. They have contented themselves, in general, with making him out to be an adherent of Auguste Comte, and classing him among the 'positivists,' which is merely a quick and ready mode of judging a cause without hearing it.

The word positivism, which is so frequently used in these days, is a very vague term, with an apparent precision about it; it is applied to ways of philosophizing which are in reality quite different, and it confounds with the pure disciples of Comte men who have more than once insisted upon their independence of thought.

Strictly speaking, there ought to be only one positivism, that of Auguste Comte, as there can be only one true Cartesianism, that of Descartes, or one true Kantism, that of Kant. But, since the doctrine of Comte, taken in its totality, is, as every one knows, rather incoherent, since his religion and his politics have done nothing but furnish arms to his opponents, and grieve his admirers, it is easily to be understood that another positivism than his has been formed. This positivism, which may be called orthodox, eliminating the subjective portion of the founder's work, restricts itself to some rigorously fixed fundamental principles, which it declares invariable; such as the suppression of all researches beyond phenomena; the law of the three conditions, theological, metaphysical, positive; the division of the sciences into concrete and abstract; and the hierarchical classification of the abstract sciences according to their order of increasing complexity and decreasing generality, thus, mathematics, astronomy, physics, chemistry, biology, sociology. Any one who does not admit these principles, with all that logically flows from them, is rejected by the School.

Mr. Mill is of the number. If he admits the law of the three states (*Comte and Positivism*, p. 33); if he eliminates all transcendental researches, it is because he holds that 'the positive mode of thinking is not necessarily a negation of the supernatural.' He thus restores to sentiment or to individual faith that which he cuts off from science. On questions of origin, he says, the philosopher is free to form any opinion he pleases; this is not one of the points on which agreement is necessary, '*but it is a mistake on the part of M. Comte to leave no open questions.*' As for the classification of the sciences, a capital point with this school, Mr. Mill, while doing justice to Auguste Comte, reproaches him for his omission of psychology and all belonging to it, logic, the theory of the criterion, etc., for his disdain of political economy,—in short, he declares that he has failed in his most ambitious work, saying 'that he has not created sociology' (*ibid.* pp. 70 and 130), which in the absence of a psychology could not but be imperfect. We have nothing to do with this discussion. But does it not seem strange that Mr. Mill, while differing so materially from them, should be classed by public opinion, at least in France, among the positivists? Whence arises this confusion? We account for it thus.

A general tendency, a method of investigation, a mode of thought which may be described as scientific, and even empirical, is common to many of the fine intellects of the seventeenth century. It consists in circumscribing as closely as possible the domain of hypothesis, and of admitting as an object of science only that which may be observed as a fact, or formulated as a law, and *verified.* This mode of thought, the work of several generations of philosophers and *savants*, and among whose promoters Mr. Mill names Bacon, Descartes, Newton,

Hume, Kant, Bentham, and even Hamilton, existed before positivism, and is not in any respect the creation of Auguste Comte.

The foundation of M. Comte's philosophy is in no way peculiar to him, but the general property of the age, and far as yet from being universally accepted, even by thoughtful minds. The philosophy called Positive is not a recent invention of M. Comte, but a simple adherence to the traditions of all the great scientific minds whose discoveries have made the human race what it is. M. Comte has never presented it in any other light. But he has made the doctrine his own by his method of treating it.[1]

Positivism is, then, a form of the modern scientific spirit, but it is only a particular form of it, it is only a wave of the great current, it is one species in the genus. Everything which the scientific mind supposes, exists in positivism, but with something more,—these are the fundamental principles which constitute the *credo* of the school. Between the positive mind, and positivism, we, for our part, discern as much difference as between the philosophic mind, and philosophy, that is to say, between that which remains and that which passes away. But as positivism is very categorical in its negations, very decided in its dogmas, very clear in its formulas, it is more imposing than the less affirmative method of the purely scientific mind. Thence the general confusion which so often makes of a *savant* or a philosopher a positivist in spite of himself.

On the contrary, that which constitutes, in our opinion, one of the principal merits of Mr. Mill, is liberty of investigation, without which there is no philosophical spirit; the taste for polemics and discussion which makes him rank so high the dialectics of a great idealist—Plato—which he values above all as a method of research; the largeness of mind which accepts all objections, the philosophical good faith with which he plainly declares what is, in his opinion, the value of each of his solutions, without concealing its incompleteness and insufficiency.

M. Littré objects to Mr. Mill's psychological and logical point of view, as opposed to the objective point of view of the positive

[1] Mill's *Auguste Comte and Positivism.*

school. He also objects to his definition of philosophy as 'the science of man as an intelligent, moral, and social being.' To us, who have only to treat of the psychologist, this is a good augury. Continuing the tradition of James Mill and of Brown, but adding to them the results of half a century of progress, he recognises them for his masters, and not Comte, from whom he has been supposed, by a retrospective illusion, to derive his inspiration. He says, in his *Examination of Hamilton's Philosophy* (ch. xiv. p. 266, note 2), 'More than half of my *System of Logic*, comprehending all its fundamental doctrines, was written before I had seen the *Course of Positive Philosophy*. My work is indebted to Comte for several important ideas, but a short list would exhaust the chapters and even the pages which contain them. As to the general doctrine (that which eliminates first or final causes), it was familiar to me in my childhood, thanks to the teaching of my father, who had learned it where M. Comte learned it, that is to say, in the method of the physical sciences, and the writings of former philosophers. Since Hume, this doctrine has been the common property of the philosophic world. Since Brown, it has entered into popular philosophy.'

A declared partisan of the psychology of association, Mr. Mill has not explained his doctrine under a systematic form, like James Mill, Herbert Spencer, or Mr. Bain. Let us now try to collect the doctrines scattered through the *Logic*, *Hamilton's Philosophy*, and the *Dissertations*, and to explain them under these three titles: Method in Psychology, Psychology strictly so called, the psychological theory of Mind and Matter.

CHAPTER I.

OF METHOD IN PSYCHOLOGY.

Of Method in Psychology.—1. The aim of psychology—2. Method of psychology: positivists, metaphysicians, and associationalists—3. The science of character, or Ethology.

I.

In every science method is of capital importance; it is all the more so in proportion as the science is less advanced, and more hesitating in its march. This is the case with psychology, and it is not rash to say that the insufficiency of its progress has been the inevitable result of the method generally employed. Mr. Stuart Mill, who justly calls attention to the little advance made in the method of the moral and social sciences, has resolutely attacked that of psychology; he returns to the charge several times,[1] and he makes his thoughts on this point perfectly clear.

'Psychology,' he says, 'has for its aim the uniformities of succession; the laws, whether primitive or derivative, according to which one mental condition succeeds another, is the cause of another, or at least the cause of the coming of another.'

It is a common opinion that the thoughts, sentiments, and actions of sensible beings cannot be the object of a science, in the same sense as the beings and phenomena of the exterior world. That opinion rests upon a confusion; all science is confounded with *exact* science. But we may conceive an intermediate case between the perfection of the science and its extreme imperfection. For example, a phenomenon may result from two sorts of causes,—from major causes accessible to observation or to calculation;—from minor, secondary causes, which are not constantly accessible to exact observation, or even which are not so at all. In such a case, we may account for the principal part of the phenomenon, but there will be variations and modifications which we cannot completely explain.

This occurs in the theory of the tides. There are the major causes, the attraction of the sun and of the moon,—all that depend on that attraction may be explained and predicted for any portion whatever, even an unexplored portion, of the earth's surface. But there are also secondary causes,—the direction of the wind, local circumstances, the configuration of the bottom of the ocean, etc., —which have a great influence on the height and the hour of the tide, and which, in most cases, cannot be calculated or predicted. Nevertheless, not only is it certain that these variations have causes which act in accordance with perfectly uniform laws,—not only is the theory of the tides, therefore, a science like meteorology, but it is more practically useful. For the

[1] See *Logic*, vol. ii. book 6, and *Dissertations and Discussions*, vol. iii. p. 97.

general laws of the tides may be established, and previsions which shall be almost entirely correct may be founded upon these laws. This is what is meant, or ought to be meant, when sciences which are not *exact* sciences are spoken of. Astronomy was a science before it became an exact science. It has only been exact since it has explained not only the planetary motions, but also their perturbations.

The science of the tides is not yet an exact science, not by a radical impossibility in its nature, but because it is very difficult to establish the derivative uniformities with precision. '*The science of human nature is of the same kind.*' It is far from being of the same exactness as our present astronomy, but there is no reason why it should not be a science like that of the stars, or even such as astronomy was, while as yet its calculations included only the principal phenomena, and not the perturbations.

1. The phenomena with which this science is conversant being the thoughts, feelings, and actions of human beings, it would have attained the ideal perfection of a science, if it enabled us to foretell how an individual would think, feel, or act throughout life, with the same certainty with which astronomy enables us to predict the places and the occultations of the heavenly bodies. It needs scarcely be stated that nothing approaching to this can be done. Hence, even if our science of human nature were theoretically perfect, that is, if we could calculate any character as we can calculate the orbit of any planet, *from given data*, still, as the data are never all given, nor ever precisely alike in different cases, we could neither make positive predictions, nor lay down universal propositions.'[1]

But the approximative generalizations are sufficiently exact for practical life; that which is only probable when it is affirmed of individuals taken at hazard, is certain when it is affirmed of the conduct of the masses; and therein lies the utility of psychology.[2]

Thus the aim of psychology is fixed: its object is the phenomena of mind. Its character is determined; it is (or may be)

[1] Mill's *Logic*, ed. 1856, p. 421.

[2] *Logic*, b. vi. ch. iii.

a science; not exact, but approximative, and sufficient for practical purposes. Let us now see the method of it.[1]

Two entirely opposite schools have contributed to its deviation from the right way,—on one side, that of Auguste Comte; on the other, that of German metaphysics. Mr. Mill writes thus of the former:—

M. Comte claims for physiologists alone the scientific knowledge of intellectual and moral phenomena. He totally rejects psychological observations properly so called, the internal consciousness. He thinks that we have to acquire our knowledge of the human mind by observing others. How can we observe and interpret the mental operations of others without previously knowing our own? He does not tell us this. But he considers it evident that the observation of ourselves by ourselves can teach us only very little concerning feelings, and nothing on the subject of understanding. 'It is not necessary,' adds Mr. Stuart Mill, 'to refute a sophism at length, whose most surprising part is, that it should have imposed on any one. Two answers may be made to it:—1. M. Comte may be referred to the experience as well as to the writings of the psychologists as a proof that the mind can not only be conscious of more than one impression at a time, and even perceive a considerable number (according to Hamilton), but even lend them all attention. 2. It might have occurred to M. Comte that it is possible to study a fact by means of memory, not at the instant in which we perceive it, but the moment after, and this is, in reality, the mode by which we acquire the best of our knowledge of intellectual actions. Besides, in fact, we know what passes in ourselves, whether thanks to consciousness or thanks to memory, but in a direct way in both cases, and not (as happens about what we do in a state of somnambulism) by their results.' This simple fact destroys the entire argument of M. Comte. Everything of which we have direct consciousness we can observe. The successions, therefore, which obtain among mental phenomena, do not admit of being deduced from the physiological laws of our nervous organization; and all real knowledge of them must continue, for a long time at least, if not for ever, to be

[1] *Logic*, loc. cit.

sought in the direct study, by observation and experiment, of the mental successions themselves. Since, therefore, the order of our mental phenomena must be studied in those phenomena, and not inferred from the laws of any phenomena more general, there is a distinct and separate science of mind.

The relations, indeed, of that science to the science of physiology must never be overlooked or undervalued. It must by no means be forgotten that the laws of mind may be derivative laws resulting from the laws of animal life, and that their truth therefore may ultimately depend on physical conditions. . . . But on the other hand, to reject the resource of psychological analysis, and construct the theory of the mind solely on such data as physiology at present affords, seems to me as great an error in principle, and an even more serious one in practice. Imperfect as is the science of mind, I do not scruple to affirm that it is in a considerably more advanced state than the portion of physiology that corresponds to it; and to discard the former for the latter appears to me an infringement of the true canons of inductive philosophy.

Thus, then, we have direct observation clearly established against positivism.[1] Let us now see how our author combats the opposite school, the metaphysicians, German or otherwise, whom he calls, in general terms, philosophers *à priori.*

The dispute between the *à priori* philosophers and the *à posteriori* philosophy, he says, goes far beyond the bounds and the bearing of psychology, and is especially concentrated on the field of ontology. I have no intention of declaring myself a partisan of either, both having done much for humanity, both requiring to be known by whoever purposes to approach philosophical questions, each having largely profited by the criticisms of the other. 'By concentrating the question simply on the ground of psychology, we find that the difference between the two philosophies consists in the *different theories which they give of the complex phenomena of the human mind.*'

Experience is not the exclusive property of one of them. They both depend on it for their materials. The fundamental difference has reference, not to the facts themselves, but to their origin.

[1] See *Logic*, book vi. chap. iv., and *Comte and Positivism*, p. 67.

We may say briefly and generally that one of these theories considers the most complex phenomena of the mind as being the product of experience, whereas the other considers them as original.

A priori psychology maintains that, in every act of thought, even the most elementary, there is an element which is not given *to* the mind, but which is furnished *by* the mind, in virtue of its own faculties. The most simple of all the phenomena, an exterior sensation, requires, according to it, a mental element to be a perception, and thus to become, instead of a passive and fugitive condition of our being, a durable object exterior to the mind. The notions of extent, solidity, number, force, etc., although acquired by the senses, are not copies of impressions made upon the senses, but creations of the laws of our minds put in action by sensations. Experience, instead of being the source and the prototype of our ideas, is itself a product of the forces proper to the mind, elaborating the impressions which we receive from without; it contains a mental as well as an external element. Experience, invoked in vain to account for our mental laws, is only possible by those laws. Now, if experience does not explain experience, *à fortiori* it does not explain the ideas of moral, *super-sensible* things; experience is their occasion, but not their source.

A posteriori psychology, on the contrary, while it recognises the existence of a mental element in our ideas, and admits that our ideas of extent, solidity, time, space, virtue, are not exact copies of impressions made upon our senses, but a product of the labour of the mind, does not consider this production as the result of particular and impenetrable laws, which cannot be accounted for. It thinks, on the contrary, that that is *possible.* It thinks that the mental element is a fact, but not an ultimate fact. It thinks that it may be resolved into simpler laws and more general facts, and that it is possible to discover the process followed by the mind in the construction of these great ideas; in a word, that their *genesis* can be determined.

Let us define the difference between the two Schools of psychology by an example. The transcendentalists examine our ideas of space and time; they find that each contains in itself in an indissoluble manner the idea of the infinite. Naturally we have no experimental knowledge of the infinite; all our ideas derived from experience are ideas of finite things. Nevertheless it is impossible to conceive of time and space otherwise than as infinite, and it is impossible to derive them from experience; these are the *necessary* conceptions of the mind. The *à posteriori* psychologist, on his side, sees clearly that we cannot think of time and space otherwise than as infinite, but he does not consider that as an ultimate fact. He sees in it an ordinary manifestation of one of the laws of the association of ideas,—the law that the idea of a thing irresistibly suggests the idea of another thing with which it has often been found by experience to be intimately united. As we have never had any experience of a point in space without other points beyond it, nor of a point in time without other points which follow it, the law of inseparable association causes us to be unable to think of any point in time or space, however distant, without immediately imagining other points yet more distant. This explains their infinitude without introducing 'necessity.' It may be that time and space have limits, but in our present condition we are totally unable to conceive of them. If we could reach the end of space, we should be apprised of it no doubt by some novel and strange impression of our senses, but of which we cannot at present form the very slightest idea.

The preceding example brings out clearly the two principal doctrines of the most advanced *à posteriori* psychology:—

1. That the most abstruse phenomena of the mind are formed of more simple and elementary phenomena.

2. That the mental law by means of which this formation takes place is the law of association.

The most complete and scientific form of *à posteriori* psychology, is that which considers the law of association as the supreme principle. Its great problem is to determine, not how far this law extends—for it extends to everything: ideas, emotions, desires, volitions, etc.,—but how many mental phenomena it is capable of explaining, and *how* it explains them. On this part of the subject there are differences of doctrine, and the theory, like every theory in an incomplete science, progresses steadily.[1]

[1] *Loc. cit.* p. 108.

This manner of interpreting the phenomena of the mind, continues Mr. Mill, has been often stigmatized as materialist. In order to see what justice there is in the accusation, we have only to remember that the idealism of Berkeley is one of the developments of this theory. If there be materialism in endeavouring to determine the material conditions of our mental operations, all somewhat comprehensive theories of the mind may, in that case, be taxed with materialism. We shall probably never know whether organization alone can produce thought and life; but we know, beyond doubt, that the mind employs a material organ. Now, this admitted, what materialism is there in following out the physiological explanations so far as they can lead us?

It is certainly true that associative-psychology represents several of the superior mental conditions as being in a certain sense the development of inferior mental conditions. But in other similar cases, as the author acutely remarks, the wisdom and the marvellous art of nature which draws the better from the worse, and good from evil, have been magnified. Besides, if those, the most noble portions of our nature, are not original, they are not therefore factitious and non-natural. The products are as much a part of human nature as the elements which compose it. Water is as much a substance of the external world as hydrogen and oxygen. It is only for vulgar minds that a great and beautiful object loses its charm in losing something of its mysteriousness, in unveiling a portion of the secret process by which nature has engendered it.'[1]

Mr. Stuart Mill requires us to be exacting with respect to explanations founded on association: we must not limit ourselves to semblances of analysis. Now nothing is more useful in getting at the bottom and into the intimate essence of complex facts, than the examination of exceptions and rare cases. Children, young animals, persons deprived of certain senses, those who, born blind, have recovered their sight, persons who have grown up in solitude like Caspar Hauser, furnish numerous sources of information, which are unhappily but rarely used.

In short, two kinds of investigations are equally necessary for

[1] *Loc. cit.* p. 111.

[2] *Mémoires des l'Académie des Sciences Morales*, tom. i. 1833.

the study of the phenomena of mind, and for that of material phenomena; the first, of which Newton's generalization is the type, applies itself, not to successions of phenomena, but to complex phenomena themselves, and resolves them into simple elements, just as chemistry resolves compound bodies. The first analyses laws into simpler laws, the second analyses subtances into simpler substances.[1]

III.

After having determined the object and the method of psychology, we have to seek whether there be not an *Art* to which this science may serve as a basis,—whether there be not some derived science applicable to practical life, which supposes, as primary science, a general knowledge of the phenomena of the mind. Every science, as soon as it is firmly constituted, comes naturally out of pure theory, and leads to practical consequences, whether they be sought for, or only found. And, in our opinion, there is no greater proof of the long lingering of psychology in its infancy, than the striking fact that no application, no useful art, has proceeded from it. Thus it was for centuries with physics and chemistry, thus with the biological sciences, whose results are even yet but dimly foreseen; nevertheless who can fail to understand that if the fundamental laws of the mind were discovered, if the circumstances which modify them were known, if, in a word, we knew the essential and the accidental, as in the case of the tides, already quoted by Mr. Mill, if we could reconstitute a psychological situation by synthesis, as we can calculate an astronomical position, if we were capable of foreseeing,—an important secret would be made known to men, available for their aid in education, politics, all the moral and social sciences, and that psychology would be the basis of those sciences, even as physics is the basis of the sciences of matter.

The possibility of this art, or, if we prefer so to style it, this derivative science, founded upon psychology, is entertained by only a few minds.[2] We shall see that Mr. Mill defines its nature

[1] Stuart Mill, Preface to James Mill's *Analysis*, p. 6.

[2] Mr. Bain has published a volume *On the Study of Character*, including an estimate of phrenology.

and its method. Let us say at once that he designates it Ethology, or the *science of character*, and that he assigns to it, as a process of investigation, the deductive method with verification.[1]

The object of psychology is the general laws of human nature, the object of ethology is the derivative laws. Psychology occupies itself with genus, ethology with species and varieties.

We employ the name psychology for the science of the elementary laws of mind; ethology will serve for the ulterior science which determines the kind of character produced, in conformity to those general laws, by any set of circumstances, physical and moral. According to this definition, ethology is the science which corresponds to the art of education, in the widest sense of the term, including the formation of national or collective character, as well as individual. . . . Ethology may be called the exact science of human nature.'[2]

But it is only exact in the affirmation of *tendencies*, not of *facts*. It declares, not that such a thing will always happen, but that the effect of a given cause will be such, so long as that cause shall operate without interruption; for instance: it is a scientific proposition that muscular strength *tends* to make men courageous, but not that it always does make them so; that experience *tends* to produce wisdom, but not that it always does produce it.

While psychology is entirely or principally a science of observation and experimentation, ethology is an entirely deductive science. The relation of ethology to psychology is analogous to that of the different branches of physics to mechanics. The principles of ethology are, properly speaking, the *axiomata media* of the science of the mind. These principles are distinct, on the one hand, from empirical laws resulting from simple observation, on the other, from lofty generalizations. As Bacon has boldly pointed out, the *axiomata media* of any science constitute the principal value of that science. Inferior generalizations, so long as they have not been explained and reduced to the *axiomata media*, whose consequences they are, possess only the precarious value of empirical laws; and the most general laws are *too* general to explain individual cases.

[1] *Logic*, bk. vi. ch. v.

[2] *Ibid.* vol. ii. pp. 445-6, 4th ed.

Mr. Stuart Mill shows very clearly that the deductive method, *with verification*, is the only one applicable to ethology. Natural laws, he says, can only be determined in two ways: by deduction or by experience. Are the laws of formation of character approachable by the experimental method? Evidently not. In fact, this method has two principal processes, experimentation and observation.

1. Is experimentation possible? It might be for an oriental despot, but even if he ventured to attempt it, how much advance would be made? It would be necessary to rear, from infancy to maturity, a number of human beings, to note each sensation or impression experienced by the subject, or to note the causes and what he thinks of them. A single apparently insignificant circumstance which might be neglected would suffice to vitiate the experiment.

2. Is observation possible? If it be not possible to know influential circumstances with entire certainty when we arrange them ourselves, *à fortiori* we cannot know them in cases beyond our control. We can only make observations *wholesale and in the lump*, that is to say, we can only aim at a purely approximative generalization. There remains, then, the deductive method, which starts from laws.

In other words, mankind have not one universal character, but there exist universal laws for the formation of character. And since it is by these laws, combined with the facts of each particular case, that the whole of the phenomena of human action and feeling are produced, it is on these that every rational attempt to construct the science of human nature in the concrete, and for practical purposes, must proceed.[1]

Ethology is still to be created. But its creation has at length become practicable; . . . though little has yet been done, and that little not at all systematically, towards forming it.[2]

The progress of this important science will depend on the employment of a double process:—

1. Given a certain particular circumstance, to deduct theoretically from it the ethological consequences, and to compare them with that which our common experience teaches us.

---

[1] *Logic*, vol. ii. p. 440, 4th edit. [2] *Ibid.* p. 450.

2. To perform the inverse operation, that is to say, to study the different types of human nature, to analyse them, to note the circumstances in which these types predominate, and to explain the characteristic features of the type by the peculiarities of the circumstances.

It is hardly necessary, says Mr. Mill in conclusion, to repeat that in ethology, as well as in every other inductive science, verification *à posteriori* ought to go *pari passu* with deduction *à priori*, the conclusions of the theory deserving no confidence except so far as they are confirmed by experience. The agreement between these two kinds of proofs is the sole sufficient basis of the principles of a science thus noted in facts, and relative to phenomena so complex and so concrete as those of ethology.

Thus a general, abstract science, founded on observation and experience, having for its object the fundamental phenomena of the human mind, and a special science, having for its object varieties of character,—such is the almost inexhaustible and almost entirely novel task which Mr. Mill has assigned to future psychology.

CHAPTER II.

PSYCHOLOGY.

Psychology.—1. Consciousness—2. Exterior perception—3. Association of ideas—4. Causality—5 Necessary truths—6. Reasoning—7. Will.

I.

We comprise under the following titles, Conscience, Perception, Association, Idea of Cause, Necessary Truths, Reasoning, Will, the principal psychological studies of Mr. John Stuart Mill.

'If the word *spirit* means anything, it signifies that which feels.' The phenomena which manifest it are sensations, ideas, emotions, and volitions.[1] Consciousness is an intuitive knowledge which constitutes the foundation of our mental conditions, which exist only in consciousness and by consciousness; to have an idea, to have a sensation, is in reality to have the consciousness of an

[1] *Logic*, book vi. ch. iv.

idea, of a sensation.[1] The verdict of consciousness is without appeal. Scepticism, which should dispute it (if such there be) would not be admissible; because in denying all consciousness it would no longer deny any. But we must not confound the knowledge which is *intuitive*, and consequently without appeal, of consciousness, with the reasonings, inductions, and interpretations of the facts of consciousness, which are fallible, and which demand verification.

Are there, beside the phenomena of which we have consciousness, unconscious mental modifications? Sir William Hamilton is probably the first of the English philosophers who has declared for the affirmative, without limiting himself to the specious pretext that an unconscious action or passion of the mind is unintelligible. This hypothesis of unconscious activity, which has since made much way in England, in Germany,[2] and in France, was sustained by Hamilton on three sorts of facts:—

1. We know a science or a language, etc. They exist i.. us in the latent state, so long as we do not make use of them.

2. Certain abnormal conditions, such as madness, delirium, somnambulism, reveal to us knowledge, or habits of action which we have no consciousness of possessing in our normal state.

3. In our ordinary life, every visible object is composed of very small portions, or *minima visibilia*. But each *minimum visibile* is composed of still smaller portions, of which each singly is to the consciousness as zero. It is the same as regards the *minimum audibile*. Finally, certain associations of ideas cannot be explained except by the intermediary associations which are produced without unconsciousness.

Mr. Mill, after having criticised the interpretation of these facts given by Hamilton, explains them by physiology:—'I am myself inclined to agree with Sir W. Hamilton, and to admit his unconscious mental modifications, in the only shape in which I

[1] *An Examination of Sir W. Hamilton's Philosophy*, chaps. viii. ix. We shall find hereafter, in Spencer and Bain, a complete and remarkable theory of consciousness, brought back to two primitive acts: the perception of a difference, the perception of a resemblance.

[2] Wundt, *Vorlesungen über die Menschen und Thierseele*, 1863.

can attach any very distinct meaning to them, namely, unconscious modifications of the nerves.'[1]

In the case of a soldier wounded in battle, and prevented by the heat of the action from feeling his wound, the most probable hypothesis is, that the nerves of the wounded part have really been affected; but that the nervous centres, being much occupied with other impressions, the affection does not reach the centres, and that consequently the sensation does not take place. So also in respect to latent association, if we admit (and physiology is making it more and more probable) that all our sentiments, like all our sensations, have for their physical antecedents a particular state of the nerves, we may easily believe that the association between two ideas can appear to be interrupted, only because it is physically continued by organic conditions of the nerves succeeding each other so rapidly that the state of consciousness appropriate to each of them cannot be produced.[2]

II.

In all probability the notion of the *ego* and the *non-ego* are not produced at the outset. We have not the notion of the *non-ego* until after we have experienced a number of sensations according to first laws and in clusters; and it is not credible that the first sensation which we experience should awaken in us the notion of an *ego*.[3] The opposition of these two terms, *ego* and *non-ego*, subject and object, spirit and matter, reduces itself to the opposition of sensation considered subjectively, and sensation considered objectively. There is, on one side, the series of states of consciousness (of which sensation forms part), which is the *subject* of sensation. On the other side, there is the

[1] Mill's *Hamilton's Philosophy*, p. 285.

[2] We refer to Leibnitz those who might be tempted to discover materialism in this mode of explanation. 'All that association makes the soul of Cæsar to do, is also represented in his body; there is a certain condition of body which responds to even the most abstract reasonings.' It is true that Leibnitz does not say that this state of body is the antecedent of it; that would have been in discord with his pre-established harmony.

[3] *An Examination, etc.*, chap. xiii. p. 258.

cluster of permanent possibility of sensation, partly realized in the actual sensation action, and which is the *object* of the sensation.[1]

Among our sensations we are in the habit of considering some subjectively, and others objectively. In the first case, we consider them principally in their relation to our various sentiments, and consequently to the subject, which is the sum of them. In the second case, we consider them principally in their relation to one or several clusters of that possibility of sensation which we call the object. 'The difference between these two classes of our sensations answers to the distinction drawn by the majority of philosophers, between the second qualities and the first qualities of matter.'

According to Mr. Mill, the first qualities are resistance, extent, and figure. These are the three principal elements of all the groups; wherever they are, there is a group; every other element of the group presents itself to our thought, less for what it is, than as a mark of those three elements. In that group of permanent possibilities of sensation which we call *object*, the permanent possibility of tactiles[1] and muscular sensations forms a group within a group, a sort of interior nucleus, conceived of as more fundamental than the rest, and on which all the other possibilities of sensation contained in the group seem to depend. This nucleus, sometimes considered as cause or substance, is our first conception of matter, which thus reduces itself to resistance, extent, and figure.

The most fundamental of these three properties is resistance, which is given to us by muscular sensations. As the sentiment of resistance is invariably accompanied by tactile sensations, by the contact of our skin with some object, it results, in virtue of the law of inseparable association, that the sensations of contact and resistance become inseparably united. An object which touches our skin, even without pressure, and without causing any muscular reaction, is spontaneously referred to some external cause. By association, our sensations of touch have become *representatives* of the sensations of resistance, with

[1] For details on this point, see chap. iii. following.

which they habitually co-exist; as the different shades of colours, and the muscular sensations, which accompany the various movements of eye, become *representatives* of the sensations of touch and locomotion.

The second of the fundamental qualities of the body is extent; a notion which was for a long time considered irreducible by the intuitive school of Reid and Stewart, but whose origin has been explained by the psychological analysis of the experimental school. We shall leave the care of expounding it to Mr. Bain and Mr. Herbert Spencer. Mr. Mill is in perfect accord with them, and quotes them at length. We must limit ourselves to a brief summary of the doctrine.

The sensation of muscular motion, unimpeded, constitutes our notion of empty space; the sensation of muscular motion, impeded, constitutes our notion of full space or extent. The idea of space is derived from a phenomenon which is not synchronized but successive. If we find this difficult to believe, it is because the eye, in contributing to produce our actual notion of extent, alters its character very much, and prevents us from recognising that the notion of extent has been, in its origin, successive.

In order to establish it categorically, it would be necessary to find a born blind psychologist, as there have been born blind geometricians and mathematicians. His declarations and interpretations would be decisive. But, in default of such a case, we have an analogous one, that of a man born blind, whom Platner, a philosopher and physician of the last century, attended and interrogated.[1] Platner tells us :—

'This observation, I say, has convinced me, that the sense of touch, by itself, is altogether incompetent to afford us the representation of extension and space, and is not even cognisant of local exteriority; in a word, that a man deprived of sight has absolutely no perception of an outer world beyond the existence

[1] Platner began this study in 1785. For a century the blind man of Cheselden has been cited in all the treatises on pyschology. Mr. Mill, besides the blind man of Platner, quotes two others, one who was operated upon by Dr. Franz of Leipsic in 1841, the other more recently, and who is mentioned by Professor Fraser in the *North British Review.*

of something effective, different from his own feeling of passivity, and in general only of the numerical diversity—shall I say of impressions, or of things? In fact, to those born blind *time serves instead of space.* Vicinity and distance means in their mouths nothing more than the shorter or longer time, the smaller or greater number of feelings, which they find necessary to attain from some one feeling to another.'[1]

In short, the idea of space is at bottom an idea of time, and the notion of distance or extent is that of a movement of the muscles continued for a greater or lesser duration.

III.

We have already seen how complete is Mr. Mill's adhesion to Associative psychology. The law of association is, in his opinion, the most general which rules psychological phenomena. 'That which the law of gravitation is to astronomy, that which the elementary properties of the tissues are to physiology, the law of the association of ideas is to psychology.'[2] It is the ultimate fact to which everything returns, the most general mode of explanation, the most powerful instrument of the experimental school in its psychological investigations.[3]

Although we do not find in Mr. Mill's works so elaborate a study of association as in those of Mr. Herbert Spencer, and especially of Mr. Bain, we shall hereafter see that he reduces the fundamental idea of cause to an inseparable and unconditional association, and that he founds on cause, that is to say, on an association, the entire theory of reasoning.

The first law of association is, that similar ideas tend to awaken each other.

The second law is, that when two impressions or ideas have been experienced simultaneously, or in immediate succession, one tends to awaken the other.

---

[1] Mill's *Examination of Hamilton's Philosophy*, p. 232.

[2] *Comte and Positivism*, p. 53.

[3] Mr. Mill quotes the *Étude sur l'association des idées*, by M. Mervoyer, as the only work on this subject which has appeared in France. M. Renouvier, in his *Année philosophique*, 1868, recently published, promises a criticism in detail of 'Associationalism.'

The third law is, that a greater intensity of one of these impressions or of both is equivalent, in order to render them likely to excite each other, to a greater frequency of conjunction.[1]

Now or later, psychology ought to be able to explain the most complex phenomena by means of the laws of association. But its task is rendered very difficult, because the combined action of different causes sometimes produces combinations in which it is difficult to find the constituent elements. In fact, when a complex phenomenon is the result of several causes, two principal cases may present themselves: that of the mechanical, that of the chemical laws. In the case of the mechanical law, each cause is to be found in the effect, as if it had acted singly. The effect of concurrent causes is exactly the sum of the separate effects of each. On the contrary, the chemical combination of two substances produces a third whose proportions are completely different from each of the two others, whether taken separately or together.

The laws of the phenomena of mind are analogous, now to mechanical, again to chemical laws. As an example of mental *combination,* we may give the colour white resulting from the rapid succession of the seven colours of the prism before our eyes. The idea of an orange, on the contrary, really results from the simple ideas of colour, form, taste, etc., because, when we interrogate our consciousness, we can discern all these sentiments in our idea. There are cases of mental chemistry in which it is more exact to say that simple ideas *produce* complex ideas, than to say that they *compose* them.[2] The knowledge of the constituent elements of a complex fact in psychological chemistry, no more dispenses us from studying the fact itself, than the knowledge of the properties of oxygen and sulphur dispenses us from studying those of sulphuric acid.

Mr. Mill (*Logic,* iii. 13; vi. 4) explains two great varieties of mind by two different modes of association.

Simultaneous (or synchronical) associations predominate in persons endowed with keen organic sensibility; because it is an acknowledged fact that all the sensations or ideas experienced

[1] *Logic,* book vi. ch. iv., and book iii. ch. vi. [2] *Ibid.*

under a strong impression are intimately associated with each other. Now this predominance of synchronical associations produces a tendency to conceive of things under concrete forms, highly coloured, rich in attributes and details; a disposition of mind which is called imagination, and which is one of the faculties of the painter and of the poet.

Successive associations predominate in less impressionable people. If they possess lofty intelligence, they will apply themselves to history or the sciences rather than to an art. The result of their inferior sensibility will be love of science, or of abstract truth, and lack of taste and warmth.

Let us now consider associative psychology in antagonism with the notion of cause.

IV.

If the theory of consciousness and of exterior perception is the basis of all psychology, the theory of cause is the key of all philosophy; it even opens up to us regions into which we are not bound to penetrate. Let us keep to psychology. Thus Mr. Mill declares that he does not concern himself with the first or metaphysical cause of anything whatever.[1]

'The causes with which I concern myself are not *efficient* but *physical* causes. They are causes in that sense alone, in which one physical fact is said to be the cause of another. Of the efficient causes of phenomena, or whether any such causes exist at all, I am not called upon to give an opinion. The notion of causation is deemed, by the schools of metaphysics most in vogue at the present moment, to imply a mysterious and most powerful tie such as cannot, or at least does not exist, between any physical fact and that other physical fact on which it is invariably consequent, and which is popularly termed its cause; and thence is deduced the supposed necessity of ascending higher into the essences and inherent constitution of things to find the true cause, the cause which is not only followed by, but actually *produces*, the effect.[2]

[1] *Logic*, book iii. ch. v.

[2] *Ibid.* vol. i. p. 359, 4th edition.

But Mr. Mill, as we may suppose, denies himself this excursion.

In his Examination of Hamilton's Philosophy,[1] he has sharply criticised that philosopher's theory of causality. According to Hamilton, the idea of cause is not a principle *sui generis* of our intelligence: it is explained by the impossibility of our conceiving of anything as absolutely commencing. It comes back to the axiom—

Ex nihilo nihil, in nihilum nil posse reverti.

It is because we cannot conceive of nothing becoming something that we are always asking the cause of every effect, that is to say, that from which the effect draws its existence, and is only a transformation. If we examine Hamilton's doctrine, we shall see that, pushed to its ultimate consequences, it would end in giving to all phenomena an eternal substratum whose causes and effects would be only manifestations in time; that is to say, that it is completely opposed in spirit and tendencies to empiricism, whereas Mr. Mill acknowledges nothing but empirical causes.

The phenomena of nature, he says, hold two different relations with respect to each other, simultaneousness and succession.[2] Causality belongs to the category of relations of succession; but every relation of succession is not a relation of causality; in order to be so, it must fulfil essential conditions which we are about to determine.

Certain facts succeed and, as we believe, always will succeed certain other facts. The *invariable antecedent* is called cause, the *invariable consequent* is called effect. The relation of cause to effect is ordinarily placed between a group of antecedents and a group of consequences, although, in general, by a quite arbitrary process, one of these antecedents is set apart under the name of cause, the others being called simply conditions. Thus a man eats of a certain aliment, and dies of it; it is said that this aliment is the cause of his death. But the true relation of causality is between the totality of the antecedents (the special constitu-

[1] *An Examination, etc.*, ch. xvi. p. 340.
[2] *Logic*, loc. cit.

tion of body, state of health, state of the atmosphere, etc.,) and the totality of the consequences (phenomena which constitute death). In the exact language proper to philosophy the cause is 'the sum of the positive and negative conditions taken together, the total of the contingencies of every nature which the consequence invariably follows, when they are realized.'

This definition of cause is, however, only partial. Invariable sequence is not the synonym of causality; the sequence must also be unconditional. There are sequences as uniform as possible, which are not considered for that reason as cases of causality: thus, night invariably succeeds day, but probably no one has ever believed that the night is the cause of the day. This succession is not unconditional; the production of the day is subject to a condition which is not the anteriority of the night, but the presence of the sun. This is what authors wish to express when they say that the notion of cause implies the idea of necessity.

Necessity signifies unconditionality. The cause of a phenomenon may therefore be defined as *the antecedent, or the collection of antecedents, of which the phenomenon is invariably and unconditionally the consequent.*

But, to say that a case of succession is necessary, unconditional, in other words, invariable in every possible change of circumstances, is not this to acknowledge in causation an element of belief not derived from experience? By no means; it is experience itself which teaches us that such a succession is conditional, and that such another is not; that the succession of day and night, for example, is a derived succession, dependent on something else; in a word, experience, without anything to go beyond it, explains our ideas of causality.[1]

As for the theory which perceives in our voluntary activity the sole source of this idea, and which even maintains that it is that voluntary activity which reveals to us what is an *efficient* cause, Mr. Mill replies that he sees in the will only a *physical* cause like any other; that it is the cause of our corporeal actions, in the same manner as cold is the cause of ice, and a spark is the cause

[1] *Logic*, book iii. ch. v.

of the explosion of powder. Volition is the antecedent, the motion of our limbs is the consequent; but we have not direct consciousness of this sequence in the sense which the theory requires. Mr Mill, agreeing with Hamilton, bids us observe that 'it is refuted by the consideration, that between the overt fact of corporeal movement of which we are cognisant, and the internal act of mental determination, of which we are also cognisant, there intervenes a numerous series of intermediate agencies of which we have no knowledge; and, consequently, that we have no consciousness of any causal connexion between the extreme links of this chain, the volition to move, and the limb moving, as this hypothesis asserts.' [2]

V.

Thus then this fundamental idea of causality, implied in the most ordinary actions as in the loftiest knowledge, the basis of all science, the 'hidden root' of all induction; that is to say, according to our author, of all reasoning, is explained by experience pure and simple; it is only invariable and unconditional succession. Mr. Mill even refers axioms and necessary truths to experience.

Let us observe, in the first place, that there are two sorts of general propositions, those which, according to everybody's belief, are born of experience and do not go beyond it, being no more than experience generalized (Example: All men are mortal); and those which, although suggested by experience, seem to go beyond it by their character of necessity (Example: Two parallels are everywhere equidistant). According to Mr. Mill, these latter propositions are neither truths *à priori*, as the rationalists would have them, nor are they mere words, as the nominalists with Hobbes at their head would have them. What are they then? Empirical propositions. This is how he establishes it.

The reasons brought forward for granting a particular origin

[1] Mill's *Logic*, book iii. chap. v.
[2] *Ibid.* book iii. vol. i. p. 389, 5th edition.
[3] *Ibid.* book ii. chap. v. vi. vii.

to these truths reduce themselves to two: they are *à priori*, they are necessary.

Axioms are not *à priori*; they are experimental truths, generalizations of observation. The proposition, 'two right lines cannot enclose a space,' is a deduction resulting from the testimony of the senses. No doubt experience gives us only an *actual* knowledge of this truth, and thence it seems insufficient to found an axiom; but, let us observe, that the imagination supplies for it; we make for ourselves a mental image of two lines, and we see that as soon as they meet each other they cease to be right lines. It is, therefore, upon an internal production and reproduction of experience that the truths called *à priori* rest.

Then there is the character of necessity. What is a necessary truth? It is a proposition, the negation of which is not only false, but also inconceivable. Mr. Mill categorically rejects this criticism of inconceivability.[1] He absolutely denies that we can say such a thing *is* not, since it is inconceivable by us. And, he adds, he has only to open the history of the sciences in order to justify his assertion. A number of propositions have been held to be inconceivable, which have now passed into science as uncontested truths, such as the existence of the antipodes, and the existence of gravitation, which the Cartesians repelled, because they regarded motion without contact as impossible. The inconceivability of the negative is but a case of inseparable association. We experience the greatest difficulty in uniting two ideas for the first time; then, by habit and repetition, they become so thoroughly associated that their disunion appears inconceivable, even to enlightened minds. Axioms are then experimental truths of which there is superabundant evidence, whose basis is experience, and whose criterion is verification. 'They are only a class, the most universal class, of inductions

[1] Mr. Mill has maintained, on several occasions, and without any variation, that the truth of a proposition is not sufficiently established by the inconceivability of its negative. On this point he combats Messrs. Spencer and Lewes.—See Mill's *Logic*, and *An Examination, etc.*, Spencer's *Principles of Psychology*, and Lewes's *History of Philosophy*.

from experience, the easiest and simplest generalizations of the facts furnished by the senses and the consciousness.'[1]

VI.

The preceding discussion has led us to the confines of logic, beyond which we will not go. Not that we hold the barrier to be impassable; it is even a little conventional, seeing that logic is contained in psychology, as the part is contained in the whole. We regret that Mr. Mill, with his great philosophical authority, should not have treated in some of his works of the relations between psychology and logic. This question is not so idle as it may appear; because clearly to determine the relations between two neighbouring sciences is to define their object with precision, afterwards to define their method, and so to render their progress possible. It is so much the more important because psychology, which is hardly constituted as an independent science, has hitherto been absorbed, now by metaphysics, and then by logic, the one debating substances and first causes, and the other considering human faculties *in abstracto* only, the science of facts, experimental psychology, was stifled, or merely vegetated.[2]

If, placing ourselves at the point of view of the school which we are considering (or even of any other, provided it gives a large share to facts), we examine the relations of psychology to logic, we shall see that logic is only a branch broken off from psychology. In fact, the latter has for its object the facts of consciousness, their immediate causes and their laws; it ought to embrace them all, whilst logic occupies itself only with the single faculty of inference and its mechanism. Besides, psychology ought to study our faculties in the entire series of their evolution, in their variations, ethnological or otherwise, whilst logic considers the faculty of reasoning only under its adult, impersonal, scientific form, and rejects the exceptions. Psychology is concrete, whilst logic, even when understood in the modern fashion—that is to say, stripped of scholastic formalism—remains abstract; a me-

---

[1] *Logic*, book ii. chap. vi.

[2] Among ancients, Aristotle must be excepted. He frequently proceeds as a naturalist, and his psychology is astonishing, considering the epoch.

chanism of reasoning being much more important to it than the matter to which it is applied. Logic is, then, only a small portion of psychology. Nevertheless it constitutes, as it is justly entitled to do, a science apart, because it can be studied separately, and because, by reason of the simplicity of its object, it is much more advanced than psychology.

We shall, therefore, lay logic aside, although we are now dealing with one of the most celebrated logicians of the nineteenth century, and we shall explain his psychological theory of reasoning only.

On this point the opposition of empiricism and idealism is remarkable. Idealism, which considers deduction as the fundamental operation, because it starts from the general, sees nothing in induction except an operation which brings it back thither. For empiricism induction is everything, because it starts from the facts, and is the experimental process; deduction supposes it, and is in many other respects no other than verification.[1] We shall not therefore be surprised at the preponderance which Mr. Mill assigns to the inductive process.

In order to reason, that is to say, in order to go from what one knows to what one does not know, a point of departure, a foundation, is necessary. This point of departure, says Mr. Mill, is the particular. 'To infer or reason is the process of the mind by which one starts from known truths to arrive at others really distinct from the first.'—(*Logic*, B. ii. p. 1.) It is generally divided into two kinds, induction and syllogism. But there is a third kind of reasoning, distinct from the preceding two, 'and which, nevertheless, is not only valid, but is the foundation of the two others.' This is inference, *which goes from the particular to the particular*.

Let us consider the first mode of reasoning. Logicians err in considering the *dictum de omni et multo* as the basis of all reasoning; in reality, 'every inference is from the particular to the particular.'[2] 'Not only may we reason from particulars to particulars without passing through generals, but we perpetually do so reason.'

[1] See Ravaisson, *La Philosophie en France au* XIX*me Siècle*, § 15, 33.

[2] *Logic*, book ii. chap. iii.

'All our earliest inferences are of this nature. From the first dawn of intelligence we draw inferences, but years elapse before we learn the use of general language. The child, who, having burnt his fingers, avoids to thrust them again into the fire, has reasoned and inferred, though he has never thought of the general maxim, Fire burns. . . . He is not generalizing; he is inferring a particular from particulars. In the same way also brutes reason.'[1]

Mr. Mill thinks that, when we draw consequences from our personal experience, we conclude more often from the particular to the particular, than by the intermediary of a general proposition.

Among the higher order of practical intellects, there have been many of whom it was remarked how admirably they suited their means to their ends, without being able to give any sufficient reasons for what they did; and applied, or seemed to apply, recondite principles, which they were wholly unable to state. This is the natural consequence of having a mind stored with appropriate particulars, and having been long accustomed to reason at once from these to fresh particulars, without practising the habit of stating to one's-self or to others the corresponding general propositions.[2]

General propositions are simple registers of inferences already effectuated, and of short formulas for the formation of others.[3] We store up our experiences in them, as it were, that we may use them at need. Reasoning from the particular to the particular bring us then naturally to induction.

Induction is, in fact, the mode of reference which goes from the particular to the general, from the known to the unknown. It may be defined as a generalization of experience,[4] or as 'the means of discovering and proving general propositions.' Its foundation is not, as the Scotch pretend, our belief in the uniformity of the course of nature, seeing that this belief itself is an example of induction, and of an induction not the easiest or most evident, since, before we reach it, we must have con-

[1] Mill's *Logic*, vol. i. p. 212, 4th edition.
[2] *Ibid.* vol. i. p. 213.
[3] *Ibid.* book iii. chap. iii.
[4] *Ibid.* book iii. chap. iii.

ceived the particular uniformities, whose general uniformity is the resultant and the synthesis. What then is the foundation of induction? It is the idea of causality. 'The notion of cause is the root of all the theory of induction.'[1] We have already seen that, according to Mr. Mill, cause is the invisible antecedent, and that the relation of causality is unconditional succession. Hence, if two facts or groups of facts are such as experience has shown them to us, up to this time (without any known exception) in a relation of irreversible and unconditional succession, it results from this, that one of the terms gives the other, with which it is indissolubly united; that if we hold the cause, we can infer the effect; that, if we know the effect, we can infer the cause; and that the passage is thus legitimately performed between the known and the unknown; and that, besides, the uniformity of causes supposing that of effects, and *vice versâ*, we pass thus from the particular to the general.

'The inductive process is essentially an inquiry into cases of causation. . . . If we could determine what causes are correctly assigned to what effects, and what effects to what causes, we should be virtually acquainted with the whole course of nature. All those uniformities which are mere results of causation, might then be explained and accounted for, and every individual fact or event might be predicted. . . . To ascertain, therefore, what are the laws of causation which exist in nature, to determine the effects of every cause, and the causes of all effects, is the main business of induction.'[2]

Deduction is thus relegated to a secondary rank. Whilst certain logicians see in it the universal type of reasoning, and think that every discursive process is reduced by final analysis to the drawing of ideas one from the others, Mr. Mill says, 'the employment of the syllogism is in reality only the employment of general propositions in reasoning.' Now, a general proposition is only a memorandum, a 'condensation' of a number of instances drawn from particular cases. 'We *can* reason without them, and we do so, in the more simple cases; they are only necessary to the advance and progress of the reasoning. They simplify it, and permit

[1] *Logic*, book iii. chap. v. [2] *Ibid.* vol. i. p. 407.

its validity to be verified.'[1] Mr. Mill, although he refuses to recognise deduction as a fundamental process, gives it a high place, holding that several sciences have hitherto made but little progress, because they have used induction in place of deduction.[2]

In short, reason, in its lowest degree, is, properly speaking, nothing but an association of ideas; for we cannot see anything else in the inference from the particular to the particular. It is because the ideas of a lighted candle, a burnt finger, and pain, are associated with one another, that later on one recalls the other.[3] True reasoning is produced only when we seize, in place of fortuitous successions, constant and unconditional successions, that is to say, relations of causality.[4]

VII.

Mr. John Stuart Mill has repeatedly and extensively treated the question of liberty.[5] Is he a fatalist? Is he a partisan of free-will? He is neither one nor the other. He believes that the question is wrongly put, and the same opinion is professed, though in different terms, by the whole of the school which we are now considering.

The partisan of necessity says: Volition is an effect; like every effect, it has its cause—motives are this cause. Who can doubt

---

[1] *Logic*, book ii. chap. iii. [2] *Ibid.* ch. vi.

[3] Leibnitz called the inference from the particular to the particular an *empirical consecution.* As, for example, that of a Dutchman who goes into a tavern in Asia, and expects to be served with Dutch beer.—*De Anima Brutorum*, vol. ii.

[4] Upon the general character of Mill's logic, and its relations to the theories of Hobbes and Hume, see Ravaisson, *op. cit.*, p. 63. Reason, he says, does not consist in Mr. Mill's drawing one thing from another thing, but simply in recalling how near to one thing another thing approaches, otherwise said to reproduce in a different order that which has been the result of observation and induction. Induction itself, in which all reason is resolved, consists but in mechanically adding to the succession of facts which experience offers, similar successions. It is an instinctive operation, by which we pass from one particular fact to another particular fact, without which there fails to be any kind of reasoning.

[5] *Logic*, book vi. chap. ii. *An Examination*, etc., chap. xxv.

that, if we thoroughly knew the character of an individual, and all the circumstances which act upon it, we could predict the resolutions of that individual with certainty? The partisan of liberty says: In the first place I have on my side the intimate sentiment of my free-will; and then my projects, my plans, even the most ordinary actions of my life show me that I am not the slave of necessity, that I do not act like an automaton, but that I participate.

These two doctrines are partly wrong and partly right. The confusion and disagreement arise from an erroneous theory of causality, which considers the relation of cause to effect as *necessary*, which imagines a mysterious constraint exercised by the antecedent upon the consequent, which could not exist, in fact, without destroying free will.

'We are certain that, in the case of our volitions, there is not this mysterious constraint. We know that we are not compelled, as by a magical spell, to obey any particular motive. We feel that if we wished to prove that we have the power of resisting the motive we could do so (that wish being, it need scarcely be observed, a *new antecedent*), and it would be humiliating to our pride, and paralysing to our desire of excellence, if we thought otherwise. But neither is any such mysterious compulsion now supposed by the best philosophical authorities to be exercised by *any* cause over its effects. Those who think that causes draw their effects after them by a mystical tie, are right in believing that the relations between volitions and their antecedents is of another nature.'[1]

The error of the necessitarians consists in understanding by the necessity which they recognise in our actions, anything more than a simple uniformity of succession which permits them to be foreseen: they have, at bottom, the idea that there is a much stricter bond between volitions and their causes.[2]

The error depends almost solely upon the associations suggested by the word necessity, and it would be avoided by abstaining from the use of a term so completely inappropriate to express the simple fact of causality. This word, in fact, implies

[1] Mill's *Logic*, vol. ii. p. 411, 4th edition. [2] *Ibid.* vol. ii. p. 420.

much more than a simple uniformity of succession; it implies *irresistibility*. If it may be applied to the natural agents which are, for the most part, irresistible, we can see how far its application to the springs of human action is inexact.

'There are physical sequences which we call necessary, as death for want of food or air; there are others which are not said to be necessary, as death from poison, which an antidote, or the use of the stomach-pump, will sometimes avert.' [2]

Human actions are in this category. In short, the question never can be understood until the improper term necessity shall have been suppressed.

'The free-will doctrine, by keeping in view precisely that portion of truth which the word necessity puts out of sight, namely, the power of the mind to co-operate in the formation of its own character, has given to its adherents a practical feeling much nearer to the truth than has generally, I believe, existed in the minds of necessarians.' [3]

Mr. Mill lays no great stress upon the proof of our free-will so frequently drawn from consciousness. To have consciousness of our free-will, he says, can only signify one thing: that I have consciousness, before I decide, that I can decide in one sense or the other.

But the use of the word consciousness, thus applied, may be criticised *in limine*. Consciousness tells me that which I feel, or do, but it does not tell me that which I may do. Consciousness has not the gift of prophecy. We have consciousness of that which is, not of that which shall or may be.

But this conviction that we are free, whether it be consciousness or belief, what is it? It consists, I am told, in this, that although I decide, I feel that I might have decided in another way. Take, for example, the alternative of assassinating or not assassinating. I am told that if I decide on assassinating, I have the consciousness that I should have been able to abstain from doing so. But have I the consciousness that I should have

[1] Mill's *Logic*, vol. ii. p. 413, 4th edition.
[2] *Ibid.* vol. ii. p. 416, 4th edition.
[3] *An Examination*, etc., chap. xxv. p. 564.

been able to abstain, if my aversion to the crime and my fear of its consequences had been weaker than my temptation? If I chose to abstain, in what case have I the consciousness that I should have been able to choose to commit the crime? In the case that my desire to assassinate should have been stronger than my horror of murder. When, by an hypothesis, we represent ourselves to ourselves as having acted otherwise than we have acted, we always suppose a difference in the antecedents of the action.

Should it be objected, that in resisting I have the consciousness of making an effort, and that if the temptation lasts long I am as sensibly exhausted by it as I should be after physical exercise? To this Mr. Mill replies: that the battle between contending motives is not decided in a moment; that their conflict may last a long time, and that when the strife takes place between violent sentiments, it exhausts nervous force to an extraordinary degree. Now, that consciousness of effort, of which we are told, is the consciousness of this state of conflict. The conflict is not between me and a strange power which beats me, or which I beat; it is between me and myself, between the self which desires a certain thing, for instance, and the self which fears remorse. The feeling of effort (a very inappropriate word to be used here) is the result of the battle: it comes from the conquered as well as from the conquerors.

The will cannot be touched without arousing the objection of moral responsibility, which, it is said, cannot exist without it. Mr. Stuart Mill has discussed it.

Suppose that there were two peculiar breeds of human beings, one of them so constituted from the beginning, that, however educated or treated, nothing could prevent them from always feeling and acting so as to be a blessing to all whom they approached; another of such original perversity of nature that neither education nor punishment could inspire them with a feeling of duty, or prevent them from being active in evil-doing. Neither of these races of human beings would have free-will, yet the former would be honoured as demigods, while the latter would be regarded and treated as noxious beasts . . . kept carefully at a distance, and killed like other dangerous creatures, when there was no other convenient way of being rid of them.[1]

We see, therefore, that if the doctrine of necessity be pushed to its most complete exaggeration, the distinction between moral good and evil must nevertheless subsist.

'We thus see that even under the utmost possible exaggeration of the doctrine of Necessity, the distinction between moral good and evil in conduct would not only subsist, but would stand out in a more marked manner than ever, when the good and the wicked, however unlike, are still regarded as of one common nature.'[2] And that he who has contrary tendencies is a natural and legitimate object of aversion; and this, whether each enjoys liberty or not.

Mr. Mill's doctrine, as we see, is, that even putting things at the worst, absolute fatalism would not suppress responsibility, that is to say, punishment.[3] We should be born good or evil, as we are born handsome or ugly, foolish or clever; but then we should compassionate crime as we pity ugliness, we should reprove it as we reprove folly, or should shut it up as we shut up madness. Let us remember that Mr. Mill is not a fatalist.[4]

The question deemed to be so puzzling is, how punishment can be justified, if men's actions are determined by motives, among which motives punishment is one. A more difficult question would be, how it can be justified if they are not so determined. Punishment proceeds on the assumption that the will is governed by motives. If punishment had no power of acting on the will, it would be illegitimate, however natural might be the inclination to inflict it. Just so far as the will is supposed free, that is, capable of acting *against* motives, punishment is disappointed of its object, and deprived of its justification.[5]

To conclude on this point, Mr. Mill distinguishes, relatively to

---

[1] Mill's *Examination of Hamilton's Philosophy*, p. 509. [2] *Ibid.*

[3] Responsibility means punishment, p. 570, *loc. cit.* On this subject, see Letter 25 of *Opera Posthuma* of Spinoza, addressed to H. Oldenburg.

[4] Page 576.

[5] Mill's *Hamilton's Philosophy*, p. 510.

the influence of motives, three doctrines, of which he rejects two, and accepts one :—

Fatalism pure and simple,—Asiatic fatalism, or that of Œdipus,—maintains that our actions do not depend on our desires. A sovereign power, an inexorable destiny, governs all our actions. Our love of good, and our hatred of evil, are of use to us as regards our conduct. Fatalism which may be called *modified*, maintains that our actions are determined by our will, our will by our desires, and our desires by the joint influence of the motives which present themselves to us, and of our individual character; but that, this character having been made for us, and not by us, we are not responsible for it, or for the actions to which it leads us, and that we should in vain attempt to modify it.

In short, the true doctrine of the causality of human actions maintains, against the two preceding doctrines, that not only our conduct, but also our character, depends in fact upon our will; that we can ameliorate it, by the use of proper means, and that, if it be such that by its nature it constrains us to do evil, it will be right to employ motives which constrain us to make an effort to improve this bad character. In other words, we are subject to the *moral* obligation to seek the amelioration of our *moral* character.

The latter solution, which is Mr. Mill's, supposes in us not only spontaneity but the possibility of regulating its development. But this directing power, this faculty of placing ourselves in circumstances favourable to our perfection, what is it at bottom? This is a capital question, it seems to us, and the school which we are considering is very vague upon the point.

CHAPTER III.

PSYCHOLOGICAL THEORY OF MATTER AND OF MIND.

Psychological Theory of Matter and Mind.—1. Matter—2. Mind—3. The phenomenism of Hume and Mill.

WE do not enter, in this place, as might be supposed, into metaphysics; at least there will be no question of matter or of mind, considered as substances. The 'psychological theory of mind and of matter,' which is the summary and the result of the preceding, is opposed to the introspective theory of Reid, Stewart, and the majority of the philosophers, inasmuch as the latter consider the subject and the object to be two fundamental terms, irreducible, revealed to us by consciousness from the beginning of life, while the experimental school hold that the notions of matter and mind are complex, and formed at a later period; and that, in consequence, by applying analysis to them, we may discover and trace their genesis. The experimental school sees a question of origin and embryological research where the rival school sees only two facts to be stated, which are inexplicable by any process. It proposes to establish that matter is nothing but the permanent possibility of our sensations, and that mind is nothing but the permanent possibility of our states of consciousness; thus approaching Berkeley on the first, and Hume on the second point.

We begin with matter.[1]

The psychological theory of the belief in an exterior world requires, in order to constitute it, some postulates, which are all proved by experience.

The first postulate is, that the human mind is capable of expectation; in other words, that after having had actual sensations, we are capable of forming the conception of possible sensations.

The second postulate is, that our ideas associate themselves according to certain laws. Among the laws of the association of ideas, those with which we are concerned at present are:—

1. There exists a tendency to think of similar phenomena together.

2. There is a tendency to think together of phenomena which have been experienced or conceived of as contiguous in time or space.

3. The associations produced by contiguity become more certain and more rapid by repetition; and thus inseparable or indissoluble association is produced.

4. When association has acquired this character of insepara-

---

[1] *An Examination, etc.*, ch. xi.

bility, not only do the two ideas become inseparable in consciousness, but the facts or phenomena which correspond to those ideas finally arrive at appearing to be inseparable in existence. We find numerous examples of this in the acquired perceptions of sight. Thus, we see artificially that a body is hot or cold, hard or soft, etc.

These postulates stated:

'Perhaps it may be objected, that the very possibility of forming such a notion of matter as Sir William Hamilton's—the capacity in the human mind of imagining an external world which is anything more than what the psychological theory makes it—amounts to a disproof of the theory. If, it may be said, we had no revelation in consciousness of a world which is not in some way or other identified with sensation, we should be unable to have the notion of such a world. If the only idea we had of external objects were ideas of our sensations supplemented by an acquired notion of permanent possibilities of sensation, we must, it is thought, be incapable of conceiving, and still more incapable of fancying that we perceive, things which are not sensations at all.'[1]

And first, what do we mean by those words: an exterior world, an external substance? We mean that our perceptions have relation to something which exists, even when we are not thinking of it, which has existed before we have thought of it, which should exist even if we should be annihilated; we mean that things exist, which neither we nor any man have ever seen, touched, or perceived. The idea of this something fixed, which is distinguished from our floating impressions by that character which Kant calls permanence, is our belief in matter. Now, according to the psychological theory, all that is only the form imposed by the known laws of association upon our notions of contingent sensations, obtained by experience.

I see a piece of white paper upon a table. I pass into another room and I no longer see it, nevertheless I am persuaded that the paper is still there, and that should I go back into that room, I should see it again. I believe that Calcutta exists, although

[1] Mill's *Hamilton's Philosophy*, p. 199.

I do not see it, and that it would still exist even though all its inhabitants should be suddenly stricken with death. Analyse my belief, and you will see that it reduces itself to this: if I were suddenly transported to the shores of the Hooghly, I should experience sensations which would lead me to believe that Calcutta exists. In these two cases (and they include the whole), my idea of the exterior world is the idea of actual or possible sensations. These different possibilities are the most important thing in the world for me. My present sensations are generally fugitive and of little importance; the possibilities, on the contrary, are *permanent;* which is precisely the characteristic which distinguishes our idea of substance or matter from our idea of sensation.

There is another important characteristic which adds to the certitude or guarantee of these possibilities of sensation; it is, that the sensations are not isolated but united in clusters. When we think of any body or material object, we think not of *one single* sensation, but of a varied and indefinite series of sensations ordinarily belonging to different senses, but so united that the presence of one generally announces the possible and simultaneous presence of all the rest. Consequently, the cluster, considered as a whole, presents itself to the mind as permanent,—the principal characteristic which distinguishes our idea of substance or matter from our idea of sensation.

In short, we do not only recognise fixed groups, but also a fixed *order* in our sensations, an order of succession which, when confirmed by experience, gives rise to the ideas of cause and effect. But this invariable succession of antecedent and consequent takes place most frequently, not between an actual antecedent and an actual consequent, but between the groups of which only one portion is actually present to us. Therefore, our ideas of cause, power, and activity unite themselves not to sensations, but to *groups of possibilities of sensations.* The whole of these sensations, considered as possible, form a permanent basis for actual sensations; the relation of the possible sensations is considered as the relation of a cause to its effects, of a canvas to the figures painted upon it, of a root to its trunk, its leaves, and its flowers, of a *substratum* to that which covers it.

Nor is this all. Having reached this point, we consider these permanent possibilities as different from sensation. We forget that they are founded in sensation, and we suppose that they are intrinsically distinct from it. Now we discover that other human or feeling beings formed their expectation or their conduct, as we do, upon the possibilities of sensations. We see that they have not exactly the same sensations as we have, but that they have their possibilities of sensations like us; that everything indicates that there is in them a possibility of sensations similar to ours, if indeed their organs do not differ from the type of ours. This agreement between ourselves and our fellows finishes and completes our idea,—that groups of possibilities are the fundamental reality of nature.

In a word, possible sensations, groups of sensations, order in these groups, and agreement between our belief and that of our fellows: in these consists our whole idea of matter.

'Matter, then, may be defined a Permanent Possibility of Sensation. If I am asked whether I believe in matter, I ask whether the questioner accepts this definition of it. If he does, I believe in matter: and so do all Berkeleians. In any other sense than this, I do not. But I affirm with confidence, that this conception of matter includes the whole meaning attached to it by the common world, apart from philosophical and sometimes from theological theories.' [1]

'It may perhaps be said, that the preceding theory gives, indeed, some account of the idea of permanent existence, which forms part of our conception of matter, but gives no explanation of our believing these permanent objects to be external, or out of ourselves. I apprehend, on the contrary, that the very idea of anything out of ourselves is derived solely from the knowledge experience gives us of the Permanent Possibilities. Our sensations we carry with us wherever we go, and they never exist where we are not; but when we change our place we do not carry away with us the Permanent Possibilities of sensation; they remain until we return, or arise and cease under conditions with which our presence has in general nothing to do. And more

[1] Mill's *Hamilton's Philosophy*, p. 227.

than all—they are, and will be after we have ceased to feel Permanent Possibilities of sensation to other beings than ourselves. Thus our actual sensations and the permanent possibilities of sensation stand out in obtrusive contrast to one another; and when the idea of cause has been acquired and extended by generalization from the parts of our experience to its aggregate whole, nothing can be more natural than that the Permanent Possibilities should be classed by us as existences generically distinct from our sensations, but of which our sensations are the effect.'[1]

II.

Let us now apply this psychological theory to Mind.[2] It is evident that our knowledge of Mind is, like our knowledge of Matter, entirely relative. We do not know what it is, outside of the manifestations of consciousness. We can neither know it, nor imagine it, under any other form than the succession of different states of consciousness. It is none the less true that our notion of Mind, like our notion of Matter, is the notion of *something* permanent, as opposed to the perpetual flux of states of consciousness which we refer to it. This 'permanent' may be, as regards mind as well as matter, only a possibility. I believe that my mind exists, even when it does not feel, does not think, and has not consciousness of its existence. To what does this reduce itself?—to believing in a permanent possibility of these conditions. Thus, then, our idea of mind is nothing more than the idea of the series of our actual sensations, and of the infinite possibilities of sensations which shall realize themselves under appropriate conditions.

But, before going further, Mr. Mill, aware that the majority of people hasten to the real or presumed consequences of a doctrine in order to judge it, proposes to examine them. This doctrine is accused, he says, of destroying our belief in the existence of our fellows, in the existence of a supra-sensible world, in God, and in immortality.

---

[1] Mill's *Hamilton's Philosophy*, p. 137.

[2] *An Examination*, etc., ch. xii.

On the first point, there is absolutely nothing in this theory which can prevent my thinking that there are other beings like me, whose minds like mine are only a series of sentiments. How am I brought to believe that the beings whom I now see walking about, whom I hear speaking, have sentiments and ideas, that they possess a mind? Evidently it is not by intuition. I go from the signs to the sentiments which they translate. My own experience is the basis of my induction. But this logical process loses nothing of its legitimacy in the hypothesis that neither mind nor matter is anything but a permanent possibility of feeling.

The psychological theory of mind leaves my certainty of the existence of my fellows exactly as it was before; and so it is as regards the existence of God. Supposing that I consider the Divine Spirit simply as the series of Divine thoughts prolonged during eternity, this would assuredly be to consider the existence of God as real as my own; this would be to do that which in reality one always does, to infer the Divine nature from the human. Belief in God has, therefore, nothing to gain or lose from the present theory.

So it is in the case of immortality. It is as easy to conceive of a succession of sentiments, a thread of consciousness eternally prolonged, as of a spiritual substance which always continues to exist; and if there are any arguments in proof, they are as capable of application to the one theory as to the other.

Thus these, the extrinsic objections, are disposed of. But the theory which resolves mind into a series of actual sentiments, with a basis of possible sentiments, contains intrinsic difficulties, which it does not appear, says Mr. Mill, that psychological analysis can resolve. In fact the thread of consciousness which constitutes the phenomenal life of the mind is composed not only of present sensations, *but also of expectations and of recollections;* it is not limited to the present, it embraces the past and the future.

'If therefore, we speak of the mind as a series of feelings, we are obliged to complete the statement by calling it a series of feelings which is aware of itself as past and future; and we are reduced to the alternative of believing that the mind, or ego, is something different from any series of feelings, or possibilities of them, or of accepting the paradox that something, which *ex hypothesi* is but a series of feelings, can be aware of itself as a series.'[1]

The truth is, adds Mr. Mill, that here we find ourselves brought face to face with that inexplicable which is necessarily to be encountered when we touch upon ultimate facts. And he thinks that if his method of explaining facts appears to be more incomprehensible than another, it is because it is less accommodated to correct language, and consequently presents occasional contradictions *in terms*.

'I think by far the wisest thing we can do, is to accept the inexplicable fact, without any theory of how it takes place; and when we are obliged to speak of it in terms which assume a theory, to use them with reservation as to their meaning.'[2]

III.

This theory of mind and matter, which in certain respects goes beyond purely experimental psychology, appears to have given rise to vehement discussion in England, if we may judge by the great number of books, pamphlets, and articles in newspapers and reviews which Mr. Mill quotes, discusses, and sometimes approves. With that taste for free criticism, and that perfect loyalty which are characteristic of him, he likes to quote his adversaries, to bring certain objections into strong relief, and even to tell us plainly what those are which he regards as insoluble.

We must first note some differences between the psychologic theory of matter and that of mind. Mr. Mill gives the former as complete, but he expressly refuses so to characterize the latter.[3]

The one would be unreservedly accepted by an idealist, the other is confined to absolute empiricism; the one touches upon Berkeley, the other upon Hume.

What is there, notwithstanding, in common between the two theories which the author ranges under the same name? There is this: as the one reduces matter to a collection of attributes,

[1] Mill's *Hamilton's Philosophy*, p. 212. [2] *Ibid.* p. 213.
[3] *Ibid.* Appendix, p. 245.

and the other reduces mind, at least in appearance, to a collection of states of consciousness, it seems that all idea of substance disappears. Now, this theory has a special name, *phenomenism.* We find it in Hume; let us see if it is to be attributed to Mr. Mill.

The author, who complains of the reception his doctrine has met with from those 'whose opinions were already formed,' acknowledges that the least unfavourable judgment has been that of the partisans of Berkeley or any other idealist. We do not see, in fact, why they should not accept his theory of matter. For, what does the idealist maintain? That all the reality of the exterior world is in the mind which knows it; that we do not know anything of matter except that which is told by our sensations and our ideas,—sensation revealing attributes, and idea revealing the order of the attributes, the first being rather ordinary consciousness, and the second scientific consciousness; but that as the whole reduces itself by final analysis to states of consciousness, we may maintain that the reality of matter is in us. But this is in no sense to deny the existence of matter; it is simply to say that we have a relative knowledge of it, and that it is not the possible cause of our sensations and our ideas. But Mr. Mill, as we have already seen, does not maintain anything else.

The debate concentrates itself upon the psychological theory of mind. Here the idealists abandon us, and the difficulty increases. We can admit, if necessary, that the exterior world is a collection of phenomena without substratum; because there still remains a mind which makes its synthesis, and serves as its support. But if the mind be also reduced to a collection of states of consciousness without any substance, we no longer find anything solid to take hold of, either in us, or out of us. Kant saw in our idea of substance a certain way of uniting and aggregating phenomena, proper to the human mind; he did not deny the possible existence of a substratum, of an inaccessible *noumenon*, a sort of mysterious stuff, on which phenomena are drawn; but here the phenomenism is absolute. In fact, says Mr. Mill, all the philosophers who have closely examined the question have decided that there is no need of substance, except as the support and the bond of phenomena. Let us, then, simply lay aside this support out of our thought, and suppose that the phenomena remain, and that they form the same groups and the same series, thanks to some other agent, or even without any agent, if this be not an internal law, and we shall arrive, without substance, at the consequences in view of which substance was supposed. The Hindus think that the earth requires to be sustained by an elephant; but the earth sustains itself perfectly in space, without being supported by anything. Descartes supposed a material *medium* between the sun and the earth, to explain their reciprocal action; but the law of universal attraction explains it much better than whirlwinds.

Still, when this first difficulty has been surmounted, there remains another more serious one, and this, Mr. Mill acknowledges, he does not solve. You reduce the *ego* to a series of states of consciousness, but there is something wanting to unite those states to one another. If you have a necklace of beads, and you remove the string, what remains? Separate beads, but no longer a necklace. Our author seems to admit that the bond, 'the organic union,' which exists between past and present consciousness, in constituting memory also constitutes the *ego*.

'I hold it to be indubitable,' he says, 'that there is something real in this bond, real as the sensations themselves; and which is not simply a product of the laws of thought without anything which corresponds to it. The precise nature of the process by which we know it is an ample subject for discussion . . . I do not attempt to decide upon it. But that original element which has no community of nature with anything answering to our names, and to which we can give no other name than its own without implying some false or unsteady theory, is the *ego*. As such, I recognise in the myself—in my own mind—a reality different from that real existence as a permanent possibility, which is the only one that I recognise in matter.'

It would be unjust, after having read the preceding, to confound this doctrine with that of Hume. The scepticism of the Scotch philosopher led to such strange conclusions, that with him there is nothing but the inexplicable, and he gets out of it with

[1] *Appendix* to chaps. xi. xii.

the words 'habit, belief, instinct.' In a world where there is, by hypothesis, nothing but attributes and states of consciousness without anything to unite them, there is really nothing astonishing but their harmony. Thus he acknowledges that, to him, the production of ideas is a miracle.

'There is, then, a kind of pre-established harmony between the course of nature and the succession of our ideas; and though the powers and forces by which the former is governed be wholly unknown to us, yet our thoughts and conceptions have still, we find, gone on in the same train with the other works of nature. Custom is that principle by which this correspondence has been effected.'[1]

The same philosopher has said that 'Physics, in its highest perfection, can do no more than remove our ignorance a little.' Might we not say that such metaphysic does but redouble it?

Mr. Mill, besides facts, admits order between minds. In addition, he grants to the bond which unites states of consciousness as much reality as to the states themselves. If he is vague, he is designedly so; it is because the obscure cannot be clearly explained. All considered, there is in his doctrine more *solidity* than in pure phenomenism; and in any case we must not forget that he means to leave the question open.

---

[1] Hume's *Essays*, 'Inquiry concerning Human Understanding,' section v., last paragraph but one.

MR. HERBERT SPENCER.

AMONG Philosophers, as among scientific men, there are original and independent minds, of an order above those who explain, comment upon, and develop truths already discovered or foreseen, and make them known to all. These original minds are, so to speak, creators, who are felt, on approaching them, to be like men of another race, in power, depth, and unity of thought. Whether their discoveries remain permanent acquisitions, or whether they only give a new aspect to insoluble problems, they are recognised in the sovereign fashion which is due to them; they cannot touch any question without setting their mark upon it. Mr. Herbert Spencer appears to us to be a man of this order. One of his countrymen, who is well entitled to be critical, Mr. Stuart Mill, unhesitatingly places him among the greatest of the philosophers, and says that the variety and depth of his encyclopedic knowledge would permit him to treat, as equal with equal, with the founder of the positivist school himself; that he is not a disciple, but a master.

'Mr. Spencer is one of the small number of persons who, by the solidity and encyclopedical character of their knowledge, and their power of co-ordination and concatenation, may claim to be the peers of M. Comte, and entitled to a vote in the estimation of him.'[1]

When we have studied his works very closely, we find ourselves impressed, not only by his superior science, by the immense variety of his precise and positive information, now

---

[1] Mill's *Comte*, p. 41.

almost indispensable to the philosopher, but especially by the firmness of his thought, by his self-mastery, by his solidity of method, and his lucidity of exposition. His mind is drilled and disciplined by scientific research; he does better than descant upon method, he practises it. He knows how to distinguish the certain from the probable, and, as he says, the *knowable* from the *unknowable.* In everything he insists on seeing clearly, he is not content with chimerical solutions, and he never confounds reasons with metaphors.

The philosophical mind is a certain manner of thinking, not acquired, but developed by culture, which has its characteristic traits, just like the poetic or the scientific mind. If there be a definition which expresses its qualities and its defects, which may be accepted by every one, and agreed to by all the schools, it appears to be the following :—

It is the mind which generalizes. The ideal would consist in laying hold, not only of the general formulas which simplify facts, but on the facts which verify the formulas; in seeing laws in facts and facts in laws. But this is an ideal, that is to say, what we may hope for, but not attain. In his study of psychological phenomena, with which only we are now occupied, Mr. Herbert Spencer has employed the fundamental processes of every method, synthesis and analysis. In our eyes, one of the greatest merits of this rare mind is his skill in handling these two different instruments, one of which distinguishes, divides, separates, while the other collects, draws together, identifies. It is with great difficulty that these two modes of thought, each of which, by its very nature, excludes the other, constitute a perfect equilibrium, so balanced that the talent of analysis may be exactly equal to the aptitude for synthesis. In Mr. Herbert Spencer synthesis predominates; he takes sensible pleasure in tracing grand outlines, in sweeping vast horizons, in seeking out simple and rich formulas, the large and comprehensive laws from whence we dominate the innumerable mass of facts; and this is his especial claim to the title of philosopher. Nevertheless, he can also handle analysis so as to satisfy the most competent and the most critical on this point.

A philosopher must have a method. This is the point common to all, from Plato and Aristotle down to Auguste Comte and Hegel. In minds of that stamp, ideas fall naturally into order; they think collectively, and not in detail, because each detail is to them a portion of the whole which they are reconstituting. This unity of method, this mode of systematic thinking, is common to Mr. Herbert Spencer and to the great masters. Let us see then, what is the governing idea of his philosophy, and the collective conception to which all the rest is attached. The great English naturalist, Professor Huxley, said on a recent occasion:—

'The only complete and methodical exposition known to me of the theory of evolution, is to be found in Herbert Spencer's *System of Philosophy*, a work that should be carefully studied by those who desire to become acquainted with the tendencies of scientific thought.'

The idea of evolution or of progress; such is in fact the fundamental idea of our philosopher; he applies it to everything, and he finds it everywhere. The formation of the worlds coming forth from a primitive nebulus, according to the hypothesis of Laplace, the unfolding of life, of thought, and of all which manifests it; science, arts, civilisation, all is explained by a progress. The hypothesis of development is the substitution of mobility for fixity, of becoming for being, but also of the relative for the absolute. No more of stable existence. We cannot say of anything that *it is*, in so far as that word implies fixity. And if everything varies and is transformed, all existence is no more than a transition, a moment between that which is ending and that which is beginning; a striking thought, because in this universal flux we feel that the infinite presses upon us on all sides, that everything holds to everything. In the human individual we see the generation which produces it, and that which shall follow; in one human generation, we see humanity; in humanity, the mysterious evolution of life; in life, the geological transformations which have rendered it possible; in them, a mode of existence so vague that it can hardly be discerned, and thus we ascend from second causes to second causes, to the point at which faith begins, and where science ends.

Is this idea of progress, such as we are about to find it in Mr. Herbert Spencer's works, a novelty in philosophy? We must be clear upon this point. It is an idea anterior to him, but which was formerly otherwise understood. Leibnitz, who in so many respects has anticipated the most recent theories, substituted the idea of a continuous progress for the geometrical mechanism of Descartes. The Hegelian dialectic, also founded on the idea of becoming, pretends to reproduce by its synthesis the evolution of the world, from void existence up to thought and absolute consciousness. But whilst the theory of Leibnitz is only a view of the future by a genius, an hypothesis not then verified by facts, while the theory of Hegel is an entirely metaphysical conception, completely subjective, encumbered with its triple movement of thesis, antithesis, and synthesis, boldly bending facts to its *a priori* conceptions, the hypothesis of development is quite otherwise presented by Mr. Herbert Spencer. It is produced objectively, the facts suggest it to the mind, the mind does not impose it upon the facts. It arises of itself, out of the study of the sciences, or at least of those in which there is movement and life: geology, botany, physiology, psychology, æsthetics, morals, linguistics, history, etc. It is supported by an almost infinite mass of facts and experiences. Besides, and this is a great point, *it claims to be only an hypothesis;* the only concession which it demands is that no other hypothesis approaches it in probability. It is, if we please, the hypothesis of Leibnitz revived, but free from metaphysics, and supported by the experience of nearly two centuries.

I have no intention of establishing a comparison which would be inexact, and which Mr. Herbert Spencer would disclaim, between him and Leibnitz; nevertheless, I wish to cite some of the points common to both, which it is impossible to fail to remark, and which relate to their dynamism.

First, the idea of continuity, or universal compenetration, whence it comes that all things hold together, that all things are 'caused and causing,' and that the process by which the human mind separates them is arbitrary, though necessary. Properly speaking, this idea and that of progress are the same, the one but another aspect of the other, because, if everything is transformed and metamorphosed, everything holds together; there is not in nature a *hiatus*, or any solution of continuity. Only, the idea of progress is dynamic, and the idea of continuity is static.

We know that Leibnitz, in his explanation of the universe, had imagined monads, a kind of metaphysical atoms, having all possible degrees, from the simple antitype to the most perfect aperception. According to their nature, they constitute brute matter, or the living being, the animal, the man, or the angel. And as, in the universe, nothing is isolated, a certain monad being given, all the universe acts upon it, and thus expresses it. Each monad is then a mirror which reflects differently. Set this grand conception free from the metaphysical phraseology which is proper to it, and there remains a positive incontestable truth. Place in the same spot different beings, a stone, a tree, a dog, a savage, an European, Newton or Shakespeare; each will reflect it according to his nature, one a little, the other much. There will exist between the being and its place that which Mr. Herbert Spencer calls *a correspondence*, and the degree of life will be measured by the degree of correspondence, the ideal mode of life being perfect correspondence. The man who could attain to that degree would reflect in himself, in a complete manner, all the reality of the universe; he would be a microcosm adequate to the microcosm. This idea of *a correspondence*, which holds the chief place in our author's psychology, as we shall see, appears to me to be a translation of Leibnitz's words into the language of experimental psychology; every monad is a mirror which reflects the universe.

One of the chief traits of the philosopher who occupies us at present is his systematic character. This is to be noted. Certainly, the country which has produced Bacon, Hobbes, Locke, Hume, without mentioning the Scotch philosophers, and Mr. Herbert Spencer's contemporaries, has done much for philosophy; but the English genius has generally preferred researches into detail to great collective views; according to Buckle, it finds pleasure in induction and analysis. In Mr. Herbert Spencer, on the contrary, there is great boldness and breadth, some would perhaps say rashness. But even that proves his power, for fertile minds err rather through audacity than through timidity. His *System of Philosophy*, of which only the two first parts have been entirely published, will embrace an immense number of facts and problems. It would be inappropriate to our subject to speak of it here, and it is not a work to be judged passingly or in haste. The *First Principles* are, as it were, the vestibule of this great building. The purpose of this work, which, if we were not afraid of being misunderstood, we would call the *Metaphysics of Positivism*, is to show that outside of science there is a region inaccessible to its processes and its methods, that outside of the knowable is the unknowable, and thus to place the old quarrel between religion and science, demonstration and faith, on new ground, by showing that there is absolutely nothing in common between them,—to endeavour, by a daring synthesis founded upon the positive sciences, to bring everything back to the law of equivalents or of correlation of forces; and to show that all phenomena are convertible between themselves, from physical manifestations, even to life, thought, and the development of history; thus to condemn spiritualism and materialism, and to reject both as vain solutions. This work is followed by the *Principles of Biology*, which traces the morphological and physiological evolution of life; the *Principles of Psychology*, now in course of publication; which will be followed by the *Principles of Sociology*, and the *Principles of Morals*. Add to these two important volumes of essays, a treatise on *Moral, Intellectual, and Physical Education*, one on *Social Statics*, in which are determined the essential conditions of human happiness, and a *Classification of the Sciences*, and we can form an idea of the various subjects which this fertile mind has entertained, and on each of which it has produced profound and original ideas sufficient to make the reputation of one less prolific.

We cannot discuss, even passingly, all these titles to fame in this place, where we are principally concerned with psychology. As, however, the fundamental doctrine of evolution is frequently expounded in the *Essays*, and applied to the most various questions, and this work is but little known in France, though it is calculated to make the philosophy of the author familiar, we propose to make a special study of it.

CHAPTER I.

THE LAW OF EVOLUTION.

The Law of Evolution. — 1. Progress consists in the passage from the homogeneous to the heterogeneous: its law—2. The hypothesis of the nebulus—3. Living organism and social organism—4. The genesis of science—5. The knowable and the unknowable.

I.

Our purpose is to explain the doctrine of progress and development, according to the *Essays*,[1] and to show how Mr. Herbert Spencer applies it to the different orders of phenomena. After having seen what is to be understood by progress, we shall follow the law of evolution in its explanation of the cosmical genesis, of the development of the social organism, and finally of the genesis of science.

The idea which is generally attached to the word *progress* is not only vague, but erroneous. Progress in itself is confounded with that which accompanies it, with the benefits and useful results which it brings to man. The vice of the current conception arises from its being teleological; facts are judged by their relation to human happiness, the only concern felt is for that which increases or tends to increase it. This process takes the shadow for the reality. In order to understand what progress is, we must study, apart from our own interest, what is the nature of the changes which produce it.

The German physiologists have established that in individual organisms progress consists in the passage from a homogeneous to a heterogeneous structure. Every germ at its origin is an uniform substance, in the double sense of its texture, and its chemical composition; by successive and almost infinite differentiations, that complex combination of tissues and organs which constitutes the animal or the adult plant is produced. This is the

[1] *Essays; Scientific, Political, and Speculative.* London, 1861. This will be found in a much more learned form in the *First Principles.*

history of every organism. Mr. Herbert Spencer proposes to show that *this law of organic progress is the law of all progress;* that the development of the earth, of the life on its surface, of society, of government, of industry, of commerce, of language, of literature, of science, and of art, supposes the same evolution of the simple into the complex by successive differentiations.

In the first place, *if the hypothesis of the nebulus be admitted* as true, the formation of the solar system furnishes us with a verification of this law. In its first condition, it consisted of a medium indefinitely extended, and almost homogeneous in density, temperature, and other physical attributes. The first progress towards consolidation brought about a differentiation between the space still occupied by the nebulous mass and the unoccupied space which it had formerly filled. At the same time differences in density and temperature are produced, between the interior and the exterior of the mass, then in the speed of the motion of rotation, which varied according to the distance from the centre. Let us reflect upon the numerous differences between the planets and satellites, with respect to distance, to the inclination of their orbits, the inclination of their axes, the time of their rotation, their density, their physical constitution, etc.; and we shall see how heterogeneous the solar system is, compared to the almost complete homogeneity of the nebulous mass from which it is supposed to have issued.

But as this is only a hypothesis, each person may take it for as much as he pleases; this does not in any way prejudice the general doctrine which we are about to verify on more solid ground. Let us take our globe. In the beginning, according to almost all geologists, the earth was a mass of matter, in a state of fusion, and consequently was of homogeneous consistence, and relatively homogeneous temperature. And now, merely looking at its surface, how heterogeneous it appears to us! Igneous rocks, sedimentary strata, metallic veins, endless irregularities, mountains, continents, seas, differences of climates, in short, such a variety of phenomena that all the geographers, geologists, mineralogists, and meteorologists put together, have not yet succeeded in enumerating them. If we pass on from the earth to the planets and the animals which are now living, or have lived, facts to verify the law are wanting; not that it is doubtful that in the individual organism progress is made from the simple to the compound; but, if we pass from the individual forms of life to life in general, we cannot say whether the modern flora and fauna are more heterogeneous than those of the past. The actual data of palæontology do not permit us to affirm anything. Nevertheless, the facts, taken together, tend to show that the most heterogeneous organisms are the last produced. To go no further than the branching off of vertebrates, the first known to us are fishes, the most homogeneous of all; reptiles appear later and are more heterogeneous; mammifers and birds appear still later, and are yet more heterogeneous. Then, the most ancient remains which we know of the class of mammifers are those small marsupials which are the lowest type of this class, whilst the highest type, man, is the most recent. We must observe, that taking the vertebrate fauna as a whole, the palæozoic period, entirely composed of fishes (in so far as we know) was much less heterogeneous than the present period, which, besides reptiles, comprehends birds and mammifers of widely various kinds.

But, if we choose to leave the question open on this point, it is at least clear that as regards man, the most heterogeneous of animals, heterogeneity has been most largely produced in the civilized subdivisions of the species; that the species has become more heterogeneous in virtue of the multiplication of races and the differentiation of races among themselves. The Papuan, whose body and arms are often well developed, has very small legs, resembling in this the quadrumanous kind, while in the case of the European, whose legs are longer and more massive, there is more heterogeneity between the upper and lower limbs. The differences between the skulls and the faces of men are greater than in any other race of animals, and greater among Europeans than among savages.[1] Ethnology, by its divisions and subdivisions of races, puts this progress in heterogeneity beyond a doubt. Within a few generations, has not the Saxon race given

[1] See Vogt, *Leçons sur l'homme*, chap. ii.

birth to the Anglo-American variety, and is not another springing up in Australia?

If we pass on to humanity considered in its social organism, we find numerous facts to sustain our law. Society in its origin, such as we find it among savage tribes, is a homogeneous aggregate of individuals having the same powers and the same functions; every man is a warrior, a hunter, a fisher, and a workman; the only differences are those which result from sex. The first differentiation is that which takes place between the governing and the governed; this increases, authority becomes hereditary, the king assumes an almost Divine character; for, at this epoch, religion and government are closely associated, and during centuries the religious and civil laws are hardly separate. Now, if we observe that among modern Europeans, not only are the State and the Church separating from each other more and more widely, but that the political organization is very complex, that it presupposes subdivisions in justice, finance, etc., we cannot doubt that in this instance progress is made from the homogeneous to the heterogeneous.

In industry it is the same; the subdivision of labour is an evident truth.

The most rudimentary form of language is the exclamation. Did it alone originally constitute simply human language? This we cannot tell. Linguistics shows us that in all languages there are words which may be grouped in families and referred to a common root. The development of idioms then also supposes heterogeneity. Whether we hold, with Max Müller and Bunsen, that all languages are derived from a single stem, or with other linguists that there are two or more, the development of the European languages, derived from one and the same source, would in itself show us that the evolution of languages is also in conformity with the law of progress.

Writing (ideographical at its origin) connects itself with painting, and both, together with sculpture, were at first simple appendices of architecture, which was itself the historical or religious art: the palaces and temples of Assyria, the monuments of Egypt or of India bear witness to this. These arts became separate in the lapse of centuries; writing was transformed into printing. 'However dissimilar they may appear to us to-day, the bust which stands upon the console, the picture which hangs upon the wall, the copy of the *Times* which lies upon the table, are related to each other, not only by nature but by origin.' Poetry, music, and dancing also originally formed an inseparable group. The dances of savage tribes, accompanied by monotonous songs, the sacred dances of the Egyptians, and of David before the ark, of the Lupercalia and the Saturnalia of Rome, the triumphal ode of Moses, accompanied by dancing and the cymbals,—these are only a few examples among thousands. These arts became separated by progress, and we may remark that in each instance that progress took place from the homogeneous to the heterogeneous. In literature, primitive works comprise everything;—the Scriptures contain the theology, cosmogony, history, legislation, morals, etc., of the Hebrews; in the *Iliad* there are religious, military, epic, lyric, and dramatic elements, which, at a later period, form so many kinds.

It is the same with science, as we shall see hereafter. Let us then fearlessly conclude, from this rapid examination of facts, that the law of progress is the passage from the homogeneous to the heterogeneous. And now, does not this uniform processus presuppose a fundamental necessity from whence it results? Does not this universal *law* imply a universal *cause?* There is no question of having an absolute knowledge of this cause: that is a mystery above the reach of human intelligence; we have simply to transform our empirical generalization into a rational generalization. Exactly as it has been possible to show the necessary consequences of the law of gravitation in the laws of Kepler, so it may be possible to show that the law of progress is the necessary consequence of some equally universal principle.

This law, which explains the universal transformation of the homogeneous into the heterogeneous, is as follows: *Every active force produces more than one change; every cause produces more than one effect.*

One body strikes another; to our eyes the effect consists in a change in the position or the motion of one or both of the two bodies. But that is a very incomplete view, because more than one sound is produced; and the vibrations of the air are produced, not only by the sound, but by the motion of the bodies; a derangement of the molecules at the point of collision has taken place; consequently condensation and disengagement of heat, sometimes even a spark, that is to say, the production of light. We have therefore at least five species of changes produced by a simple shock.

Some one lights a candle, that is a simple fact; but there results from it a production of light, a production of heat, an ascending column of hot gases, currents established in the surrounding air, a continuous formation of carbonic acid, water, etc. Besides, each of the changes thus produced gives rise in its turn to other changes. The disengaged carbonic acid will combine itself little by little with some basis, or, under the influence of the solar light, it will give out its carbon to the leaf of a plant. The water will modify the hygrometric condition of the surrounding air, etc.

A small quantity of virus from smallpox, introduced into the system, may cause, during the first period, stiffness, heat of the skin, acceleration of the pulse, loss of appetite, thirst, gastric disturbance, vomiting, headaches, etc.; during the second period, cutaneous eruption, cough, etc.; during the third period, œdematous inflammation, pneumonia, pleurisy, diarrhœa, etc. A living species, animal or vegetable, in proportion as it spreads itself out, and occupies a more extended area, finds itself exposed to very different conditions of climate, sun, light, and heat, and thus we see it give birth to numerous varieties. This happens even in the case of domestic animals.

We have now mentioned a sufficient number of the various examples which the author borrows from geology, linguistics, ethnology, chemistry, industry, and commerce, to elucidate his thought. He always calls upon us to observe that if there be in reality complex causes of which we have spoken as simple causes, it still remains true that these causes are much less complex than their results. 'Finally, the facts tend to show that each kind of progress is from the homogeneous to the heterogeneous, and that this is because each change is followed by several changes.'[1]

[1] Perhaps it may be objected, that it is not in reality *one single* cause which produces several effects; that in the case of the shock, for example, there must

II.

In a long essay upon the hypothesis of the Nebulæ, the author attaches the hypothesis of Laplace to the doctrine of evolution, defending it against the objections to it raised by science. Lord Rosse's powerful telescope having enabled astronomers to solve the hitherto insoluble Nebulæ, it has been concluded that if we had sufficiently powerful instruments, we could resolve every nebulus into stars. Is this a sufficient reason for rejecting the hypothesis? By no means. *A priori*, it was very improbable, if not impossible, that nebular masses should still remain uncondensed when others have been condensed for millions of years.

In comparison with the doctrine of finality, or, as Mr. Herbert Spencer calls it, *manufacture*, the hypothesis of the nebulus has a great deal of probability and many facts in its favour. It explains much better the necessities of constitution and of the motions of the planets, the anomalies in the distribution and the motion of the satellites, the speed of the planetary rotation; and then in these later times, the spectrum analysis has arisen to corroborate the hypothesis of a community of origin between all the parts of our universe. Into this purely scientific domain, otherwise outside our limits, the conclusion draws us. It is this: 'It remains only to point out that while the genesis of the solar system, and of countless other systems like it, is thus rendered comprehensible, the ultimate mystery continues as great as ever. The problem of existence is not solved; it is simply removed further back. The Nebular Hypothesis throws no light on the origin of diffused matter, and diffused matter as much needs accounting for as concrete matter. The genesis of an atom is not easier to conceive than the genesis of a planet. Nay, indeed, so far from making the universe a less mystery than before,

exist, besides the shock, certain conditions of the bodies concerned which render the production of sound, heat, etc., possible. There would also be, besides the visible cause, virtual causes acting with it, and the passage from the homogeneous to the heterogeneous would be the actualization of these virtual causes. We think Mr. Spencer would reply that to put the question thus would be to transfer it to the ground of the noumena, which he does not wish to approach; and that if a simple statement of facts be adhered to, *one* shock is followed by *several* effects.

it makes it a greater mystery. Creation by manufacture is a much lower thing than creation by evolution. A man may put together a machine, but he cannot make a machine develop itself. . . . That our harmonious universe once existed potentially as formless diffused matter, and has slowly grown into its present organized state, is a far more astonishing fact than would have been its formation after the artificial method vulgarly supposed. Those who hold it legitimate to argue from phenomena to noumena, may rightly contend that the Nebular Hypothesis implies a First Cause as much transcending the mechanical God of Paley, as this does the fetish of the savage.'[1]

III.

The result of the idea of evolution, applied to social and political phenomena, is to bring out the analogy between society and the organized body. It may be thought that the author's comparisons in his *Essay upon Social Organization* are far-fetched. At least it cannot be denied that his combinations are ingenious, in many respects sustainable, and, taken collectively, incontestable. Nothing being true except within certain limits, the danger for a correct idea is that of being pushed to extremes. We must, therefore, in observing the following combinations, confine ourselves to the consideration of them as an *illustration*, a throwing of light upon social phenomena by biological phenomena.

The social body, like the living body, is not a simple aggregate of parts, it supposes a *consensus* between them. Both are subject to the same law of evolution, to the same varieties of form; there are rudimentary societies, just like coarse organisms; there are learned and complex social organizations, just like the organisms whose mode of life is rich and complex. For ages this parallelism was felt by the philosophers. Thus Plato drew his ideal republic upon the model of the faculties of the human soul. Hobbes goes farther; his city is an immense body (*Leviathan*), whose sovereign is the soul, the magistrates are the articulations, the sanctions are the nerves, the wealth of the whole is the strength, their concord is the health, etc. But, in the absence of really comprehensive

[1] Spencer's *Essays*, vol. i. p. 55-6, edition 1863.

physiological generalizations, these comparisons necessarily remained vague. So little was the natural and necessary law of development conceived of, that that true saying of Mackintosh: 'constitutions are not made, they make themselves,' at first caused only surprise. Has not history been explained by supernatural interventions; by the preponderating action of great men, instead of its being understood that the great man can only disturb, retard, or aid the general evolution, but that, taken in its totality, it remains out of his reach. Mr. Herbert Spencer reduces the principal resemblances which exist between social organization and living organism to four :—

1. That, commencing as small aggregations, they insensibly augment in mass; some of them eventually reaching ten thousand times what they originally were.

2. That while at first so simple in structure as to be considered structureless, they assume in the course of their growth a continually-increasing complexity of structure.

3. That though in their early, undeveloped states, there exists in them scarcely any mutual dependence of parts, their parts gradually acquire a mutual dependence; which becomes at last so great, that the activity and life of each part is made possible only by the activity and life of the rest.

4. That the life and development of a society is independent of, and far more prolonged than, the life and development of any of its component units; who are severally born, grow, work, reproduce, and die, while the body politic composed of them survives generation after generation, increasing in mass, completeness of structure, and functional activity.

On the other hand, the leading differences between societies and individual organisms are these :—

1. That societies have no specific external forms. This, however, is a point of contrast which loses much of its importance, when we remember that throughout the vegetable kingdom, as well as in some lower divisions of the animal kingdom, the forms are often very indefinite.

2. That, though the living tissue whereof an individual organism consists, forms a continuous mass; the living elements of a society do not form a continuous mass.

3. That while the ultimate living elements of an individual organism are mostly fixed in their relative positions, those of the social organism are capable of moving from place to place, seems a marked disagreement. But here, too, the disagreement is much less than would be supposed. For while citizens are locomotive in their private capacities, they are fixed in their public capacities. . . . Each great centre of production, each manufacturing town or district, continues always in the same place; and many of the firms in such town or district are for generations carried on either by the descendants or successors of those who founded them.

4. The last and perhaps the most important distinction is, that while in the body of an animal only a special tissue is endowed with feeling, in a society all the members are endowed with feeling. Even this distinction, however, is by no means a complete one. For in some of the lowest animals, characterized by the absence of a nervous system, such sensitiveness as exists is possessed by all parts. It is only in the more organized forms that feeling is monopolized by one class of the vital elements. Moreover, we must remember that societies, too, are not without a certain differentiation of this kind. Though the units of a community are all sensitive, yet they are so in unequal degrees. The classes engaged in agriculture, and laborious occupations in general, are much less susceptible, intellectually and emotionally, than the rest; and especially less so than the classes of highest mental culture.[1]

In short, the resemblances are fundamental, essential; and the differences all exterior, and, strictly speaking, contestable. The analogy is much more striking if we consider them in their development, if we remark how closely the lower forms of life resemble the lower forms of social organization. Are there not analogies between the almost structureless protozoa, such as rhizopodes, the foraminifera, the vorticellæ, which form aggregates of cells, without subordination of parts, and inferior races, such as the Bushmen, among whom society is sometimes reduced to two or three families, and division of labour exists only between the sexes?[1]

[1] Spencer's *Essays*, 2d ed., vol. i. p. 391.

Physiological division of labour appears in the common polype; this is a progress. In the same way a less rude society comprehends warriors and a chief council invested with authority. Certain zoophytes, like the hydra, produce others by a process of germination; a tribe also produces its slips; jealousies, quarrels, cause divisions, a chief takes the initiative of the rupture, and the members part, and emigrate.

In the germ of a polype, as in the human egg, the aggregate of cells whence the animal is to come forth, gives birth to a peripherical layer of cells which afterwards subdivides itself into two, the one interior, called mucous or endodermous; the other, exterior, called serous or ectodermous. From the latter come the digestive and respiratory organs; from the former the nervous, muscular, and bony systems. In the social evolution we sce an analogous first differentiation of species, that of the governing and the governed, of masters and of slaves, of nobles and of serfs. And in the same way that at a later stage, between the mucous and the serous layer, a third is formed, called vascular, whence come the blood-vessels; so, when a society is growing up, an intermediate class forms itself, a class given to industry and commerce, which is also the distributing organ of that society, as the blood-vessels are the distributing apparatus of the body.

The lower animals have no blood or circulating channels in the bulk of the body, thus uniting the different portions; but as soon as the being becomes more complex, they are a necessity; each portion of the organism must receive the materials which it assimilates. An inferior society has no roads, no way of communication; but the development of civilisation necessarily supposes them. Where civilisation is only beginning there are some rude tracks traced out by use, like those *lacunæ* which serve in the inferior animals for the distribution of the nutritive fluids.

Again, if we come to the nervous system, we find ganglions in the inferior organisms which are sometimes almost independent, just as in feudal society we see the barons and the other lords governing without any control; sovereignty, almost local, exercised within narrow limits. The superior animal, on the contrary, has his nerves, his cerebro-spinal axis of a complicated structure; just as England has her parliament, her ministers, her sheriffs, and her judges, animated by the same thought and obedient to a common impulsion.

IV.

Thus, in a few words, we have explained how the law of evolution draws together social and biological phemomena. If we go into another domain, that of science, we shall find there also continuity in development. It is organically produced; its genesis is the work of an inherent progress; it comes out of vulgar knowledge, as the oak comes out of the acorn. If we consider the current opinions, we find science regarded as a kind of knowledge apart, *sui generis*, placed in an almost inaccessible region, having processes of research proper to itself, totally foreign (save in its applications) to the reasonings and the habits of common life. The doctrine of evolution, on the contrary, shows that between science and common knowledge any line of demarcation is impossible; that they differ *in degree*, not *in kind*, and that any absolute separation between them is illusory and chimerical. More than this, as development implies continuity, all the sciences hold by each other; they are the parts of one whole, there is between them *unity of composition*, and each influences the others; one progress renders new discoveries possible, which shall throw more light upon that which has been already acquired. Everything coheres; high civilisation is possible only through the culture of the sciences; but let it be borne in mind that the culture of the sciences is only possible through civilisation; thus, cause becomes effect and effect becomes cause, because in everything that lives the supreme law is reciprocity of action.

We shall now leave it to Mr. Herbert Spencer to trace back the Genesis of Science (*Essays*, vol. i. p. 166-193); that is to say, its evolution.

If we oppose to science under its most precise form, that of mathematics, our everyday modes of thought, in which there is no method, the contrast is striking. But only a little reflection is required to see that in the two cases the same faculties are brought into play, and that their mode of operation is the same at bottom. Shall we say that science is *organized knowledge?* But all knowledge is more or less organized; the commonest domestic actions presuppose facts observed, inferences drawn, results expected. Shall we say that science is a *prevision?* The definition would then be too extended; for the child who sees an apple, *foresees* that it will be resistant, soft to the touch, and of a certain flavour. Shall we say that science is an *exact* prevision? But there are sciences which are not and which never can become exact, like physiology, and there are exact previsions which we do not regard as science; for instance, that a light will be extinguished in water, and that ice will melt on the fire. Logically, then, the distinction between scientific knowledge and common knowledge is not justifiable.

If they do not differ in kind, what relation is there between them? (1.) That which science reveals is more distant from perception than that which is given by common knowledge: the prediction of an eclipse of the moon by an astronomer differs, in this respect, from the prevision of a servant that fire will make water boil. It may be said, from this point of view, that science is *an extension of the perceptions by means of reasoning.* (2.) Science, undeveloped, is a *qualitative* prevision; science developed is a *quantitative* prevision. To foresee that a piece of lead will weigh more than a piece of wood of the same size; and to foresee that at a certain moment two specified planets will be in conjunction—that is the difference between qualitative and quantitative prevision. There is no true science except where the phenomena are *measurable.* Space is measurable, thence geometry; force and space are measurable, thence statics; time, space, and force are measurable, thence dynamics. No measure is possible for our sensations; thus, there is no science of flavours or of odours.

In proportion as we pass from qualitative to quantitative prevision, we pass from inductive to deductive science. While science is purely inductive, it is purely qualitative; when it becomes imperfectly quantitative, it comprehends deduction and induction; when perfectly quantitative, it is completely deductive.

Every science, at its origin, has been qualitative, and has sometimes taken thousands of years to arrive at its quantitative period; chemistry has entered it only recently. It must not be lost sight of that science and ordinary knowledge are of the same nature, and that the one is only the extension and perfection of the other.[1]

Since science, by its processus of evolution, comes out of common knowledge, that which is given us by reason and our senses reduced to themselves merely; and that common knowledge itself proceeds from simple perceptions; the genesis of science ought, strictly speaking, to take the origin of knowledge as its point of departure. At the risk of beginning after an abrupt fashion, let us take the adult savage.

In order to live, it is necessary that he should know what will nourish him, what may hurt him, what he ought to avoid; he must distinguish a great variety of substances, plants, animals, tools, persons, etc. But what does this distinction or *classification* of objects presuppose? A recognition of the resemblance or the dissimilarity of things. By a natural progress, classification goes from rude resemblances to more subtle ones; sub-classes, according to degrees of dissimilarity, are formed in the classes; and the mind, always eliminating the dissimilar, seeking more and more close resemblances, finally tends towards the notion of complete resemblance which supposes *non-difference.*

---

[1] Here Mr. Herbert Spencer examines the classification of the sciences by Hegel, Oken, and A. Comte. He is not favourable to 'the bastard *a priori* method' of the two first. As for the third, while making much of his doctrine, he criticises him for having said that the order of decreasing generality is that in which the sciences are historically produced. In fact, algebra, which is more general than arithmetic, is posterior to it; there is an increasing generality of arithmetic in the differential calculus. The solution of A. Comte is a half-truth; the progress of science is double; it goes from the general to the special, and from the special to the general. Its *serial* arrangement of the sciences is a vicious conception; there is a *consensus* between them, which Comte has been wrong in not acknowledging. Each discovery of a science influences the others. Mr. Spencer has developed these ideas in his *Classification of the Sciences*, a special work; and M. Littré has discussed at length the objections of the English philosopher in his work on *Auguste Comte and Positivism.*

That which we have just seen in the perception and classification of objects is produced in the same way in the genesis of reasoning. To class, is to group together *similar things;* to reason is to group together *similar relations.* It is of the essence of reasoning to perceive *a resemblance* between cases, and the idea which is at the bottom of all our processes of reasoning, is the idea of *resemblance.* And in the same way as the final progress of classification consists in forming groups of completely similar objects, so the perfection of reasoning consists in forming groups of completely similar *cases.*

It is now possible for us to understand how the passage from qualitative to quantitative knowledge takes place. The processus of classification, by a progress proper to itself, tends towards complete resemblance, or *equality;* when it has attained that, science has become quantitative.

Whence comes the notion of equality? From experience. The things which we call equal (lines, angles, weights, temperatures, sounds, colours) are those 'which produce in us sensations which we cannot distinguish from one another,' the idea of equality is drawn by abstraction from artificial objects. Afterwards experience separates the idea of equality into two ideas, *equality of things; equality of relations* (two equal triangles and two similar triangles). The first idea is the concrete germ of the exact science; the second is the abstract germ, and both come from that resemblance of things and that resemblance of relations which we have already seen.

At the same time and in the same way distinct ideas of *number* are produced. Number, equality, resemblance, these are notions which are intimately related. Simple enumeration is a registration of experiences repeated in a certain way; in order that they may be susceptible of enumeration, they must be more or less similar; and in order that *absolutely true* numerical results should be obtained, the units must be *absolutely equal.* We apply number on occasion to unequal units, like the animals on a farm, but every calculation supposes the *perfect equality* of the units, and reaches exact results only in virtue of that hypothesis; the first ideas of number are those derived from equal or similar magnitudes, especially in inorganic objects; and consequently geometry and arithmetic have a simultaneous origin. We should also remark that several nations, who do not seem to have any relation between them, have adopted *ten* (the ten fingers) as the basis of their enumeration, or five (the five fingers of one hand), or twenty (the fingers and toes), which shows that the fingers have been the original unit of numeration.

Thus, then, we know the idea of equality as the basis of all science, but how do we apply it? How do we pass from the vague perception of equality to the exact perception proper to science? By the juxtaposition of the things compared. Hence it arises that if we wish to judge of two shades of colour, we place them side by side; that if we wish to estimate two weights, we take one in each hand, and compare their pressure, making our thought pass rapidly from one to the other, and 'as of all greatnesses, those of linear extension are those whose equality may be most easily ascertained, it results that it is to those we should reduce all others.' It is the property of linear extension that it alone admits of absolute juxtaposition or coincidence, such as befalls two mathematical lines, *equality* then becoming *identity*. 'Thus it is that all exact science is reducible by final analysis to results measured in equal units of linear extension.'

The idea of measure by juxtaposition is suggested to us by experience. We must all have remarked that when two men, two animals, any two objects, are near one another, the inequality becomes more visible. This experience, repeated constantly, has given us our first lessons.

In short, all knowledge, whether scientific or vulgar, presupposes resemblances which may vary from the vaguest analogy to perfect equality, which alone constitutes quantitative science; equality being given and verified by an empirical juxtaposition. The terms foot, thumb, finger, pace, and others of a similar kind used in the origin of almost all languages, are they not facts which come to the support of the empirical origin of the idea of measure, if it be disputed by sceptics?

We should exceed our limits did we follow Mr. Herbert Spencer through his picture of the production of the various sciences. He brings out, by numerous facts, their close relations and their reciprocal dependence. In our time, he says, the *consensus* between the sciences has become such, that there is no considerable discovery in one order of facts which does not soon lead to important discoveries in others. And each serves the others; the observation of a star supposes the employment of highly-perfected instruments, and the assistance of optics, thermology, hygrometry, barology, electricity, for the registration of certain minute observations, and even of psychology itself, to correct the 'personal equation.' Such is the complication of sciences involved in so seemingly simple a thing as fixing the position of a star.

V.

Here we leave the law of evolution. No doubt the author will at some future time carry it into questions of morals, whither it would have been interesting to follow him; for the hypothesis of progress alone can produce an agreement between those who maintain against all evidence that morals do not vary, and those who maintain against all reason that there is nothing in morals but the mobile and the arbitrary. A short essay on *Anthropomorphism* (vol. i. p. 440) shows how the idea of development can also transform the study of religions, from that of the grossest fetichism to that of monotheism under its purest forms.

But what it behoves us thoroughly to understand is, that the idea of evolution, whether it explains cosmical and biological phenomena, or whether it penetrates the world of thought and of history, never explains first causes. Everything which goes beyond experience escapes it. We shall let the author state his conclusions on this point himself.

'Probably not a few will conclude that here is an attempted solution of the great questions with which philosophy in all ages has perplexed itself. Let none thus deceive themselves. Only such as know not the scope and the limits of science can fall into so grave an error. The foregoing generalizations apply not to the genesis of things in themselves, but to their genesis as manifested to the human consciousness. After all that has been said, the ultimate mystery remains just as it was. The explanation of that which is explicable does but bring out into greater clearness the inexplicableness of that which remains behind. However we may succeed in reducing the equation to its lowest terms, we are not thereby enabled to determine the unknown quantity; on the contrary, it only becomes more manifest that the unknown quantity can never be found.

'Little as it seems to do so, fearless inquiry tends continually to give a firmer basis to all true religion. The timid sectarian, alarmed at the progress of knowledge, obliged to abandon one by one the superstitions of his ancestors, and daily finding his cherished beliefs more and more shaken, secretly fears that all things may some day be explained, and has a corresponding dread of science: thus evincing the profoundest of all infidelity—the fear lest the truth be bad. On the other hand, the sincere man of science, content to follow wherever the evidence leads him, becomes by each new inquiry more profoundly convinced that the universe is an insoluble problem. Alike in the external and the internal worlds, he sees himself in the midst of perpetual changes, of which he can discover neither the beginning nor the end. If, tracing back the evolution of things, he allows himself to entertain the hypothesis that all matter once existed in a diffused form, he finds it utterly impossible to conceive how this came to be so, and equally, if he speculates on the future, he can assign no limit to the grand succession of phenomena ever unfolding themselves before him. On the other hand, if he looks inward, he perceives that both terminations of the thread of consciousness are beyond his grasp; he cannot remember when or how consciousness commenced, and he cannot examine the consciousness that at any moment exists, for only a state of consciousness that is already past can become the object of thought, and never one which is passing. When, again, he turns from the succession of phenomena, external or internal, to their essential nature, he is equally at fault. Though he may succeed in resolving all properties of objects into manifestations of force, he is not thereby enabled to realize what force is, but finds, on the contrary, that the more he thinks about it the more he is baffled. Similarly, though analysis of mental actions may finally bring him down to sensations as the original materials out of which all thought is woven, he is none the forwarder; for he cannot in the least comprehend sensation—cannot even conceive how sensation is possible. Inward and outward things he thus discovers to be alike inscrutable in their ultimate genesis and nature. He sees that the materialist and spiritualist controversy is a mere war of words; the disputants being equally absurd—each believing he understands that which it is impossible for any man to understand. In all directions his investigations eventually bring him face to face with the unknowable, and he ever more clearly perceives it to be the unknowable. He learns at once the greatness and the littleness of human intellect—its power in dealing with all that comes within the range of experience; its impotence in dealing with all that transcends experience. He feels, with a vividness which no others can, the utter incomprehensibleness of the simplest fact, considered in itself. He alone truly *sees* that absolute knowledge is impossible. He alone *knows* that under all things lies an impenetrable mystery.'[1]

CHAPTER II.

PSYCHOLOGY.

Psychology.—1. The principles of psychology—2. Continuity and correspondence. Progress of correspondences, their co-ordination and integration—3. The law of intelligence—4. Unity of composition of psychological phenomena. Consciousness reduced to a double processus of assimilation and dissimilation—5. Summary—6. Is Mr. Herbert Spencer a Positivist?

THE law of evolution is about to appear to us under a new aspect. The *Principles of Psychology*, the study of which we are approaching, have for their object the establishment, by a double process of analysis and of synthesis, the unity of composition of the phenomena of mind, and the continuity of their development. As the word 'principles' indicates, there is no question here of a simple description of the facts of consciousness, of a complete

[1] Spencer's *Essays*, p. 58, 2d edition, 2 vols., 1868.

enumeration of phenomena, of a review in which nothing shall be omitted; this would be to set up a psychological repertory, in which every fact should be described, almost as melodies are described in pathological and plants in botanical treatises. Such a task would be of great utility, but Mr. Herbert Spencer has not proposed to fulfil it. His enterprise is more philosophical and more systematic. He does not pretend to exhaust his subject, whether it be biology, psychology, sociology, or morals; he aims only at the establishment of *principles*, accompanying them with sufficient elucidation and example to render their relations and their results comprehensible.

The first result of the law of continuity is that there is no *precise* line of demarcation between physiological and psychological facts, and that every *absolute* distinction is illusory. Sensations, sentiments, instincts, intelligence, all constitute a world apart; but which comes out of the animal world, in which it is rooted, of which it is, as it were, the efflorescence. Between the most humble function and the most lofty thought there is no opposition of nature, but there is difference in degree, each being only one of the innumerable manifestations of life. 'The life of the body and mental life are species, of which life, properly so called, is the genus' (*Principles of Psychology*). While ordinary psychology, founded exclusively upon interior observation and the employment of the subjective method, restricts itself to the study of man, without any care for the inferior forms of intellectual life, experimental psychology aspires to describe and to classify the various modes of sensation and of thought, to follow their slow and continuous evolution, from the infusoria to the civilized white man. It is, then, not only a static but a dynamic study; it not only establishes facts, it studies their genesis, their development, their transformations. This is not all; while vulgar psychology separates the thinking being from its mechanism, thus reducing itself to abstraction, experimental psychology never separates these two terms. Between the external and the internal world there is a constant and necessary correspondence. It is only by the action of the without on the within, and by the reaction of the within on the without, that mental life is possible. It is in the material world that we must seek the ultimate reason of the nature of our thoughts, of the order of their succession. Where is the source of our ideas of simultaneousness and of succession if not in external co-existences and sequences? What should be the cause of the mode by which our ideas are linked together if not anterior experience? By and bye all this will be made clear.

The work which now occupies us comprehends an analytical and a synthetical study.

The synthetical study sets out with purely physiological life, and shows how intellectual life, which is not to be distinguished from it at first, begins its slow evolution, and constitutes itself little by little by successive additions; how mental activity, which at first reproduced only the simplest, most elementary modifications of the external world, arrives at explaining the most varied and complex relations with completeness.

The aim of the analytical study, which might also be called subjective as contrasted with the preceding, which is rather objective, is to reduce every kind of knowledge to its ultimate elements. It examines the most complicated reasonings, and, by successive decompositions, resolving that which is more into that which is less complex, getting down to that which is simple, primitive, irreducible, it finally reaches the constitutive principles and the indispensable conditions of all thought.

Before we enter upon this double study, it will be well to state briefly how the author understands psychology and its object.

The object of psychology is 'not the connexion between internal phenomena, nor the connexion between external phenomena, but the connexion between these two connexions.'

A psychological proposition is necessarily composed of two propositions, one of which concerns the subject and the other the object: consequently it implies four terms. Let us suppose that *A* and *B* are an internal connexion—the flavour and the colour of a fruit. So long as we only occupy ourselves with this connexion we are dealing with physics. But suppose that *a* and *b* are the sensations produced in the organism by these two external conditions. So long as we study the action of *A* upon the optic centres, and of *B* upon the organs of taste, we are dealing with physiology. We pass into the domain of psychology from the moment at which we examine how there can exist in the organism a relation between *a* and *b* which corresponds in one way or another to the relation between *A* and *B*. Psychology occupies itself solely with the connexion between *a b* and *A B*, in its nature, its origin, and its signification.

Thus phenomena constitute the object of psychology, and especially the relations between phenomena. As for 'the substance of the mind,' considered independently of its modes, we can know nothing about it, for such knowledge is altogether out of the reach of human intelligence. But although the sensations and emotions, real or ideal, which form consciousness, seem to be simple, homogeneous, not to be analysed, they are not so. In endeavouring to analyse them we can attempt a genesis of mind, considered under its phenomenal form. This is one of the most curious and original portions of the work of Mr. Herbert Spencer.

The elements of which mind is composed are of two sorts—feelings, and the relations between feelings. Each of these feelings, which seems simple to consciousness, decomposes itself into elements still more simple, into simple nervous shocks, and it is from the integration of those nervous shocks that sensation, properly so called, results.

Let us take as an illustration the seemingly simple sensation which we call musical sound. We know that if the vibrations do not exceed sixteen in a second, each may be considered as a distinct noise; but if they become more rapid, the noises, instead of being each known as a distinct state of consciousness, melt into an unique and continuous state of consciousness, which is the musical sound. If the rapidity of the vibrations increases, the quality of the sound varies, it becomes sharper; and if the rapidity continues to increase, it attains such a degree of acuteness that soon it is no longer appreciable as a sound. This is not all; the researches of Helmholtz have shown that the difference of tone between instruments (violin, horn, clarionet, flute) is due to the addition of various harmonies to the fundamental sound. These differences of sensation, known as difference of tone, are then due to the simultaneous integration of other series, having other degrees of integration with the primitive series.

This analysis may make us understand how illusory is the apparent simplicity of the phenomenon called sensation, because the same applies to savours, colours, scents, and all the sensations in general. Sensation is, then, a composite phenomenon. But what is its primordial element? Can it be discovered?

Mr. Herbert Spencer believes that it can. 'The last unit of consciousness is what we may call a nervous shock.' If we examine our various feelings we shall see that notwithstanding their specific differences, there is something in common in them, and that the nervous shock is at the bottom of them all. The effect produced upon us by a sudden cracking noise which has no appreciable duration is a nervous shock. An electric discharge which traverses the body, a flash of lightning which strikes the eyes, are also to be assimilated to a nervous shock. The state of consciousness thus produced is comparable in quality to the state of consciousness caused by a blow (abstracting from it the pain which ensues), so that this may be taken for the primitive and typical form of the nervous shock. It is then possible and even probable that something of the same order as that which we call a nervous shock is the final unit of consciousness, and that all the differences between our feelings result from different modes of integration of this final unit. We must remark that there is a perfect agreement between this opinion and the well-known character of nervous action. Experience shows that the nervous current is intermittent, that it consists of waves. The external stimulus does not act continually on the sensitive centre, but it sends towards it a series of *pulses* of molecular motion. Consequently, in concluding that its subjective effect, that is to say the *feeling*, is composed of a succession of mental shocks, we simply conclude that there is a resemblance between the effect and its objective cause.[1]

This being established, it is easy to understand that the evolution of the mind consists in a progressive integration. We

[1] *Principles of Psychology*, 2d edit. p. 60.

cannot follow the author through this very long and delicate analysis, in which he traces the genesis. We must limit ourselves to a few words.

The result of the first integration, as we have seen, is to unite together a certain number of nervous shocks, and make a sensation of them. Each integration of this kind supplies what we call a simple sensation. But these sensations themselves may be mingled together, and produce by their integration a composite sensation. Now, similar sensations become integrate among themselves. Again, a sensation unites itself so as to form an aggregate with other sensations which limit it in time or space. Finally, the integrate clusters which result therefrom enter into the higher integrations of one kind and the other. Let us remark in support of the preceding, that in the domain of mind we hardly comprise these series of states of consciousness whose integration is imperfect, and that, on the contrary, the series whose integration is pushed the furthest possible are those which we consider as belonging especially to mind. For instance, hunger, thirst, sickness, all the visceral sensations in general, and even feelings like love and anger, which have but little cohesion between them, which form badly integrated clusters, are regarded as occupying only a subordinate place in what we call mental life. Mental acts, on the contrary, are those which belong to the order of tactile, auditive, visual sensations, which have much cohesion, and are remarkably integrate. Our intellectual operations are almost always restricted to the sensations of hearing (integrate in words) and to visual sensations (integrate in impressions, objects, and their relations).

The nature of mind being thus conceived, it will be elucidated by comparing it with the nature of matter, and this fact, that there exists a parallelism between that which chemists have established relatively to matter and that which we suppose here relatively to mind, will aid us to justify our conception.

It is established that a great number of substances which seem homogeneous and simple, are in reality heterogeneous and composite, and it is shown by analysis that many which seem entirely without relation to each other are in truth analogous. There is a large class of salts formed by sulphuric acid, another large class formed by nitric acid, and another large class formed by acetic acid, and so on in succession. These classes of acids are different in many respects, but it has been discovered that the former have a characteristic common to them with many others, the possession of oxygen as an active element. Further, there is reason to suspect that the substantives called simple are themselves composite, and that there is finally only one ultimate form of matter, of which all the other forms are only compositions more and more complex.

So it is with regard to mind. We can conceive that these innumerable forms of spiritual life, which are given to us at different states of consciousness may be finally composed of simple units of feeling, and even of units which are at bottom of the same kind. But these homogeneous units produced by integrations of a different sort produce feelings relatively simple, then feelings more and more complex and different, and thus continually.

It must not, however, be supposed that all that has just been said about mind is in disagreement with the preceding assertion of the author. We know nothing about mind. When those two modes of existence which we call subject and object have been reduced, each to its ultimate expression, it only remains for us to endeavour to assimilate those two ultimate expressions to each other. But the distinction of subject and object in itself implies the impossibility of any assimilation, 'for this distinction is the consciousness of a difference which surpasses all other differences.' On this important point we shall let the author himself speak :—

'Here, indeed, we arrive at the barrier which needs to be perpetually pointed out, alike to those who seek materialistic explanations of mental phenomena and to those who are alarmed lest such explanations may be found. The last class prove by their fear almost as much as the first prove by their hope, that they believe Mind may possibly be interpreted in terms of Matter; whereas many whom they vituperate as materialists are profoundly convinced that there is not the remotest possibility of so interpreting them. For those, who, not deterred by foregone conclusions, have pushed their analysis to the uttermost, see very clearly that the conception that we form to ourselves of matter is but the symbol of some form of power absolutely and for ever unknown to us, and a symbol which we cannot suppose to be like the reality without involving ourselves in contradictions (*First Principles*, p. 16, etc.) They also see that the representation of all objective activities in terms of motion is but a representation of them and not a knowledge of them, and that we are immediately brought to alternative absurdities if we assume the power manifested to us as motion to be in itself that which we conceive as motion.'[1]

When, to these conclusions, that matter and motion, such as we think them, are only the symbols of unknowable forms of existence, we join the recently drawn conclusion that mind is also unknowable, and that the most simple form under which we can think substance is only a symbol of something which can never come under thought, then we see that the whole question reduces itself to knowing whether these symbols may be expressed in terms as symbols of so-and-so, a question which is hardly worth decision, since either reply leaves us as entirely ignorant of the reality as we were before.

Nevertheless it may be well to say, once for all, that if we were constrained to choose between the alternative of translating mental into physical phenomena, or physical into mental, the latter would seem the more acceptable of the two. Mind, such as it is known to be by him who possesses it, is a circumscribed aggregate of activities, and the cohesion of these activities one with the other postulate a something of which they are the activities. But the same experiences which make him know this coherent aggregate of mental activities make him simultaneously know activities which are not included in the aggregate—activities placed outside, which are only known by their effects on this aggregate, but which, as experience proves, have no cohesion with the aggregate, though they have cohesion between themselves (*First Principles*, pp. 43, 44). As, by their definition, these external activities cannot be comprised in the aggregate of activities designated under the name mind, they must always remain

[1] Spencer's *Principles of Psychology*, 2d edition, p. 158.

for him the unknown connotations of their effects on that aggregate, and they cannot be thought except in terms furnished by that aggregate. Consequently, if he considers his conceptions on these activities placed outside of mind as constituting knowledge of them, he deceives himself; he does no more than represent these activities to himself in expressions of the mind, and he cannot do otherwise. He is obliged to admit that his ideas of matter and motion, pure symbols of unknowable realities, are complex states of consciousness produced by units of sensation. But if, after having admitted this, he persists in asking if units of consciousness are of the same nature as units of force distinguished as external; or if the units of force distinguished as external are of the same nature as the units of sensation, then the answer, always fundamentally the same, must be, that it will advance us no further to conceive of the units of external force as identical with the units of sensation, than to conceive of the units of sensation as identical with the units of external force. It is clear that if the units of external force are regarded as absolutely unknown and unknowable, then, to translate the units of sensation into them is to translate the known into the unknown, which is absurd. And if they are only what they are supposed to be by those who identify them with their symbols, then the difficulty of translating units of sensation into units of force is insurmountable. If force, such as it exists objectively is absolutely foreign in its nature to that which exists subjectively as sensation, then the transformation of force into sensation is unthinkable; that is to say, it is impossible to interpret intimate existence by terms of external existence. But if, on the other hand, units of force such as they exist objectively are essentially the same in nature as those which manifest themselves objectively as units of sensation, then a becoming hypothesis remains open. Each element of that aggregate of activities which constitutes a consciousness is known as belonging to the consciousness only by its cohesion with the rest. Beyond the limits of that coherent aggregate of activities, there are other activities completely independent of it, and which cannot enter into it. We can imagine then that by their exclusion from the circle of those activities which constitute consciousness, the external activities, although of the same intrinsic nature, assume an antithetical aspect. Being separated from consciousness, and cut off by its boundaries, they become foreign to it. Not being incorporated with the activities of consciousness, nor united with them, as they are among themselves, consciousness cannot, so to speak, traverse them, and thus they are figured as unconscious; they are represented as having the nature called material, in opposition to that which we call spiritual. Nevertheless, although this shews that it is possible to imagine that the units of external force are identical in nature with the units of force known as sensation, we do not, by representing them thus, arrive at understanding external force any better, because, as it has already been seen, in supposing that all forms of mind be composed of homogeneous units of sensation differently aggregated, this resolution into units leaves us as incapable as before of understanding how the substance of mind can consist of such units; and thus, when we could even really figure to ourselves all the units of external force as being essentially the same as the units of force known as sensation, so that they should constitute a universal sensibility, we should still be for ever as far off from forming an idea of this universal *sensorium.*

Consequently, though it seems more easy to translate that which we call matter into that which we call mind, than to translate that which we call mind into that which we call matter (an operation which is, in fact, completely impossible) nevertheless our translation cannot lead us further than our symbols. Those vast conceptions which we see from afar are illusions evoked by the false connotation of our words. The expression 'substance of mind,' regarded as anything by the x of our equation, leads us inevitably into error, for we cannot think a substance except in terms which imply material properties. All our progress consists in acknowledging that our symbols are only symbols, and that our constitution necessitates the unknowable such as it manifests itself within the limits of consciousness and under the form of sensation, no less impenetrable than the unknowable such as it manifests itself outside these limits and under other forms. We do not arrive at understanding it better by translating the second into the first. The conditional form in which being is presented in the subject, cannot, any more than the conditional form in which being is presented in the object, be the unconditional being common to the two.

II.

Two fundamental ideas rule the psychology of Mr. Herbert Spencer: that of the continuity of psychological phenomena; that of the intimate relation between the being and its medium. These two points virtually contain his doctrine. We have seen that the idea of progress, evolution, development tends to prevail in modern sciences. In nature, as in history, nothing is isolated; everything is linked to something else, and forms a series; each phenomenon proceeds from those which precede, and contains the germ of those which are about to follow it. But the human mind is so constructed, that it cannot lay hold of objects except when they offer themselves to it under defined, discontinued forms, when they present sufficiently marked characteristics. Every science must settle the boundaries of its object; it is only possible on this condition; but that settlement is frequently arbitrary, and phenomena do not allow themselves to be imprisoned within our conventional divisions. Thus mental life comes out of physiological life, in virtue of this law of continuous progress slowly step by step, by infinitesimal transformations, and without our being able to say,—There is its place of birth.

'Though we commonly regard mental and bodily life as distinct, it needs only to ascend somewhat above the ordinary point of view, to see that they are but sub-divisions of life in general; and that no line of demarcation can be drawn between them otherwise than arbitrarily. Doubtless, to those who persist, after the popular fashion, in contemplating only the extreme forms of the two, this assertion will appear incredible. . . . It is not more certain that, from the simple reflection by which the infant sucks, up to the elaborate reasonings of the adult man, the progress is by daily infinitesimal steps, than it is certain that between the automatic actions of the lowest creatures, and the highest conscious actions of the human race, a series of actions displayed by the various tribes of the animal kingdom may be so placed as to render it impossible to say of any one step in the series,—Here intelligence begins.' [1]

If, from the *savant* who pursues his researches with the full consciousness of the processes of reasoning and induction which he employs, we descend to the man of ordinary education, who reasons well and intelligently, but without knowing how; if from him we descend to the villager, whose highest generalizations do not go beyond local facts; if from thence we go to the inferior human races, whom we cannot regard as thinking creatures, whose numerical conceptions hardly go beyond those of the dog; if we put aside the most elevated in the race of quadrumanes whose actions are as reasonable as those of a little schoolboy, if from them we reach the domestic animals, and thence pass on from the more to the less sagacious quadrupeds; that is to say, those which cannot modify their actions according to circumstances, but are guided by an immutable instinct; then, if we remark that instinct, which at first consisted of a complicated combination of motions produced by a complicated combination of stimulus, takes lower forms in which stimulus and motions become less and less complex; if from thence we come to reflex action, and 'if we descend from the animals in whom this action implies the irritation of a nerve and the contraction of a muscle, to the animals unprovided with a nervous and muscular system, and that we discover that in them too, it is the same tissue which manifests irritation and contractibility, which tissue likewise fulfils the functions of assimilation, secretion, respiration, and reproduction; and if, finally, we remark that each of the phases of intelligences enumerated here is founded upon the neighbouring one by modifications too numerous to be specifically distinguished, and too imperceptible to be described, we shall have to some extent shown the reality of this fact, that no precise separation can be effected between the phenomena of intelligence and those of life in general.' [2]

The other basis of the doctrine is the necessary correlation of being and its medium, which the author expresses by saying that life is a *correspondence*,—'a continuous adjustment of internal

[1] Spencer, *Principles of Psychology*, p. 349. [2] *General Synthesis*, chap. ii.

to external relations.' The living being, whatever he may be, tree, infusoria, or man, cannot subsist if there be not harmony between his organism and his medium; and, if to physical life be added psychical life, the adjustment becomes more complex. In order that the game may escape the falcon, there must be inside of it certain modifications which correspond to the modifications outside of it, there must be correspondence between its flight and the pursuit of its enemy. And so, when Newton conceives the system of the world, it is necessary that the nature and the sequence of his ideas should correspond with the nature and the concatenation of the real phenomena; that which is within him must be adjusted to that which is without him. Life is then truly a correspondence, under both the highest and the lowest forms. Thus the degree of life varies, like the degree of correspondence. Life is rich or poor according as it reflects the universe, or the simple mechanical modifications of some neighbouring molecule. From the entozoa, confined in a tissue, to the thought of Shakespeare or of Newton, which reproduces the concrete or abstract reality of the world, there is room for every possible degree of correspondence; but parallelism always exists between the being and its medium. The author retraces for us the various stages of this progress, which is nothing else than the history of the passage from physical to psychical life. We see the latter, feeble at the commencement, becoming firm and strong by degrees. Let us follow him step by step in this synthetical exposition.

At the lowest step, the correspondence between the living being and its medium is *direct* and *homogeneous*. As the highest life is to be found in the most complicated medium, so the lowest is only to be found in the simplest. Such are the germ of yeast, the mushroom called *protococcus novilis*, the parasite cellule which causes smallpox, the *gregarina*, a monocellular animal which lives in the intestines of certain insects, is moistened by the nutritive fluid which it assimilates, which is kept at an almost constantly equal temperature, and can only continue to exist as long as its special medium exists. Here there are few changes, and they relate only to a homogeneous medium.

Above this is *direct* but *heterogeneous* correspondence, of which the zoophyte offers us an example, when its tentacles are extended and touched. To a relation of co-existence between the properties, tangible and otherwise, presented by the surrounding medium, there corresponds in the organism a relation of sequence between certain tactile impressions, and certain contractions. But correspondence between distant internal and external relations is absent in all these forms of life.

Let us now see how correspondence extends itself *in space.* The special senses are constituted and gradually developed by a continuous progress. Take, for example, sight. In the zoophyte, where the entire tissue has the property of responding to the marked changes in the quantity of light which falls upon it, there is, as it were, a stretch of the visual faculty and of the correspondences which result from it.

'The rudimentary eye, consisting, as in the *Planaria*, of a few pigment grains beneath the integument, may be considered as simply a part of the surface more irritable by light than the rest. We may form some idea of the impression it is probably fitted to receive, by turning our closed eyes towards the light, and passing the hand backwards and forwards before them.' [1]

Nevertheless, even this little specialization of function implies a progress in correspondence. If, from the polyp, which stirs only when it is touched, we go on and up to the articulated mollusca, to the vertebrates which inhabit the water, and thence to the more elevated animals which dwell in a more rarefied medium, we shall find, under varied forms and modifications, a more complex visual apparatus, and an increasing distance in the extension of the correspondence. We cannot in this place follow the details of this progress which leads to such astonishing results in the case of civilized man.

'A ship guided by compass and stars and chronometer brings him from the other side of the Atlantic information by which his purchases here are adapted to the prices there. An examination of the surface-strata, from which he infers the presence of coal below, enables him to bring his actions into correspondence with the co-existences a thousand feet underneath. Nor is the range of environment through which his correspondences reach con-

[1] Spencer's *Principles of Psychology*, p. 406.

fined to the surface and the substance of the earth. It stretches into the surrounding sphere of infinity. It was extended to the moon when the Chaldeans discovered how to predict eclipses; to the sun and nearer planets when the Copernican system was established; to the remoter planets when an improved telescope disclosed one and calculation fixed the position of the other; to the stars when their parallax and proper motion were measured; and, in a vague way, even to the nebulæ when their composition and forms of structure were ascertained.'[1]

To correspondence in space, correspondence *in time* adds itself. The living being at first seizes upon the simplest and shortest mechanical sequences, then by successive conquests, he adjusts himself to longer and longer periods; he takes possession of the future; he foresees future events, like the dog who hides a bone for the time when he shall be hungry.

'This higher order of correspondence in time, which, for the reasons assigned, is impossible to creatures of inferior type, which is but vaguely discernible in the higher animals, and which is definitely exhibited only when we arrive at the human race, has made marked progress in the course of civilisation. Among the lowest tribes of men, who are without habitations, and who wander from place to place as the varying supplies of wild animals, roots, and insects dictate, a year is the longest period to which their conduct is adapted. Hardly yet worthy to be defined as creatures "looking before and after," they show by their utter improvidence and their apparent incapacity to realize future consequences, that it is only to the conspicuous and often-recurring phenomena of the seasons that their actions respond. But in the succeeding stages of progress, we see, in the building of huts, the breeding and accumulation of cattle, and the storing of commodities, that longer sequences are recognised and measures taken to meet them. And gradually, as we advance to higher social states, men show, by planting trees that will not bear fruit for a generation, by the elaborate education they give their children, by building houses that will last for centuries, by insuring their lives, by all those struggles for future wealth or fame, which

[1] Spencer's *Principles of Psychology*, p. 409.

now mainly occupy the educated classes, that in them internal antecedents and consequences are habitually adjusted to external ones that are extremely long in their intervals. More especially, however, is this extension of the correspondence in time displayed in the progress of science. Beginning with a recognition of the sequences of day and night, men next advanced to those monthly ones exhibited by the moon, next to the sun's annual cycle; next to the cycle of the moon's eclipses, afterwards to the periods of the superior planets; while modern astronomy determines the vast interval after which the earth's axis will again point to the same place in the heavens, and the scarcely conceivable epoch in which planetary perturbations repeat themselves.' [1]

Fresh progress consists in the *growth in speciality* of the correspondence. The organism is in a condition to foresee smaller and smaller differences. In the evolution of the visual faculty, for instance, a growing aptitude to distinguish the various intensities of colours, intermediate shades, and tints of light and shade is produced. This progress of correspondence in specialty leads in the course of human development to the passage from ordinary knowledge to science, from the quantitative provision which is vague to the quantitative provision which is precise.

The living being can now seize no longer differences only, but resemblances, forming within him groups of interior relations which respond to the groups of external relations and attributes; correspondence grows in *generality and in complexity*. The impression which the organism receives from each object becomes more and more heterogeneous. The eye not only seizes colour, size, and form, but distance in space, motion, species, direction, rapidity.

'It suffices to cite an extreme case, such as that afforded by the mineralogist, who, in identifying a mass of matter as of a kind fitted for a certain use, examines its crystalline form, its colour, texture, hardness, cleavage, fracture, degree of transparency, lustre, specific gravity, taste, smell, fusibility, magnetic and electric properties, etc., and is decided in his conduct by all these taken together.' [2]

---

[1] Spencer's *Psychology*, p. 419.

[2] *Ibid.* p. 447.

Correspondence between the being and its medium is thus fully constituted by successive conquests; it remains only to co-ordinate these different elements. The *co-ordination* of correspondences goes through every possible degree, from that of the hunted animal which flies to its earth, to that of quantitative science, which embraces the most precise relations and the most complex data.

From the co-ordination of correspondences springs their *integration;* that is to say, the simplest correspondences melt into one another and become intimately united, so that they become separable only by analysis. Thus, in the case of an adult, a glance cast upon a visible object awakens simultaneously the idea of tangible extent, of resistance, of texture, of weight; all these various elements are associated, integrated, by repetition. It is thus we learn to understand a foreign language, thus the child, at first hesitating over the letters and the syllables, comes to interpret the words and the phrases fluently.

We are, then, led to this necessary conclusion that intelligence has not distinct degrees, that it is not formed of really independent faculties; but that the most elevated phenomena are the effects of a complication which has come out of the simplest elements by insensible degrees.

'Evidently, then, the classification current in our philosophies of the mind can be but superficially true. Instinct, reason, perception, conception, memory, imagination, feeling, will, etc. etc., can be nothing more than either conventional groupings of the correspondences, or subordinate divisions among the various operations which are instrumental in effecting the correspondences. However widely contrasted they may seem, these various forms of intelligence cannot be anything else than either particular modes in which the adjustment of inner to outer relations is achieved, or particular parts of the process of adjustment.'[1]

III.

After having sketched in outline the genesis of psychical life, after having seen it proceed, little by little, from organic and

[1] Spencer's *Psychology*, p. 486.

animal life, and constitute an order of facts sufficiently vast to become the object of a special study, we must now consider this study itself, and see how the most complex psychological problems come out of the most simple, in virtue of a natural processus. This is the object of *special synthesis.*

At the point which we have now reached, we may endeavour to define the characteristics which distinguish physical from mental life. Let us be on our guard against any misapprehension. This distinction is only approximately possible, and only a wholesale truth; there is nothing set or absolute about it; the law of continuity does not admit of exceptions.

'The two great classes of vital phenomena which physiology and psychology respectively embrace are broadly distinguished in this—that while the one class includes both simultaneous and successive changes, the other includes successive changes only. While the phenomena forming the subject-matter of physiology exhibit themselves in an immense number of different series bound up together, those forming the subject-matter of psychology exhibit themselves as but a single series. The briefest consideration of the many continuous actions constituting the life of the body at large suffices to show that they are synchronous—that digestion, circulation, respiration, excretion, secretion, etc., in all their many subdivisions, are going on at one time in mutual dependence. And the briefest introspection serves to make it clear that the actions constituting thought occur, not together, but one after another. Should a rigorous criticism demand qualifications of this statement, they cannot be such as to diminish its general truth. Life being the definite combination of heterogeneous changes, both simultaneous and successive, in correspondence with external co-existences and sequences, the two great divisions of life must ever be distinguished as, the one a correspondence that is both simultaneous and successive, and the other a correspondence that is successive only.

'At first sight this may be supposed to constitute an impassable distinction between the two. Such, however, is by no means the fact. Even were the highest psychical life thus *absolutely* distinguished from physical life, which we shall presently see reason to doubt, it would still be true that psychical life, in its earlier and lower phases, is not thus distinguished; but that the distinction arises only in the course of that progression by which life in general attains to its more perfect forms.'[1]

Thus, then, the two great divisions of life consist—one of a correspondence both simultaneous and successive, the other of successive correspondence only. And this is a necessity. For the most essential characteristic of psychological phenomena is that of being conscious, and as a state of consciousness necessarily excludes every other, these states must produce themselves under the form of a simple series. This tendency of the psychical phenomena to form themselves into a successive chain is, however, true only in theory, and never reaches a complete realization. 'The vital actions which are the object of psychology, though they are distinguished from all the others by their tendency to take the form of a simple series, never attain this form in an absolute manner.' At the beginning, the different manifestations of mental activity are rather simultaneous than successive, consequently more physical than psychological. Here are the proofs of this: Among the radiates of the highest order each of the similar parts which form the body is bound to a ganglionic centre, which seems to serve only for the functions of that part which belongs to it, consequently the psychical changes which are produced in the animal localize themselves simultaneously in the different portions of its body. Among mollusca, the actions of the various ganglions are very imperfectly co-ordinated. Finally, the articulates have a structure which fits them to demonstrate this dispersion of psychical life. If the head of a centipede be cut off while it is in motion, the body will continue to advance by the movement of the feet alone, and the same thing will take place in the separated portions, if the body be divided into several distinct sections. Analogous experiments made on the *Mantis religiosa* have often been quoted (See Dugès, *Physiol. Comp.* vol. i. p. 337).

Little by little the simultaneous form decreases before the successive, thus bringing about new progress in the psychical life.

[1] Spencer's *Psychology*, p. 491.

Besides, in order that correspondence between the being and its medium should be possible, it is necessary that in proportion as the organism is exposed to more numerous impressions, these impressions should become co-ordinate, should be centralized, and constantly tend to unity. The serial form is thus the special characteristic of intelligence. 'A continuous series of changes being thus the subject of psychology, its work is to determine the law of their succession. That these changes are not produced by chance is manifest. That they follow one another in a special manner, the very existence of intelligence testifies. The problem consists, then, in determining their order,' that is to say, in determining *the law of intelligence.*

Intelligence, like life, consists in a correspondence. There must be a parallelism between the thinking being and the co-existences or external sequences which his thought reflects. But these co-existences and sequences have all kinds of relations between them. There are some which are assisted by fixed immutable relations, known without exception; there are some so slightly linked that they have been perhaps only once given by experience as associated. Between these two kinds of relations, the one intimate, the other fortuitous, there are all possible degrees of cohesion. In order that the correspondence may be realized, the intelligence must also reproduce all these degrees. To fortuitous sequences and co-existences, or those which are simply possible, a very weak attraction between the internal conditions which represent them will answer, and so on. In a word, the law of intelligence may be formulated as follows:—

'The law of intelligence, therefore, is that the strength of the tendency which the antecedent of any psychical change has to be followed by its consequent, is proportionate to the persistency of the union between the external things they symbolize.

'To say, however, that this is the law of intelligence, is by no means to say that it is conformed to by any intelligence with which we are acquainted. It is the law of intelligence in the abstract; and is conformed to by existing intelligences in degrees more or less imperfect.' [1]

[1] Spencer's *Psychology*, p. 510.

Intelligence, considered at its foundation, reduces itself then to the association of its ideas, which is, so to speak, its fundamental property. On this point, Mr. Herbert Spencer agrees with Mr. John Stuart Mill and Mr. Alexander Bain.

After having defined the law of intelligence, let us now examine the successive phases of its development. In its lowest degree it is *reflex action*, it then becomes *instinct;* from which proceed, on one side, the cognitive manifestations, *memory and reason*, and on the other the affective powers, *sentiment and will.*

Reflex action is hardly a mode of psychical life. It has however its importance, from the point of view which occupies us, in that it forms the transition from purely physical life to instinct. In employing the word instinct, not as it is commonly used, to designate all kinds of intelligence other than that of man, but in restricting it to its proper signification, instinct may be defined as a *composite reflex action.* Strictly speaking, we cannot draw any line of demarcation between it and the simple reflex action, from which it issues by successive complications. While, in simple reflex action a single impression is followed by a single contraction; while, in all the more developed forms of reflex action, one single impression is followed by a combination of contractions; in that which we distinguish by the name of instinct, a combination of impressions produces a combination of contractions; and in the highest form, in the most complex instinct, there are co-ordinations which tend at once to direct and to execute. The transformation of simple reflex action into composite reflex action, that is to say, into instinct, is explained by the accumulation of experiences, and *hereditary transmission.*[1] But instinct, in proportion as it grows in complexity, approaches its end; for, as the instincts become more elevated, the various psychical changes which compose them become less coherent, co-ordinate themselves less and less perfectly, and the time comes when their co-ordination will no longer be regular. Then these actions begin to lose the automatic character which distinguishes

[1] The author devotes a long and interesting chapter, which, however, is not susceptible of analysis, to Instinct. We therefore refer the reader to it. Part iv. ch. 5.

them, and that which we call instinct will gradually become lost in something higher.

Thence results memory. These two modes of intelligence are transformed one into the other. As instinct may be considered a kind of organized memory, so memory may be regarded as a dawning instinct. Let us see how memory becomes instinct. To remember the colour red is to be to a slight degree in the psychical state which is produced by the presentation of the colour red. To remember a movement made with the arm is to feel, in a slight degree, the repetition of those internal conditions which accompany the movement; it is a commencement of the excitement of all the nerves whose stronger excitement has been experienced during the movement. Recollection is then a commencement of nervous excitement. It consists in feeling, to a slight degree, a movement, a sensation, an impression. But when instinct becomes too complex to produce itself with the automatic certainty proper to it, there results a conflict between all the movements. Those which do not succeed in realizing themselves remain in the condition of simple tendencies, that is to say, of movements simply conceived; those internal impressions arouse others; and thus that succession of regular, or irregular, ideas which we call memory is formed.

Let us now see how memory becomes instinct again, that is to say, how it returns to its point of departure. Examples of this are easily found. The pianist who plays instinctively, and with automatic precision, certain pieces of music which he has learned, is a ready case in point.

It is clearly implied by all the preceding that the line of demarcation generally traced out between instinct and reason does not exist. Each is an adjustment of internal to external relations, with this single difference, that in the case of instinct the correspondence is very simple and very general, while, without reason, the correspondence is between internal and external relations which are complex, or abstract, or rare. The experimental hypothesis also suffices to explain the progress from the lowest to the highest forms of reason. From that reasoning, from the particular to the particular, which is the reasoning of children, of domestic animals, and, in general, of the superior mammifers, to inductive or deductive reasoning, progress is determined by the accumulation of experiences. And the case is the same as regards the progress of all human knowledge, even to its widest generalizations.

Every one is acquainted with the famous disputes which have arisen concerning the nature of reason, and how idealism and empiricism have fought over the question from the days of antiquity to our own. Mr. Herbert Spencer is neither for Locke, nor for the contrary doctrine of 'forms of thought.'

'To rest with the unqualified assertion, that, antecedent to experience, the mind is a blank, is to ignore the all-essential questions—whence comes the power of organizing experiences? whence arise the different degrees of that power possessed by different races of organisms and different individuals of the same race? If, at birth, there exists nothing but a passive receptivity of impressions, why should not a horse be as educable as a man? or, should it be said that language makes the difference, then why should not the cat and dog, out of the same household experiences, arrive at equal degrees and kinds of intelligence? Understood in its current form, the experience-hypothesis implies that the presence of a definitely organized nervous system is a circumstance of no moment—a fact not needing to be taken into account. Yet it is the all-important fact—the fact to which, in one sense, the criticism of Leibnitz and others pointed—the fact without which an assimilation of experiences is utterly inexplicable.'[1]

On the other hand, if the doctrine of *forms of thought* is unacceptable in the transcendental sense of Leibnitz and of Kant, it contains a foundation of truth, and only needs to undergo a physiological transformation. That innateness on which so much stress has been laid is explained by inheritance. In the sense then that certain pre-established relations corresponding to relations in the surrounding medium exist in the nervous system, there is truth in the doctrine of forms of thought, not the truth maintained by its supporters, but a truth of a parallel order. These pre-established internal relations, although independent of

[1] Spencer's *Psychology*, p. 580.

the experience of the individual, are not independent of general experience; they have been established by the accumulated experience of preceding organisms. They are legacies, both capital and interest. And thus the European arrives at having some cubic inches more brain than the Papuan; that savages, incapable of counting beyond the number of their fingers, and speaking a formless language, have, in the course of ages, Newtons and Shakespeares for their descendants.

The intimate relation between sentiment and reason has long been established; every emotion implying knowledge, and all knowledge some sort of emotion. The evolution of the sentiments also consists in a development of correspondences, and their progress is made by additions and by increase of complexity. The lowest degree is *desire*, then some simple impulsions corresponding to only slightly complex impressions; then the simple sentiments form groups; then the groups aggregate themselves. Place a child in the midst of great mountains, he remains insensible to the sublime spectacle, but he will look at a toy with pleasure. If he is older he may experience an agreeable emotion while looking at a field, a street, his house, his garden. But in youth, and in mature age:—

'The various minor groups of states that have been in earlier days severally produced by trees, by fields, by streams, by cascades, by rocks, by precipices, by mountains, by clouds, are aroused together. Along with the sensations, immediately received, there are partially excited the myriads of sensations that have been in times past received from objects such as there presented; further, there are partially excited the various incidental feelings that were experienced on all these countless past occasions, and there are probably also excited certain deeper, but now vague combinations of states that were organized in the race during barbarous times, when its pleasurable activities were chiefly among the woods and waters. And out of these excitations, some of them actual, but most of them nascent, is composed the emotion which a fine landscape produces in us.' [1]

[1] Spencer's *Psychology*, p. 599.

Hence, we must conclude that the emotions will be strong in proportion as they shall include a greater number of actual or dawning sensations. And this it is which explains the irresistible character of love.

'As supplying a marked illustration of this truth, I may cite the passion which unites the sexes. This is habitually, but very erroneously spoken of as though it were a simple feeling, whereas it is in fact the most compound, and therefore the most powerful, of all the feelings. Added to the purely physical element of it, are first to be noticed those highly complex impressions produced by personal beauty; around which are aggregated a variety of pleasurable ideas, not in themselves amatory, but which have an organized relation to the amatory feeling. With this there is united the complex sentiment which we term affection—a sentiment which, as it can exist between those of the same sex, must be regarded as in itself an independent sentiment; but which assumes its highest activity between lovers. Then there is the sentiment of admiration, respect, or reverence, in itself one of considerable power, and which in this relation becomes in a high degree active. Next there must be added the feeling which phrenologists have named love of approbation. To be preferred above all the world, and that by one admired beyond all others, is to have the love of approbation gratified in a degree passing every previous experience; especially as to this direct gratification of it there must be added that reflex gratification of it which results from the preference being witnessed by unconcerned persons. Further there is the allied emotion of self-esteem. To have succeeded in gaining such attachment from, and sway over, another, is a practical proof of power, of superiority, which cannot fail agreeably to excite the *amour propre.* Yet again the proprietary feeling has its share in the general activity, there is the pleasure of possession; the two belong to each other—claim each as a species of property. Once more, there is involved an extended liberty of action. Towards other persons a restrained behaviour is requisite: round each there is a certain subtle boundary which may not be crossed—an individuality on which none may trespass. But in this case the barriers are thrown down; the freedom of another's individuality is conceded, and thus the love of unrestrained activity is gratified. Finally, there is an exaltation of the sympathies, purely personal pleasures are doubled by being shared with another, and the pleasures of another are added to the purely personal pleasures. Thus, round the physical feeling forming the nucleus of the whole, there are gathered the feelings produced by personal beauty, that constituting simple attachment, those of reverence, of love of approbation, of self-esteem, of property, of love of freedom, of sympathy. All these, each excited in the highest degree, and severally tending to reflect their excitement on each other, form the composite psychical state we call love. And as each of these feelings is in itself highly complicated, uniting a wide range of states of consciousness, we may say that this passion fuses into one immense aggregation nearly all the elementary excitations of which we are capable; and that from this results its irresistible power.'[1]

Those who have followed the synthesis so far will clearly perceive that the will cannot be anything but another aspect of the same general processus, from which sentiment and reason have come forth :—

'When, as a result of the organization of accumulating experiences, the automatic actions become so involved, so varied in kind, and severally so infrequent, as no longer to be performed with unhesitating precision—when, after the reception of one of the more complex impressions, the appropriate motor changes become nascent, but all prevented from passing into immediate action by the antagonism of certain other nascent motor changes appropriate to some nearly allied impression, there is constituted a state of consciousness which, when it finally issues in action, exhibits what we term volition.'[2]

The phenomena of affective life are then the source of voluntary development, and the root of our volitions is in desire. At the point which we have reached, says the author, it is very easy to see that the work is in complete disagreement with current opinions upon free will. But, whence does the general illusion proceed?

---

1 Spencer's *Psychology*, p. 601.

2 *Ibid.* p. 613.

'Considered as an internal perception, the illusion appears chiefly to consist in supposing that at each moment the *ego* is something more than the composite state of consciousness which then exists. A man who, after being subject to an impulse consisting of a group of psychical states positive and nascent, performs a certain action, usually asserts that he determined to perform the action, and performed it under the influence of this impulse: and by speaking of himself as being something separate from the group of psychical states constituting the impulse, he falls into the error of supposing that it was not the impulse alone which determined the action. But the entire group of the psychical states which constituted the antecedent of the action, also constituted himself at that moment—constituted his psychical self, that is, as distinguished from his physical self.'[1]

In other words, we say that an action is free, because we consider it as our work, as proceeding from our *ego*. But the *ego*, anterior to the resolution, is not and cannot be anything but the sum of our actual psychical conditions, which are determined by experience:—

'Thus it is natural enough that the subject of such psychical changes should say that he wills the action; seeing that, psychically considered, he is at that moment nothing more than the composite state of consciousness by which the action is excited. But to say that the performance of the action is, therefore, the result of his free-will, is to say that he determines the cohesions of psychical states by which the action is aroused; and as these psychical states constitute himself at that moment, this is to say that these psychical states determine their own cohesions, which is absurd.'[2]

This cohesion results from character and inheritance.

IV.

If we now pass from the synthetical to the analytical study of the phenomena of consciousness, we are led to the same results. The analysis verifies the synthesis, and the conclusion which it necessitates as certain, or at least suggests as very probable, is again that of the law of continuous progress, the doctrine of

[1] Spencer's *Psychology*, p. 617. [2] *Ibid.* p. 618.

evolution. That it may only be an hypothesis the author grants. He claims only one concession in its favour, which is, that of all theories it is the most simple, the most natural, and that which is supported by the greatest number of positive facts.

The fundamental idea which governs Mr. Herbert Spencer's analytical psychology is that there exists between all the phenomena of intelligence an *unity of composition.* There is identity of nature between the process followed by the *savant*, in his most lengthened and complicated reasonings, and that by which a dawning consciousness essays thought. Both consist in seizing upon resemblances and differences, only that the *savant* perceives them by hundreds and thousands, where the child or the animal sees only a few. There is only a difference of degree. The entire task of analytical psychology is to prove this truth, or to speak more precisely, to discover it, for it is a voyage of discovery.

Its ultimate result is, that intellectual life consists of two fundamental processes, one which verifies, the other which differentiates; one which seizes upon analogies, equalities, identities, the other which attaches itself to oppositions and contrasts; one which *assimilates* impressions, the other which *disassimilates* them; one which consists in an *integration*, the other in a *disintegration*.

Let us see how the author reaches this result—how he establishes this unity in the composition of intellectual phenomena—and how this double processus, by its incessant working, and its immeasurable complications, constitutes our mental life.

We must, in the first place, keep in mind that we are about to follow a system totally opposed to that of synthesis:—

'An analysis, conducted in a truly systematic manner, must commence with the most complex phenomena of the series to be analysed; must seek to resolve these into the phenomena that stand next in order of complexity; must proceed after like fashion with the less complex phenomena thus disclosed; and so, by successive decompositions, must descend step by step to the simpler and more general phenomena, reaching at last the simplest and most general.' [1]

[1] Spencer's *Psychology*, p. 71.

We are going to take this edifice of human intelligence to pieces, beginning from the top, pulling down each successive storey, until we reach the foundations, and the immutable earth which supports them. We are going from the adult tree to the germ whose fruit it is. In our retrogression we descend from our intellectual phenomenon to that which is its immediate condition and support. Let us sketch the various phases of this decomposition.

The most complex intellectual action, says Mr. Herbert Spencer, is *composite quantitative reasoning*. It is so for several reasons; first, because the knowledge in this case must be precise, it does not admit of the *almost*, or the *nearly*, and then because the relations are very numerous. Here is an example of this mode of reasoning. An engineer, after having built an iron tubular bridge, is commissioned to build another, of double strength. He knows that it will not suffice to double all the dimensions, but he arrives at this negative conclusion only by taking count of a great number of elements, and of defined relations, of several precise laws taught by physics and mechanics. In algebra and geometry, in all quantitative reasoning whatever, the intelligence passes through a series of identities. The relations which it perceives, adds, transforms, compares, are homogeneous. More than that, their resemblance is the highest possible; it is that which is called equality or identity.

Composite quantitative reasoning resolves itself into *simple quantitative reasoning:* the object of the first being 'the quantitative relations of quantitative relations;' the second reducing itself to a direct and immediate intuition of relation of quantity. But, in simplifying itself, the process remains identical and always consists in the perception of identities.

'Ability to perceive quality implies a correlative ability to perceive inequality; neither can exist without the other. But though inseparable in origin, the cognitions of equality and inequality, whether between things or relations, altogether differ in this, that whilst the one is essentially definite the other is essentially indefinite. There is but one equality; but there may be numberless degrees of inequality.'[1]

[1] Spencer's *Psychology*, p. 93.

From this results a new sort of reasoning, which operates upon inequalities; this is *quantitative reasoning, simple and imperfect.* That which gives to quantitative reasoning, under all its forms, a character of incontestable rigour is its applicability, not to relations of every kind, but to a restricted number. Identity of nature in the objects compared, identity of co-existence in time, identity of co-extension in space,—these are the only notions perfectly defined by us, and consequently the only notions which permit exact conclusions. If we pass from the comparisons of sizes to that of intensities—'from co-extension to co-intensity,'—precision disappears. We operate no longer on quantities, but on qualities; the reasoning has become *qualitative.* Its object is to determine 'the co-existence or non-co-existence of things, attributes, or relations which are identical in nature with certain other things, attributes, or relations.'

We cannot however trace a strict line of demarcation between the reasoning which has quantity for its object, and that which applies itself to quality, any more than between the two kinds ot quantitative reasoning, the *perfect* and the *imperfect.* All the difference consists in our passing from equality to simple resemblance. The compared relations are no longer considered as *equal* or *unequal,* but as *like* or *unlike;* and as resemblance is of all possible degrees, the probability of the conclusions varies in the same relation. It is to qualificative reasoning that induction, analogy, and the syllogism belong; on the subject of the latter it would be difficult to explain how so many logicians have maintained that it represents the process of mind by which we habitually reason, but for the immense influence of authority on human opinions. The author shows clearly that it is only a process of verification.

In short, we must add a third mode of reasoning to that which goes from the general to the particular, and that which goes from the particular to the general, a mode which Mr. Mill has called reasoning from the particular to the particular, proper to children and the higher animals.

The whole study of reason may be defined as a classification of relations. But what does the word classification signify? It signifies the act of grouping together the *similar* relations, and the act of separating the similar from the *dissimilar.* To infer a relation is to think that it is similar or dissimilar in certain other relations. All reasoning, then, reduces itself to an assimilation or a disassimilation.

From reasoning to *classification* there is only one step. The unity of composition of the two processes is manifest. If it be true to say that all reasoning is a classification, it is equally true that all classification supposes reasoning. A simple example is sufficient. The image of a yellow spherical fruit is produced upon my retina; I class it with others like it, which I have previously seen, under the name of orange. But this classification implies something more than the actual sensation, it implies tangible attributes, an odour, a flavour, an interior structure, which are only inferred consequently to the visual sensation. And the proof of this is that the object may be a mere imitation, in which case touch, taste, and smell rectify my inference, and the object is no more classed among oranges.

Transition from classification to perception is equally easy; because there is identity of nature between these two processes, which, strictly speaking, are inseparable. Every classification supposes perception, and every perception is a classification. To perceive a special, defined, concrete object, is to range it in the same category with those which resemble it; and as this classification is effected spontaneously, and co-ordinates attributes by a natural process, perception may be called *an organic classification.* To say that a thing *is*, is to say what is like it,—to what class it belongs. Here is, then, a double process of assimilation and differentiation.

The relation which establishes itself between the subject and the object in the act of perception is of a triple kind. It takes three distinct aspects, according to the activity which exists on the part of the object, on the part of the subject, or on the part of both:—1. If, while the subject is passive, the object produces an effect upon him (Ex.: radiation of heat, emission of odour, propagation of sound), there results in the subject a perception of what is commonly called a secondary property of the body; but which may be more correctly called a *dynamic* property. 2. If the subject acts directly upon the object, by seizing it, drawing, pushing, or subjecting it to some other mechanical process, and if the object reacts in an equal measure, the subject perceives those kinds of resistance which have been called second-primaries, but which I prefer to class under the name of *statico-dynamics.* 3. If the subject only is active; if that which occupies consciousness is not an action or a reaction of the object, but something which has been known by means of these actions and reactions (such as face, form, position), then the property is of the kind generally called primary, but which we shall here call *Statics.*[1]

The author, in a long and minute analysis, through which we cannot follow him, descends from the dynamic and statico-dynamic attributes to the static attributes, which are the fundamental elements of perception. He shows that the figure is resolvable in reference to size, size in reference to position, and that all the relations of positions may be finally reduced to positions of perceiving subject and perceived object. Briefly, the visual or tactile perception of each static attribute of the body is resolvable into perceptions of relative positions which are acquired by movement.

Let us now pass from the perception of real extended objects to the perception of space, which is their receptacle; and of time, which is their condition. First of all, let us set aside the hypothesis of Kant, on the transcendental origin of these two notions. Placed on the ground of facts, the question reduces itself to this: How can the experience of an occupied extent, that is to say, of the body, give us the notion of unoccupied extent, that is to say, of space? How do we come, from the perception of a relation between resistant positions, to the perception of a relation between non-resistant positions? It is by a complicated process, although repetition and habit have rendered it simple. We only know two relative positions *A* and *B*, by the number of intermediate positions, and this knowledge is due to our sensations. To perceive between these two points, no longer a concrete extent, but a void extent simply possible, a space, there must be produced in us, in a dawning condition, the idea of the different muscular, tactile,

[1] *Special Analysis*, chap. x.

and visual sensations which have been previously given by experience between *A* and *B*.

'If the reader, whilst looking at his hand, or any equally close object, will consider what kind of knowledge he has of the space lying between it and his eyes, he will perceive that his knowledge of it is, as it were, exhaustive. He is conscious of the minutest differences of position in it. He has an extremely complete or detailed perception of it. If now he will direct his eyes to the farther side of the room, and contemplate an equal portion of that more remote space, he will find that he has but a comparatively vague cognition of it. He has nothing like so intimate an acquaintance with its constituent parts. If, again, he will look through the window, and observe what consciousness he has of a space that is a hundred yards away, he will discover it to be a still less specific consciousness. And, on gazing at the distant horizon, he will perceive that he has scarcely any perception of that far-off space—has rather an indistinct *con*ception, than a distinct *per*ception. This now is exactly the kind of knowledge that would result from the organized experiences above described. Of the space that is so close to us as to be within the range of our hands, we have the most complete perception, because we have had myriads of experiences of relative positions within that space. And of space as it recedes from us we have a less and less complete perception, because our experiences of the relative positions contained in it have been fewer and fewer.' [1]

The strange feelings which accompany certain abnormal actions of the nervous system furnish similar evidence. De Quincey tells, in his *Confessions of an Opium-Eater*, that there appeared to him buildings and landscapes of proportions so vast that the bodily eye is not capable of taking them in. Space stretched itself out, and became of an infinite inexpressible vastness. It is not at all uncommon to find, among nervous subjects, persons who have illusory perceptions, in which the body seems to extend itself enormously, sometimes so as to cover an acre of ground. Now the state in which these phenomena are produced

[1] Spencer's *Psychology*, p. 240.

is one of exaggerated nervous activity,—a state in which De Quincey describes himself as seeing, in their smallest details, the long-forgotten facts of his childhood. And, if we consider that an effect must be produced upon our consciousness of space by an excitement which resuscitates our forgotten experiences in great abundance, we shall see that it would cause the illusion of which he speaks. Evidently, we only recall a portion of the innumerable experiences of surrounding positions which we have accumulated during our life. They tend, like all other experiences, to disappear from the mind, and the perception of space would end by becoming indistinct, if they were not refreshed each day, or replaced by new ones. Let us now imagine that these innumerable experiences of relative positions are suddenly revived, that they become present in a distinct manner to consciousness. What must be the result? That space would become known to us in relatively microscopic detail; that a much greater number of positions would be perceived in it; that, as De Quincey says, it would become swollen.

The idea of *time* is inseparable from that of sequence, as the idea of space is inseparable from that of co-existence. The doctrine that time is only known to us by the succession of our mental conditions is so ancient and so well established that it is useless to explain it. Time *in abstracto* is a relation of position between states of consciousness. Our notion of a certain period of time varies according to the number of our states of consciousness. Thus, every one knows that a week passed in travelling, and which consequently excites much activity of mind, appears to us retrospectively much longer than a week passed at home. A road by which one travels for the first time seems much longer than when it has become familiar. The phenomena which accompany certain morbid conditions of the brain furnish analogous examples. In his description of his dreams caused by opium, De Quincey says that he has seemed to live fifty or one hundred years in a single night; and again, that he has had feelings which seemed to him to have lasted a thousand years, or rather for a lapse of time which exceeded the limits of all human experience. Have we not known what it is, during the swoon of a few minutes, to have dreams which seem to have lasted for a considerable time? All these facts, to which we may add many others, show us plainly that our notion of a period of time is defined by the series of states of consciousness which we recall.

Analysis finally leads us to fundamental experience. By successive decompositions of our knowledge into elements more and more simple, we must finally arrive, at the most simple, at the ultimate material element or substratum. What is this substratum? It is the impression of *resistance.*

'It is primordial, alike in the sense that it is an impression of which the lowest orders of living beings show themselves susceptible, and in the sense that it is the first species of impressions received by the infant—alike in the sense that it is appreciated by the nerveless tissue of the zoophyte, and in the sense that it is presented in a vague manner even to the nascent consciousness of the unborn child.

'It is universal, both as being cognizable (using that word not in a human, but in a wider sense) by every creature possessing any sensitiveness, and usually as being cognizable by all parts of the body of each—both as being common to all sensitive organisms, and in most cases as being common to their entire surfaces. It is ever present, inasmuch as every creature, or at any rate every terrestrial creature, is subject to it during the whole of its existence. Excluding those lowest animals which make no visible response to external stimuli, and those which float passively suspended in the water, there are none but what have, at every moment of their lives, some impressions of resistance, proceeding either from the surfaces on which they rest, or the reaction of their members during locomotion, or both. Thus impressions of resistance, as being the earliest that are appreciated by the sensitive creation regarded as a progressive whole, and by every higher creature in the course of its evolutions, and as being appreciated by almost all parts of the body in the great majority of creatures, are necessarily the first materials put together in the genesis of intelligence, and as being the impression continuously present in one form or other throughout life, they necessarily constitute that thread of consciousness on which all other impressions are strung.'[1]

[1] Spencer's *Psychology*, p. 265.

If, after having analysed the various forms of perception, we now seek for that which is common to all, we are led to conclude that perception, considered with respect to all that is most general in it, consists in catching the relations of the senses to each other, in perceiving a relation or relations between actual or previous states of consciousness, in a word, to perceive is to classify relations.[1]

Mr. Herbert Spencer examines in detail the various relations of cointensity, coexistence, and connature. He shows that they all lead back, in final analysis, to the relations of *resemblance* and of *difference*. But difference may be called *change*, and resemblance *non-change*. In fact, in order that two objects may be known as different, there must be two corresponding states in the consciousness, and consequently a change from the first to the

[1] Among the lengthy analyses made by Mr. Herbert Spencer, of different relations, one of the most remarkable and often quoted, is that which resolves the relation of co-existence or simultaneousness into a relation of sequence. It is as follows:—

'So that the relation of co-existence is to be defined as a union of two relations of sequence, such that while the terms of the one are exactly like those of the other in kind and degree, and exactly the reverse in their order of succession, they are exactly like them in the feeling which accompanies that succession. Or, otherwise, it may be defined as consisting of two changes in consciousness, which, though absolutely opposite in other respects, are perfectly alike in the absence of strain. And of course the relation of non-co-existence differs in this, that though one of the two changes occurs without any feeling of tension, the other does not.

'It may be worth while to point out, that these conclusions are indicated even by *a priori* considerations. For if, on the one hand, the great mass of outward things are statical, are persistent, are not manifesting any active change, and if, on the other hand, perpetual change is the law of the inner world—is the primary condition under which only consciousness can continue,—there arises the questions,—How can the outer statical phenomena be ever represented by the inner dynamical phenomena?—How can the no-changes outside even be symbolized by the changes inside? That changes in the *non-ego* may be expressed by changes in the *ego* is comprehensible enough, but how is it possible that objective rest can be signified by subjective motion? Evidently there is only one possibility, a consciousness ever in a state of change can represent to itself a no-change only by an inversion of one of its changes—by a duplication of consciousness equivalent to an arrest—by a regress which undoes a previous progress—by two changes which exactly neutralize each other.'—*Psychology*, p. 308.

second; the perception of similitude, on the contrary, does not imply any internal change. Here we reach the *final term* of the analysis. The most simple relation which intelligence can perceive, is a relation of sequence or of succession; this is the primordial relation which constitutes the foundation of consciousness, and consequently the condition of all thought is change, succession, dissimilarity.

A homogeneous or continuous state of consciousness is an impossibility, a non-consciousness. A being in a state of total repose, a being who undergoes absolutely no change, is dead, and a consciousness which has become stationary is a consciousness which has ceased. Nevertheless a succession of changes does not suffice to constitute consciousness. This succession must be *regular*. Changes form only the raw material of consciousness, it is necessary in addition that they be *organized*, that is to say, classed according to resemblances and differences. In fact, then, the first act of consciousness, the most simple of all, is the perception of a difference, the second act is the perception of a resemblance. Henceforth, intelligence is constituted. To assimilate and to differentiate, therein is the whole mechanism of thought; and all its progress consists in accumulating resemblances and differences. The *unity of composition* is established and verified by analysis. From the humblest act of consciousness up to the most complicated reasoning, from the intuition of a coarse resemblance, which is only a distant analogy, to the intuition of that perfect resemblance which is an identity, the processus invariably remains the same.

We will let the author himself explain these important results, and bring together the double psychological processus of the double processus which constitutes physical life :—

'We have seen that the condition on which only consciousness can begin to exist, is the occurrence of a change of state, and that this change of state necessarily generates the terms of a relation of unlikeness. We have seen that not simply does consciousness become nascent only by virtue of a change—by the occurrence of a state unlike the previous state; but that consciousness can continue only so long as changes continue—only so long as relations of unlikeness are being established.

Hence, then, consciousness can neither arise nor be maintained without occurrences of differences in its state. It must be ever passing from one state into a different state. In other words, there must be a *continuous differentiation* of its states.

'But we have also seen that the states of consciousness successively arising can become elements of thought only by being known as like certain before-experienced states. If no note be taken of the different states as they occur—if they pass through consciousness simply as images pass over a mirror, there can be no intelligence, however long the process be continued. Intelligence can arise only by the organization, by the arrangement, by the classification of these states. If they are severally taken note of, it can only be as more or less like certain previous ones. They are thinkable only as such or such; that is, as like such or such before-experienced states. The act of knowing them is impossible, except by classing them with others of the same nature—assimilating them to those others. Hence then, in being known, each state must become one with certain previous states—must be integrated with those previous states. Each successive act of knowing must be an act of integrating. That is to say, there must be *a continuous integration* of states of consciousness.

'These, then, are the two antagonistic processes by which consciousness subsists—the centrifugal and centripetal actions by which its balance is maintained. That these may be the material for thought, consciousness must every moment have its state differentiated. And for the new state hence resulting to become a thought, it must be integrated with before-experienced states. This perpetual alteration is the characteristic of all consciousness, from the very lowest to the very highest. It is distinctly typified in that oscillation between two states, constituting the simplest conceivable form of consciousness; and it is illustrated in the most complex thinkings of the advanced man of science.

'Nor is it only in every passing process of thought that this law is displayed: it is traceable also in the general progress of thought. Those minor differentiations and integrations that are going on from moment to moment, result in the greater differentiations and integrations which constitute mental development. Every case in which an advancing intelligence distinguishes between objects, or phenomena, or laws, that were previously confounded together as of like kind, implies a differentiation of states of consciousness. And every case in which such advancing intelligence recognises, as of the same essential nature, objects, or phenomena, or laws, that were previously thought distinct, implies an integration of the states of consciousness.

'Under its most general aspect, therefore, all mental action whatever is definable as the *continuous differentiation and integration of states of consciousness.*

'The only further fact of importance here needing to be pointed out is, the harmony which subsists between this final result and that reached by a kindred science. The widest truth disclosed by the inquiries of physiologists is parallel to the one at which we have just arrived.

'As there are two antagonistic processes by which consciousness is maintained, so there are two antagonistic processes by which bodily life is maintained; and the same two antagonistic processes are common to both. By the action of oxygen every tissue is being differentiated; and every tissue is integrating the materials supplied by the blood.

'No function can be performed without the differentiation of the tissue performing it; and no tissue is enabled to perform its function save by the integration of nutriment. In the balance of these two actions the organic life consists. By each new integration, an organ is fitted for being again differentiated: each new differentiation enables the organs again to integrate. And as with the physical life, so with the physical—the stopping of either process is the stopping of both.'[1]

V.

The Physical Synthesis is one of the most original portions of the work, but, especially on its physiological side, it exceeds the limits of our present study. The theory of evolution is put forth

[1] Spencer's *Psychology*, p. 332.

there, under its boldest aspect, since it serves to explain the genesis of even the nervous system, that is to say, of the indispensable condition of all mental life.

Founding his argument upon the principle, 'that motion follows the line of the greatest traction, or the line of the least resistance, or the resultant of the two,' and that 'motion, when once it has begun along a line, itself becomes a cause of subsequent motion throughout that line,' the author explains, in his *Principles of Biology*, and again, with much more detail, in his *Principles of Psychology*,[1] how a nerve may be produced in an extremely simple primitive organism. And as evolutions always go from the simple to the complex, from the homogeneous to the heterogeneous, from the indefinite and the incoherent to the definite and the coherent, systems more or less complicated may have come out of this primitive genesis. Following this ascending evolution through the entire animal kingdom, Mr. Herbert Spencer retraces for us successively the genesis of the simple nervous systems, of the compound nervous systems, and the doubly compound nervous systems, with the variations of functions which are in relation with these variations of structure. These functions have a psychological character, at which we ought to pause, in order to examine how the three essential states of consciousness, *perception*, *idea*, and *emotion*, are formed.

Between a perception considered physiologically and a perception considered psychologically there is a manifest relation. Perception, that is to say consciousness of an external object, cannot result from the excitement of a simple fibre, or of a single cellule; it requires the excitement of a plexus of fibres and cellules. How can this excitement of so restricted a number of elements produce the almost infinite variety of the perceptions? An example will make us understand.

A good piano comprises, taking the demi-notes into account, between eighty and ninety notes; let us, for the sake of the calculation, say one hundred. If each note be separately struck, the piano can yield only one hundred different tones. If two be struck at a time, the different possible combinations rise to 4550,

[1] *Biology*, p. 302; *Psychology*, Part v.

if three be struck together, to 1,617,000; if four, to 3,922,225; if five, to 75,287,250. The numbers may then be indefinitely increased. Now, instead of the notes of a piano, let us suppose sensitive bodies like those which form the retina, instead of vibrating chords, excited ganglions, and we can easily see how a limited number of cellules and of fibres become the seat of a relatively unlimited number of perceptions. And yet this is only a rough comparison, because how can a dead instrument like a piano resemble a living instrument?

Let us now pass from perceptions to *ideas* properly so called. That which characterizes the latter, when they are completely developed, is their *detachableness.* But to return to our comparison. A being who should be composed after such a fashion that he should not be capable of conceiving ideas except when impressions suggest them, would resemble a piano which remains dumb so long as the musician does not touch it. When are ideas really born? They are born when compound co-ordination passes into doubly compound co-ordination. So long as internal impression remains linked with external impression, it is completely dependent upon it, but when clusters of internal impressions become united among themselves, for example, a group of visual sensations with a group of tactile sensations, the relation, the co-ordination established between these psychical conditions permits them to recall, to excite one another; and thus ideas, that is to say detachable independent phenomena, are formed. The process which gives birth to them is then, at bottom, the law of association.

We have seen what is to be understood by *emotions*, and how inheritance plays a great part in their formation. Emotions are formed in the same way as ideas, and by an analogous co-ordination. Placing ourselves at the point of view proper to *Physical Synthesis*, which considers the emotions as a function of the nervous structures, we may say that each plexus has been inherited under the form of a series of well-organized connexions, in the midst of many less defined, and a multitude of slight connexions,—that is to say, between the plexus, which are such that one is habitually excited after the other. The subjective results which ensue are these:—If, for example, a body approaches an animal, producing sounds and emotions of a certain kind, the consciousness in the animal of this phenomenon is followed by disagreeable sensorial and motor conditions; in short, a complex emotion, fear, is produced.[1]

VI.

Such is, in the briefest form, and reduced to essentials, the psychology of Mr. Herbert Spencer. Let us endeavour to summarize it.

We may give the title Genesis of Psychological Life to the whole of the synthetical portion. It appears to us to be the most original part of the book, because of its strict connexion and the novelty of its method. It is the first truly scientific attempt at a history of the different phases through which the evolution of mental life passes. If we compare it with the attempts of Locke and Condillac on this subject, the sensualist genesis will seem to be infantine simplicity. The author, taking pyschological life at its lowest degree, leads it up by successive additions to its fulness; its fundamental characteristics being a correspondence which, in proportion as it completes itself, reproduces subjectively the objective reality of the world. It is successively direct and homogeneous, direct and heterogeneous; it extends to space, to time; it grows in speciality, in generality, in complexity; it finally co-ordinates its different elements, and thus produces an integration, that is to say, a fusion of originally separate elements. Such are the periods traversed by psychological life in order to constitute itself. Considered no longer in its mode of formation but in its manifestations, it is at first reflex action, then instinct, which is only composite reflex action. There, properly speaking, conscious life commences, which is on one side memory and reason, on the other, sentiment and will.

If therefore we take an adult human soul in the full exercise of its faculties, that is to say, the most elevated type which we can know of the psychological life, we resolve it by analysis into its elements, going from the more to the less compound, from the

---

[1] Pp. 245, 247.

compound to the simple, from the simple to the very simple and to the irreducible, we traverse a descending progression, thus: —compound qualitative reasoning, simple qualitative reasoning qualitative reasoning simple and imperfect, perfect qualitative reasoning, imperfect qualitative reasoning, reasoning in general. Reasoning is classification of relations, perception is classification of attributes. The concrete object of perception submitted to analysis is, in the first place, stripped of its dynamic attributes, and afterwards of its statico-dynamic attributes. The fundamental perception is that of resistance. Generally considered, perception is an *organic* classification of relations, the two simplest are those of similarity and dissimilarity, and that of succession, so that the most simple act of consciousness is, first, the perception of a difference, and afterwards the perception of a resemblance.

We shall limit ourselves to observing that it is perhaps to be regretted that Mr. Herbert Spencer has not included volitions and emotions in his analysis, and has not shown us how this branch unites itself to the common truth. By doing so, he would have supplied a new verification of his principle of unity of composition.

VII.

If we bear in mind that we have sketched only a very small portion of the work of our philosopher, and if we have been struck, as we ought to be, with the vigour of his thought and the originality of his method, we shall not be surprised to find it said by a contemporary:—

'It is questionable whether any thinker of finer calibre has appeared in our country, although the future alone can determine the position he is to assume in history. . . . He alone of British thinkers has organized a system of Philosophy. Seeing that he adopts the positive method, is thoroughly imbued with the positive spirit, and constructs his system solely out of the positive sciences, one cannot but raise the question,—What is his relation to the Positive Philosophy?' [1]

[1] Lewes, *History of Philosophy*, vol. ii. p. 653 (Spencer).

In a small work entitled *Reasons for Dissenting from the Philosophy of M. Comte*,[1] Mr. Herbert Spencer has clearly asserted his independence with regard to that school.

A common error, he says, consists in confounding those who follow the method of the sciences with the positivists, and setting them down as disciples of Auguste Comte. The enemies of this philosopher, as well as his friends, have contributed to keep up the confusion of the two terms, 'savants' and 'positivists.' That Comte has given a general explanation of the doctrine and the method of sciences is true. But it is not true that those who accept that doctrine and follow that method are disciples of Comte. As the *savant* limits himself to studying the facts and deducing from them their laws as immediate causes, he is 'positivist' in a certain sense, and in this sense positivism existed before Auguste Comte, and will exist so long as human science shall endure. But this scientific positivism is not identical with the positive philosophy.

'A thinker who re-organizes the scientific method and knowledge of his age, and whose re-organization is accepted by his successors, may rightly be said to have such successors for his disciples. But successors who accept this method and knowledge of his age, *minus* his re-organization, are certainly not his disciples. How then stands the case with M. Comte? There are some few who receive his doctrines with but little reservation; and these are his disciples truly so called. There are others who regard with approval certain of his leading doctrines, but not the rest; these we may distinguish as partial adherents. There are others who reject all his distinctive doctrines, and these must be classed as his antagonists. The members of this class stand substantially in the same position as they would have done had he not written. Declining his reorganization of scientific doctrine, they possess this scientific doctrine in its pre-existing state, as the common heritage bequeathed by the past to the present; and their adhesion to this scientific doctrine in no sense implicates them with M.

[1] Published in 1864, with reference to an article by M. Aug. Laugel, upon the *First Principles* in the *Revue des Deux Mondes*, 15th February 1864. New edition, 1869.

Comte. In this class stand the great body of men of science, and in this class I stand myself.'[1]

Going still further, Mr. Herbert Spencer declares that the points on which he agrees with Comte are not proper to that philosopher, and that on those which are proper to him, he disagrees with him. I acknowledge, he says, with Auguste Comte, that all knowledge comes from the senses,—that all knowledge is relative,—that it is a false explanation which assigns distinct entities as the cause of phenomena,—that there are in nature invariable laws. But these doctrines had entered into the domain of philosophy long before him.

As to the dissent of Mr. Herbert Spencer from the doctrines proper to M. Auguste Comte, they are ascertainable from the following examples :—

AUGUSTE COMTE.	HERBERT SPENCER.
Each branch of our knowledge passes through three different and successive states,—theological, metaphysical, positive.	There are not three radically opposed manners of philosophy, but one method, which remains in its essence the same.
The perfection of the positive system would be to consider all researches into *first* and *final* causes as absolutely devoid of sense, and inaccessible.	The idea of cause will govern at the end, as it has done at the beginning. The idea of cause cannot be abolished, except by the abolition of thought itself. (*First Principles*, p. 26.)
There are six fundamental sciences, with an order of filiation between them.	There are three categories of sciences: 1. Abstract (mathematics, logic). 2. Abstract concretes (mechanics, physics, chemistry, etc.). 3. Concrete (geology, biology, psychology, etc.). There is no order of filiation between them.

[1] Spencer's *Reasons for Dissenting from the Philosophy of M. Comte*, p. 30, 3d edition, 1871.

All researches into the origin of beings and species is useless.

The part of biology which treats of these questions is the most important of all, the others are only subsidiary.

All subjective analysis of our ideas is impossible.

One half of the *Principles of Psychology* is devoted to a subjective analysis.

The ideal of government is to subordinate the individual to society, etc.

The ideal of government ought to be a *minimum* of government, and a *maximum* of liberty, etc.

We refer the reader for further details of this dissent to the *First Principles.* Perhaps we have already exceeded the limits of our subject. But the great philosopher of whom we now take leave is so little known in France that we fear we have been too brief.

MR. BAIN.

The Chair of Logic in the University of Aberdeen, a city celebrated in the history of the sciences and of philosophy, is occupied by Mr. Bain, who has been placed in the first rank of English psychologists by his two works, *The Senses and the Intelligence*, *The Emotions and the Will.* The most illustrious representatives of the Scotch school, could they return to the world, would not disown their successor. There would be grave disagreement on more than one point, but they would have to acknowledge that he has followed that sure method which led them to sound discoveries, and that he has continued the tradition of the school, better than the metaphysicians, like Ferrier, or than the Kantists, like Hamilton. The Scotch philosophy, which has been by turns too much praised and too much criticised in France, has done real service. The timidity which is its ruling characteristic explains both its merits and its defects. Among the merits of the school I place reserve in metaphysics which has preserved them from a rush into the region of ideas, and from dangerous constructions. This reserve, which was rather an instinct than a system, has permitted them to observe patiently. They have a taste for the small facts, for the curiosities of psychology, for rare cases, for exceptions, without which one cannot get to the bottom of things; and yet they have not had taste enough. Among their defects is an excessive anxiety to be always 'in accord with common sense,' a horror of doubt, singular among philosophers, and which has often led them on to empty and ridiculous declamation (see Reid on the *Human Understanding*, chap. i. sects. 3 and 6). They have not had sufficient ability for generalization and synthesis; from whence it arises that their analyses are often made by chance, and that they and their disciples have provided us with an indefinite number of sub-faculties, without having taken the trouble to simplify and reduce all this feudal psychology. Still, everything compared, no school has done more for experimental psychology, in virtue of which principally Mr. Bain belongs to it.

Nevertheless, we should form an erroneous idea of the author, if we saw in him only one of the Scotch school, in the ordinary acceptation of the word. The philosophy of Leibnitz has been defined as 'a Cartesianism in progress and movement.' This formula might be applied to Mr. Bain. His is a Scotch psychology which goes with the age, that is to say, much modified, and upon many points. If Reid or Dugald Stewart were, by a miracle, to revisit Edinburgh, Aberdeen, or Glasgow, and to read the books which we are now considering, this is what would probably occur:—First, they would be profoundly astonished upon several points, then profoundly indignant upon others, and Reid would perhaps even contemplate a rupture. But, instead of a hurried reading of these books, let us suppose that the two illustrious resuscitated philosophers had been initiated beforehand into the progress of the biological sciences, and into the metamorphoses of philosophical thought during the last half-century, and we should find their language very different. I cannot help thinking that if Dugald Stewart (born in 1753) had been born sixty years later, he would have written a psychological treatise analogous to that of Mr. Bain.

The Scotch school says that the method of the *physical* sciences ought to be applied to psychology. Mr. Bain says the method of the *natural* sciences ought to be applied to it, and in that consists all his superiority.

'The object of this treatise is to give a full and systematic account of two principal divisions of the science of mind,—the Senses and the Intellect. The remaining two divisions, comprising the Emotions and the Will, will be the object of a future treatise.

'While endeavouring to present in a methodical form all the important facts and doctrines bearing upon the mind, considered as a branch of science, I have seen reason to adopt some new views, and to depart in a few instances from the most usual arrangement of the topics. . . .

'However imperfect may be the first attempt to construct a natural history of the feelings, upon the basis of a uniform descriptive method, the subject of mind cannot attain a high scientific character until some progress has been made towards the accomplishment of this object.'[1]

We must then expect to find the author frequently speaking as a physiologist. Besides some purely physiological chapters, he has made it a rule from which he never departs to consider all the phenomena which he studies under their double physical and mental aspect. He has thought, rightly, that purely psychological study is abstract and incomplete; that an agreeable or painful emotion, for example, is so intimately connected with the corporeal conditions which express it, that analysis which separates them is arbitrary, and in many respects erroneous.

'Mr. Bain,' says Mr. Stuart Mill, 'has pushed analytical research into mental phenomena, by the method of the physical sciences, to the farthest point which it has yet attained, and has worthily inscribed his name beside those of the successive builders of an edifice to which Hartley, Brown, and James Mill have contributed their share of toil.'

In an article specially devoted to Mr. Bain's work, after having shown that it belongs essentially to the associationist school, which he has helped to popularize, to illustrate, and to reinforce by new proofs, Mr. Mill adds that he has caused associative psychology to advance considerably. This progress consists in bringing the spontaneity of mind into relief.

'Mr. Bain's theory, the germ of which is in a passage cited by him from the eminent physiologist Müller, stands in nearly the same relation to Hartley's as Laromiguière's to that of Condillac. . . . He holds that the brain does not act solely in obedience to im-

[1] Bain's *Senses and Intellect*, ed. 1855, Preface.

pulses, but is also a self-acting instrument, that the nervous influence, which, being conveyed through the motory nerves, excites the muscles into action, is generated automatically in the brain itself, not of course lawlessly and without a cause, but under the organic stimulus of nutrition, and manifests itself in the general rush of bodily activity which all healthy animals exhibit after food and repose, and in the random motions which we see constantly made without apparent end or purpose by infants, and his doctrine, of which the accumulated proofs will be found in Mr. Bain's first volume (pp. 73 to 80), supplies him with a simple explanation of the origin of voluntary power.'[1]

Thus sensation, memory, association, are passive facts; the mind is simply their recipient. A theory of association which stops there seems sufficient to explain our dreams, our reveries, our fortuitous thoughts, but not all our nature; because the mind is active as well as passive. This appearance of absolute passiveness in the theory has helped to alienate from it certain minds who had really studied it. Among them Mr. Mill quotes Coleridge, who was at first attracted by the mechanism of Hartley, but whom it could not finally satisfy.

Activity cannot come forth from passive elements; a primordial active element must be found somewhere. Mr. Bain, who has found it, is therefore greatly in advance of Hartley's theory. In France, adds our critic, the progress made from Condillac to Laromiguière is frequently cited; the first making sensation, a passive phenomenon, the basis of his system, the second substituting attention, an active phenomenon.

'Those who have studied the writings of the Association-Psychologists must often have been unfavourably impressed by the almost total absence, in their analytical expositions, of the recognition of any active element, as spontaneity, in the mind itself.'[2]

[1] Mill's *Dissertations and Discussions*, Art. 'Bain.'

[2] *Ibid.* Bain's *Psychology*, p. 119.

CHAPTER I.

OF THE SENSES, THE APPETITES, AND THE INSTINCTS.

The Sensations.—1. Muscular sense—2. Sight and Touch—3. Instinct, germ of Will.

I.

EVERY study of experimental psychology, whose object is the exact description of facts, and research into their laws, must henceforth set out with a physiological exposition, that of the nervous system. Mr. Bain has done this, and also Mr. Herbert Spencer (in his latest edition of the *Principles of Psychology*). This is the obligatory point of departure, not resulting from a passing fashion, but from nature itself, because the existence of a nervous system being the condition of psychological life, we must return to the source, and show how the phenomena of mental activity graft themselves upon the more general manifestations of physical life. Mr. Bain describes the brain, the cerebellum, the marrow, the spinal cord, and the spinal and cerebral nerves. The nervous force acts upon these different portions of the body after the manner of a current.

'It is nevertheless manifest that the nervous power is generated from the action of the nutriment supplied to the body, and is therefore of the class of forces having a common origin, and capable of being mutually transmitted,—including mechanical momentum, heat, electricity, magnetism, and chemical decomposition. The power that animates the human frame and keeps alive the currents of brain, has its origin in the grand primal source of reviving power, the sun.'[1]

If our means of observation and of measurement were perfect, we could see how nourishment is consumed in the human being, one part being attributed to the animal heat, another to the action of the viscera, another to the activity of the brain, and so on. The nervous force which thus results from the expenditure of a given quantity of nourishment may be converted into every other form of animal life.

Hence we must conclude, contrary to the received opinion,

[1] Bain's *Senses and the Intellect*, edit. 1855, p. 59.

that the brain alone does not constitute the *sensorium*, that it is not the only seat of the mind; but that that seat is wherever there are nervous currents, including the brain, the nerves, the muscles, the organs of the senses, and the viscera.

From this completely physiological beginning we pass on to the first class of phenomena properly belonging to mind. This is not, as it might at first be supposed, the study of our various sensations. There are more general phenomena, hitherto neglected by psychology, which the author describes and examines with that wealth of details, that abundance of facts, which characterize true experimental study.

These are the phenomena of *spontaneous activity*, known to us by *muscular sense.* This sense, whose objects are sensations attached to the movements of the body, or to the action of the muscles, must not be confounded with the five ordinary senses; it is generally admitted that it ought to be studied separately.

The chapter which the author devotes to this subject affords a specimen of his learned and scrupulous method. Always in search of experiences, bent on obtaining completeness, he illustrates by his fine and ingenious remarks a great number of curious and common facts which metaphysics, looking down upon them from its height, does not seem to have observed. I cannot, however, attempt to analyse his minute analyses.

We generally see in our own activity, interpreted by our movements and our desires, the result of some anterior sensation or knowledge; but prior to the former, there is a spontaneous activity coming from ourselves—coming from within, and no' from without, which acts of itself, and not by reaction against the exterior world. The facts which best establish the existence of this is the tonicity of the muscles, the state of permanent closing of the sphincter muscles, the morbid activity and excitement which it causes, the extreme mobility of childhood, and of second childhood, which can only be explained by a surplus of activity. This spontaneity, to which psychology is apparently indifferent, nevertheless contains, as we shall see, the germ of the development of the will.

Muscular sensation, although it very nearly approaches sensation properly so called, differs from it in this, that the one is associated with an internal stimulus, the other with an external stimulus. United to the organic condition of the muscles, it reveals to us the pains and the pleasures which result from exercise, the different modes of tension of the organs in movement; and it gives the measure of the effort. We might perhaps especially call it the sense of our movements, and of that which relates to them.

The muscular sensations have a double character, affective or emotional, and intellectual; each in an inverse ratio to the other.[1]

In considering these under their emotional aspect we find two great classes of movement, whence very different muscular sensations result. Slow movements induce sleep; they produce calm after morbid agitation; they inspire gravity and sadness. After a day of exertion and tumult we recover tranquillity by the sympathetic effect of measured movements, such as music and the conversation of calm persons. Thence also the slow pronunciation in exercises of devotion—the melancholy sounds of the organ. Quick movement, on the contrary, causes great excitement of the nerves. These rapid movements are in fact a sort of mechanical intoxication. Every organ in a state of rapid motion communicates its excitement to all the other organs in motion. If we walk quickly, still more if we run, the mental tone is excited, our gestures and speech become hurried. As examples of this class of muscular excitement and movement, we may cite hunting, dancing, the orgie-like worships of the East, and the rites sacred to Dionysus and Demeter. Finally, muscular sensation may be given to us simply by effort, and independently of all movement; for example, carrying a weight, sustaining one's body, are cases of *dead tension.*

Considered under their intellectual aspect, the muscular sensations are very important from the point of view of knowledge. If to a weight of four pounds held in the hand we add another

[1] It is a psychological law that in a complex phenomenon like a sensation, knowledge is clear and complete in proportion as pleasure and pain have been slight, and *vice versa.*

pound, the state of consciousness changes : this change of constitution is discrimination, or the faculty of discerning, and it is the foundation of our intelligence. Let us note this definition of our author; later on we shall discover its import.

The different modifications of muscular action make us know three things: first, *resistance*, which is the fundamental experience; secondly, *continuation of effort*, accompanied by movement or not; finally, *rapidity* of contraction of the muscle corresponding to the rapidity of the movement of the organ. We have only to reflect a little in order to see that these are important notions, whence several others are derived. Thus the degree of effort or of force expended gives not only the measure of resistance, but the inertia, the weight, and the mechanical properties of matter. The continuation of muscular action gives ideas of duration and extent.

'The difference between six inches and eighteen inches is expressed to us by the different degrees of contraction of some one group of muscles, those for example that flex the arm, or in walking, those that flex or extend the lower limb.' [1]

Finally, the knowledge which we have of the degree of rapidity of our movements permits us to estimate the speed of other bodies in motion, the measure being at first borrowed from our own movements.

II.

We will now pass on to the study of sensations. They are distributed into six classes : sensations of organic life, of taste, of smell, of touch, of hearing, and of sight. The three latter are especially intellectual. Mr. Bain gives the pre-eminence to sight, and even places hearing above touch. His analysis, ample and detailed as it always is, is largely indebted to chemistry and psychology. We shall confine ourselves to selecting three essential points in this study, which are treated with originality and depth : the nature of organic sense, the perception of the exterior world by touch, and by sight.

Even in France we begin to consider the sensations of organic

[1] Bain, *Senses and Intellect*, p. 114.

life as a separate group.[1] Spread over the whole body, particularly in the viscera, they have no organs proper to themselves. Their obscure and continuous action exercises an incontestable influence over our psychological life. Distinct from muscular sensations which especially reveal to us the movement and the effort of the muscles, they reveal themselves to us by the pleasure or the pain which they cause us; they are most frequently affective. Mr. Bain particularizes seven species.

The sensations due to the condition of the muscles, the pain experienced by their being cut, the suffering caused by excessive fatigue, broken bones, torn ligaments; in a word, all the violent damage which can be done to the muscular system.

The nervous system is not only the instrument proper to the faculty of feeling, it also has organic sensations resulting from the condition of its tissue; for instance, neuralgia, nervous exhaustion, and tic-douloureux are examples of pain proceeding from the tissue itself.

Circulation and respiration, with the sensations of hunger, thirst, and suffocation, which belong to them, the pleasure of breathing pure air, the uneasiness produced by a confined atmosphere, have considerable influence upon our condition.

The state of consciousness which results from a healthy circulation may be considered as the characteristic sensation of animal existence.

Digestion, like respiration, presents all the conditions of a sense; an external object, nourishment, and a special organ, the alimentary canal. To it we owe the agreeable sensations produced by a good condition of the digestive organs, the malignant influence exercised by their deranged condition, the sensations of nausea and disgust, and the melancholy caused by diseases of the stomach and intestines.

We may add the sensations of cold and of heat, their influence upon the activity of the organic functions; and, finally, the sen-

[1] See in particular M. A. Lemoine, *L'Ame et le Corps*, and M. L. Peisse *La Médecine et les Médecins*. The sensations, says the latter, proper to headache, indigestion, and palpitation prevent our being ignorant of where our organs are, apart from the aid of dissection.

sations of an electrical condition, whether they result from the employment of machines, or have a natural cause, such as the state of uneasiness which precedes a storm.

From the preceding, the writer will see how much the author excels in this naturalist method, which consists of classification and description; but there are analyses of a more difficult order, whose object is the perception of exteriority and extension.

Touch is the most general sense; it is probable that it is not wanting in any being endowed with sensibility, and its intellectual importance is great. It gives us notions of size, form, direction, distance, and situation. Touch, considered as a source of these ideas, is not a simple sense; it supposes, in addition, the sense of motion. Our appreciation of the weight of a body depends very much upon the exercise of the muscles, although it may result from a simple sensation of pressure exercised upon the skin. Weber shows this by an experiment. If we lay a weight of thirty-two ounces upon a motionless and supported hand, we may vary the quantity of this weight from eight to twelve ounces without the variation being perceptible to the subject of it; on the contrary, if the muscles of the hand are in action, no imperceptible variation, except between one and a half to four is possible. Whence Weber concludes that the valuation of the weight is more than doubled by the play of the muscles.

Muscular sense is no less important for the perception of extension. Properly speaking, this quality, and those of size, form, etc., which belong it, are revealed to us, as we have seen, by the movements which they cause in us; the feelings which they produce are the feelings of motion or of the condition of the muscles. What we have now to ascertain is to what point the sense of touch contributes to our fundamental notion of the exterior world; that is to say, to extension, of which distance, direction, position, and form are only modifications.

Let an arm be moved in empty space, and see what is the result. The absence of determinate marks to limit the beginning and the end of the muscular movement leaves a certain vague character upon our sensation of motion. But *if to the sense of motion we add the sense of touch*, if the movement takes place, for instance, from one side of a box to the other, there we get resistance, and two distinct conditions, which constitute a mark in consciousness. In the same way, if we pass our hand over a surface, we feel at the same time a tactile sensation and a sensation of continued motion. It must also be remarked, that the movement of the arm in empty space not being determined by any contact, renders us incapable of distinguishing the successive from the co-existent (or time from space). Now, so long as this distinction is impossible, we cannot know extension, the foundation of which is co-existence. Time and space are two correlatives, one of which cannot be known without the other, but which are distinct the one from the other. Succession is a simple fact, co-existence is a complex fact. When the serial order of our sensations can neither be changed nor replaced, that is a succession. When it can be replaced, taken in an indifferent order, there is co-existence. Mr. Herbert Spencer is quoted on this subject by Mr. Bain as follows :—

'The chain of states of consciousness, A to Z, produced by the motion of a limb, or of something over the skin, or of the eye along the outline of an object, may with equal facility be gone through from Z to A. Unlike the states of consciousness constituting our perception of sequence, which do not admit of an unresisted change in their order, those which constitute our perception of co-existence admit of their order being inverted—occur as readily in one direction as the other.'[1] It is not without interest to compare this explanation with that of Kant.

The combined sensations of movement and of touch give us notions of length, of surface (extension to two dimensions), *solidity* (extension to three dimensions). *Distance* supposes two fixed points which may be recognised by a movement of the hand, the arm, or the body. *Direction* implies a marking point, our body is the most natural; it serves to measure the right, the left, the back, and the front. *Situation*, that is to say relative position, is known if direction and distance are known. Form depends upon muscular movements, made in order to follow the outlines of a material body.

It has been more than once discussed, whether the superior

---

[1] Spencer's *Psychology*, p. 384. Bain.

sense is sight or touch. The two solutions may be found in Condillac. Most psychologists have declared for touch; most physiologists for sight. Mr. Bain is of opinion of the latter; we have seen that he even places touch below hearing. Without stopping at the physiological study of the sense of sight, and of the mechanism of the muscles which regulate its adaptation, let us examine three disputed questions, that of binocular vision, of reflex images, and of the complex perceptions of sight.

How does it happen that although the image of each object paints itself in the depth of each eye, upon each retina, the object is nevertheless perceived as simple, and not as double? This so often discussed problem has assumed a new aspect since the communication made by Wheatstone to the Royal Society on presenting his stereoscope. When we regard a distant object, says this physiologist, the two visual axes are sensibly parallel, and the images which depict themselves in each eye are *similar;* in this case there is no difference between the visual appearance of an object in relief and its projection upon a plane surface. Upon this the diorama is founded. On the contrary, when the object is near, as the visual axes must converge, the images become *dissimilar*, and they are the more unlike as their convergence becomes greater. It is this dissimilarity, of images which is, in optics, the indicator of solidity or of the three dimensions. The greater the dissimilarity, the more clearly the third dimension is suggested. The stereoscope gives the illusion of solidity by presenting to the eye two dissimilar images; by these means it imitates nature, and produces the same effects, while painting, which produces two similar images, cannot be confounded with solid objects. And now, if we remark that the images painted on the retina are the materials of vision, that they serve to suggest to us a mental construction, which alone constitutes sight properly so called, that there is produced in the mind, by the sight of an exterior object, an aggregate of past impressions which the impression of the moment suggests and does not constitute, we understand that it matters very little whether these materials which serve to the ulterior working of the mind be furnished by two images, as in man, or by thousands, as in insects. The difference or the resemblance of images only teaches us whether the object is distant or near.

As to that frequently offered difficulty, how images reversed upon the retina can appear straight to us,—it only shows that one is completely mistaken concerning the processes proper to the sense of sight. Our ideas of high and low are due to our sense of movement, and in no way to optic images.

The complex sensations of sight result from the combination of optic effects, and the sensations of movements produced by the muscles of the globe of the eye. Here, as in the case of touch, the *combination* of visual perceptions and of movements is the groundwork of our perception of the exterior world. If we follow a moving light with the eye, we experience at the same time two sensations: one of light, the other of movement. The latter varies according as the right or left muscles are employed to move the eye, as a consequence of the direction of the light. The combined sensations of sight and movement give us speed, distance, succession, and co-existence. The particular movements of the muscles cause us to know the circle, angles, complex angles, surfaces, and solids. In short, all that has been stated of the combined sensations of touch and motion applies, *mutatis mutandis*, to the combined sensations of sight and motion.

III.

Before ascending into the higher region of psychology, by passing from sensation to thought, we have to review in as complete a manner as possible all the phenomena which are the raw material of intelligence and of will. Such are the appetites and the instincts.

Instinct is defined as the opposite to that which is acquired by education or experience.[1] We may say that it is an unlearnt power of accomplishing actions of every sort, particularly those which are necessary and useful to the animal. This study of the instincts, which Mr. Bain justly claims as one of the most original portions of his work, has not hitherto been the object of any important researches by psychologists. Psychologists are

[1] *Senses and Intellect*, chap. iv.

indeed very incomplete upon many points. Several explanations, however, are to be found in the germ in Müller, and the author states in many instances that he has taken advantage of them.[1] In our opinion the word instinct tends to produce errors. In the first place, it may be thought that it is a question of those curious phenomena proper to the lower animals, whose origin and cause still remain impenetrable; and thus we immediately get the idea of a general and comparative psychology which shall embrace all the manifestations of mental life. This is in no wise the case. The author keeps to man, and this instinct which he is about to study may be illustrated by the clearer term *instinctive movements*. Taken in their entirety, they constitute a complete order of primitive dispositions, a complete primordial structure, which serves as a basis for what the human being shall become at a later stage, on the development of sentiment, of volition, and of intelligence. These instinctive acts form five groups:—

First, Reflex actions.

Secondly, The special mechanism of the voice.

Thirdly, The primitive arrangements which render harmony and combination of certain actions possible.

Fourthly, The union of feeling with its physical manifestations.

Fifthly, The instinctive germ of volition.

The author treats of the two first points as a simple physiologist, and I have regretted for my part that language has been nowhere studied in his work as a psychological faculty.

What are the actions which are due to the primitive impulses of the nervous and muscular mechanism? That is what we are about to find out. Let us first remark movements which are associated among themselves prior to all experience, and to all volition. Such is the alternate movement of a child's two legs, even before he knows how to walk. Other associated movements are simultaneous; for example, that of the child's two arms and two eyes. It may be said that there is a general law of harmony in the whole muscular system, from whence it arises that when we look or listen attentively the body stops,

[1] See Müller, *Manual of Physiology*, vol. i. p. 632.

the features of the face remain fixed, the mouth is open, our elocution accords with our gestures; rapid walking awakens thought, etc. Let us also remark the intimate relation which exists between taste, smell, and the stomach, and we shall conclude from all these facts that natural harmony between our movements exercises a great influence upon our mental life.

The expression of feeling has also its distinctive and original mechanism. It translates itself: first, by the movements produced by the muscular system, especially by the different muscles of the face, whence results the play of the physiognomy;[1] Secondly, by the organic effects, that is to say, by an influence on the viscera. Grief troubles the digestion, joy exhilarates it; fear dries up the saliva and causes cold sweat; the heart, the lacteal gland in women, feel the shock of the emotions; the lachrymal gland, which constantly secretes its liquid, lets it escape with more abundance in the fervour of tender emotions. All these facts, and a number of others, may be reduced to the following principle: the conditions of pleasure are united with an increase, the conditions of pain with a diminution of all or some of the vital functions. Nevertheless, if we submit this formula to a verification in detail, we shall see that it admits of exceptions. It is not true that augmentation of the vital energy is always coexistent with augmentation of the degree of pleasure. A sweet flavour, an agreeable contact, do not cause an increase of activity; a smart, on the contrary, excites a momentary development. It is the same with those narcotics which, while they cause pleasure, weaken vital power. In fact, neither the doctrine which unites pleasure to self-preservation, nor that which unites pleasure to the increase of activity, is sufficient if taken separately; they must be united in order to arrive at a complete explanation.

This portion of the work, a little vague in expression, is rather touched upon than treated. The question which lies at the bottom of it is this: all our pleasures and all our pains, whatever be their nature, may they be explained by one single principle?—

[1] Müller; see Lemoine, *La Physionomie et la Parole*, chap. iii. *et seq.*

are they reducible to one or two fundamental laws?[1] This is by no means an idle question, because the progress of a science consists in uniting particular causes and derivative laws in a formula which shall contain both. The descriptive and analytical method of Mr. Bain seems to us insufficient. His study upon the emotions, which we shall explain hereafter, though excellent in detail, is only a succession of fragments, whose connexion is not shown with sufficient clearness; and this defect is in our opinion referable to the following cause. It is in that obscure region of the primitive phenomena of affective life, that the germs of pleasures, pains, and passions of every kind, which the play of life breeds, transforms, and incessantly refines, ought to be sought for.

The author has done this in the case of the will. He has sought for its germ in that spontaneous activity which has its seat in the nervous centres, which acts without any impressions from without, or former sentiment of any kind. This is the essential prelude of every development of voluntary power; this activity is one of the terms or elements of volition; volition, in a word, is a compound, formed of this spontaneous activity, and of something beside. It is in Müller's work that we must seek for this.[2] No previous psychologist had demonstrated the part played by these instinctive movements, and their influence upon the will. This physiologist points out that the fœtus produces motions which evidently cannot depend upon the complex circumstances which give rise to the same in the adult; if the fœtus moves his limbs, it is therefore because he *can* move them. Let us remark, besides, that nervous force cannot be equally distributed, and that the nervous centres are not equally charged; but that there is a condition of constitution or nutritive vigour which impels the fœtus to move one foot rather than the other. Spontaneous excitement gives birth to movements, to changes of position, consequently to sensations; there is thus established

[1] We know that Spinoza refers all our inclinations to the self-love of each individual. The most complete treatise on this subject is the Monograph of M. Bouillier, *Du Plaisir et de la Douleur*.

[2] Müller, vol. ii. p. 312.

in the still empty mind a connexion between certain sensations and certain movements; and later, when the sensation shall be excited by some exterior cause, the mind will know that a certain movement will be executed, in consequence, by that part of the body. The nervous system may thus be compared to an organ whose pipes are constantly full of air, which discharges itself in such and such directions, according to the particular stops which are employed. The stimulus produced from our sensations and from our feelings does not furnish the internal power, but it determines the method and the place of the discharge.

What is there in Will more than this discharge of spontaneous impulses? There is this, that spontaneous activity is regulated by physical circumstances and not by the final well-being of the animal. The dog, who in the morning runs wildly about, and expends his superabundance of activity, follows his instinct only; but it is just at the moment when he becomes exhausted that he feels the need of food, and that he is obliged to exert himself to procure it. Pure spontaneity falls short of that which it ought to do for self-preservation. Will, on the contrary, knows the end and the means, and does not expend itself by chance. Let us take account of the existence of this spontaneity, of this instinctive activity, which will aid us hereafter to a better comprehension of the nature of Will.

CHAPTER II.

INTELLIGENCE.

Intelligence.—1. Association of ideas—2. Of consciousness—3. Association by contiguity: exterior perception—4. Association by resemblance: scientific processus—5. Compound association—6. Constructive association, or imagination.

'In treating of intelligence,' says the author in his Preface, 'I have abandoned subdivision into faculties. This explanation is entirely founded upon the laws of association; very small details have been given as examples, and they have been followed up in the variety of their applications.' The treatment of this portion of the work is masterly, as excellent in synthesis as it is in analysis. The collecting an innumerable multitude of facts around some fundamental principles, and submitting principles to verification by facts, is a truly experimental method. Thus, notwithstanding long enumeration of details and examples, the mind keeps a clear impression of this explanation, because it always has a clue to guide it. It knows that each illustration is a proof in support of some particular form of association of ideas; above the facts, it sees partial laws; above partial laws, a general and fundamental law, that irreducible property of intelligence by virtue of which our ideas direct each other and form a succession.

When we see that Stuart Mill, Herbert Spencer, and Bain, in England; with the physiologists Luys and Vulpian, in France, and previous to them Herbart and Müller,[1] in Germany, attach all our psychological acts to different methods of association between our ideas, feelings, sensations, and desires, we cannot help believing that this law of association is destined to become preponderant in experimental psychology, to remain for some time at least the ulterior mode of explanation of psychical phenomena; and thus it will take in the world of ideas a position analogous to that of attraction in the world of matter. It is strange that this discovery should have been arrived at so late. Nothing is more simple in appearance than to remark that this law of association is a realistic, fundamental, irreducible phenomenon of our mental life; that it is at the bottom of all our actions; that it admits of no exception; that neither dreams, reveries, mystic ecstasy, nor the most abstract reasoning can dispense with it; that its extermination would be the suppression of thought itself; and nevertheless no ancient has understood this, for we cannot seriously maintain that the few lines collected here and there from Aristotle and the Stoics constitute a theory and a distinct view upon the subject.[2] It is to Hobbes, Hume, and Hartley that we must refer the origin of these studies on the connexion of our ideas. The discovery of the final law of our psychological acts has this in

[1] Müller, vol. ii. p. 512.

[2] See, for the history of the question, Mervoyer, *Etude sur l'association des idées*, and Hamilton, in his edition of Reid.

common with many other discoveries, that it has come late, and every one is astonished at its apparent simplicity.

Perhaps it is not superfluous to ask in what this method of explanation is superior to that of the faculties. The most general mode consists, as we know, of dividing the intellectual phenomena into classes, of separating those which differ, and grouping together those of the same nature, giving them a common name, and attributing them to one and the same cause; thus we have arrived at distinguishing those different aspects of intelligence which are called judgment, reasoning, abstraction, perception, etc. This method is exactly the same as that followed in physics, in which the words heat, electricity, weight, designate the unknown causes of certain groups of phenomena. If we do not lose sight of the fact that the various faculties are also only the unknown causes of known phenomena, that they are only a convenient means of classifying facts and speaking of them; if we do not fall into the common error of making them substantial entities, personages who form a little republic in intelligence; we do not see that there can be anything reprehensible in this distribution into faculties, in conformity with the rules of a healthy method and a good natural classification. In what then is Mr. Bain's manner of proceeding superior to the method of the faculties? In that the latter is only a classification, while his is an explanation. There is the same difference, in our opinion, between the psychology which attaches intellectual facts to certain faculties, and that which reduces them to the single law of association, as there is between the system of physics which attributes phenomena to five or six causes, and that which attaches weight, heat, light, etc., to motion. The system of the faculties explains nothing, since each of them is no more than a *flatus vocis*, only valuable for the phenomena which it contains, and signifying nothing less nor more than these phenomena. The new theory, on the contrary, shows that the different processes of intelligence are only the different forms of an unique law; that to imagine, to deduct, to induct, to perceive, etc., is to combine ideas in a definite manner; and that the differences of faculties are only differences of association. It explains all intellectual facts, not after the fashion of metaphysics, which insists upon the ultimate and absolute reason of things, but after the fashion of physics, which seeks only their secondary and proximate cause.

We may regret that Mr. Bain has not endeavoured to show in detail how his explanation is to replace the ordinary theory of the faculties, and how each of the latter is attached to a particular method of association. The materials for this study being scattered about in his book, I shall endeavour to indicate it in few words. Consciousness is the fundamental mode of intellectual activity. Who says consciousness, says change, succession, series; it consists of an uninterrupted current of ideas, sensations, and desires; it is therefore the linking together, the association of our internal conditions which constitutes it.

The perception of an exterior object is founded upon associations by contiguity in time and space. It is because we associate the data of our various senses; that is, of sight, touch, muscular feeling, smell, etc., that we perceive concrete objects, which are exterior. To perceive a house is to associate in a single group the ideas of form, height, solidity, colour, position, distance, etc., by a repetition, and by habit these notions are combined in a whole which is perceived almost instantaneously. Mr. Herbert Spencer, in his *Principles of Psychology*, calls these associations *organic*, or organized, and in another place, *integrate*, because they, so to speak, enter one into the other.

That which Mr. Bain calls constructive association is *imagination*. To imagine is to associate ideas or sentiments previously acquired in order to produce some construction which resembles reality. It is by association that I can imagine the drunkenness produced by opium, or the feudal system of the thirteenth century.

Association, founded no longer upon contiguity, but upon resemblances, explains classification, abstraction, definition, induction, generalization, judgment, reasoning, deduction, analogy; all these operations reducing themselves to the associating of ideas, which resemble each other, which differ from each other, or which resemble and differ at the same time.

II.

Before we enter into a detailed explanation of the various forms of the law of association, let us examine the fundamental properties of intelligence. This prior examination is in reality an analytical study of consciousness.[1]

'The word consciousness signifies mental life, with its various energies, in so far as it is distinguished from the purely vital functions, and from the conditions of sleep, torpor, insensibility, etc.' It also indicates that the mind is occupied with itself, instead of being applied to the exterior world; because those pre-occupations whose objects are external present an anæsthetic character.

The primitive and fundamental attributes of intelligence are *consciousness of difference*, *consciousness of resemblance*, and *retentiveness*, which includes memory and recollection.

1. The most primitive fact of thought is the sense of difference or *discrimination;* it consists of seeing that two sensations are different in nature or in intensity. To thoroughly comprehend the thought of the author, we must remark that consciousness is entirely produced by change. So long as the living being has no consciousness, he leads a purely psychological life. If we imagine in any one a single and invariable sensation, there is not yet consciousness. If there are two successive sensations, with a difference of nature between them, still less a simple *hiatus* between two moments of the same sensation, still less a difference of intensity, then we have a more or less clear consciousness: psychological life is born. It is impossible for us to be conscious without experiencing transitions or changes. There are in us many changes, which are slight, or even *nil*, so far as pleasure or pain is concerned, but which are important as transitions, that is to say, as differences.

Discrimination is the foundation of association by contrast.

2. When intelligence is awakened to life, so as to grasp a difference, what does it do? It retains it. Retentiveness is then the condition which immediately succeeds to the consciousness of

[1] This study is to be found in three parts of Mr. Bain's work, vol. i., on *The Senses*, Introduction; *The Intellect*, Introduction; vol. ii. concluding chapter.

difference. It consists of the persistence of mental impressions, after the disappearance of the external agent; we can live a life in ideas, added to our actual life. We can revive sensations and sentiments long past, under the form of ideas. How is that done? Impressions which have always accompanied each other become as it were inseparable.

Retentiveness is the foundation of memory, almost entirely; and of association by contiguity.

3. The third fundamental property of mind is agreement, or consciousness of resemblance. An impression which constantly remains without variation, ceases to affect us; but if it produces another, and that this first impression returns afterwards, then we recognise it, we have consciousness of resemblance. It is owing to this power of recognising the similar in the dissimilar, that what we call general ideas or principles are produced.

Consciousness of resemblance is the foundation of abstraction of reasoning, and association between the similar.

This analytical study of consciousness is, as we see, substantially identical with that of Mr. Herbert Spencer. Let us now observe its consequences.

The fundamental property of intelligence or discrimination implies the *law of relativity*, which may be thus explained: as a change of impression is an indispensable condition of all consciousness, our mental experience is necessarily double. We can neither know nor feel heat except by a transition from cold to heat. In every feeling there are two opposite conditions; in every act of knowledge there are two things which are known together. No mental impression can be called knowledge, unless it co-exists with some other which is compared with it. These are like the two electricities, or the two poles of a magnet, which cannot exist the one without the other. 'A simple impression is equivalent to a non-impression.' The applications of this law of relativity are numerous and important; it applies itself to the useful arts, to the fine arts, to the communication of science, and 'in metaphysics it combats the doctrine of the absolute.'[1]

[1] Vol. i. p. 10.

Mr. Bain, who has very little taste, as we may perceive, for metaphysical excursions, declares that he will not approach the problem of the nature of knowledge, difficult in itself, and obscured by centuries of discussion. The little which he says about it, however, shows that his solution might be brought into relation with that of Mr. Herbert Spencer, who reduces perception to a classification. To feel is not to know; it is erroneous to believe that knowledge can have as much extension as sensation or consciousness. We may say that a child feels all which occurs to him through his eyes or his ears, that he is conscious of it; but to make out of these elements knowledge, choice, classification, and specialization are required. That which we call attention, observation, concentration of mind, must be added to the act of discrimination, in order that knowledge may begin. 'The process of knowledge is essentially a process of selection.' The essential elements of knowledge may be thus summarized.

1. To know a thing is to know that it resembles certain others, and differs from certain others.

2. When knowledge is an affirmation, two known things are required, which two must be brought together under a third general property; for example, co-existence or succession.

3. Into these affirmations an active condition, that disposition called belief, must enter.

III.

In approaching the study of the various forms of the law of association, I think it will be useful to summarize them in the following table, which may serve as a guide for the reader :—

I. *Simple Associations.*
- 1. By contiguity { conjuncts. / successive.
- 2. By resemblance.

II. *Compound Associations.*
- 1. Contiguity.
- 2. Resemblance.
- 3. Contiguity and resemblance.

III. *Constructive Associations.*

A primary species of associations has contiguity for its foundation. This mode of mental reproduction may be established after the following fashion :—

'Actions, sensations, and sentiments which are produced together, or succeed each other immediately, tend to spring up together, to adhere in such a fashion that when, afterwards, one of them presents itself to the mind, the others are also represented.'

The associated conditions may be either of the same nature (as sounds with sounds, movement with movement, etc.), or of a different nature (as colour with resistance, movement with distance, etc.). The following are examples of both cases.[1]

Association by contiguity plays a great part in our movements. All those which are voluntary present great difficulties during early childhood. Each of them is produced separately and with effort. It is by association that series or aggregates of mechanical motions produce themselves rapidly. Such are all those necessary for writing, playing the piano, knitting, etc. The physiological condition of these associations by contiguity is a fusion of the nervous currents. It is in the cerebral hemispheres that the cohesion of associated acts is produced; two currents of nervous force call two muscles into play, one after the other; these currents, flowing together to the brain, form a partial fusion, which in time becomes total fusion. What is still more curious than this fusion of real movements, is the fusion of simple ideas of movements. They associate themselves perfectly according to the law of contiguity. 1st, What relation is there between the reality and the idea? The idea is weakened reality; between conceiving a sensation and really perceiving it, there is only a difference of degree. And as sensation has its seat in one position of the organism, as is generally supposed, which is not the brain only, but also the affected nerves,—the idea, or the ideal sensations, must have the same seat. The continuation of an impres-

[1] It is almost needless to say that the author remains faithful to his complete method, that each group is separately examined, and then in its relations with the others. The study of the Law of Contiguity extends over no less than 130 pages.

sion being the continuation of the nervous circuit, its reproduction must be of the same nature. The idea of an impression is then a reproduction in a feebler form of those nervous conditions which cause the impression itself. This explains why the idea of a movement, when it becomes very lively, induces a movement spontaneously of itself, without the intervention of our will, the excited nervous current being as intense as in the case of a real impression coming from without.[1]

'The tendency of the idea of an action to produce the fact, shows that the idea is already the fact in a weaker form. Thinking is restrained speaking or acting. . . . The tendency of an idea of the mind to become the reality is one of the controlling forces of our constitution, it is a distinct source of active impulses. Our chief active faculty is expressed by the will, or volition, whose nature it is to urge us *from* pain *on* to pleasure. But the disposition to pass from a mere recollection, imagination, or idea to the action that it represents—not merely to think an act, but to do it—is also a determining principle of human conduct.' [2]

The author shows how many curious facts in psychology are explained by this tendency of the idea to realize itself; the fascination exerted by a precipice, the phenomena produced by fixed ideas, by magnetic sleep, and the sensation caused by sympathy.

Let us now examine a case of association by contiguity, between the data of the various senses: a subject already handled by the author, and again resumed. These repetitions, hardly justifiable in a literary work, appear to me to be useful in this case; they permit us to see the different aspects of the question more clearly. We already know that knowledge of the exterior world is due to the associated sensations of touch, sight, and the muscular sense.

'The relations between these four distinct facts—namely, ocular adjustment for seeing an object, the extent of the image on the retina, the distance, and the true magnitude of the object,

---

[1] On this mechanism of the idea returning to its starting-point, see Lélut, *l'Amulette de Pascal*, Introduction. See also Chevreul, *Du Pendule explorateur*.

[2] Bain, *The Senses and the Intellect*, p. 346.

are what we have to consider, for we find that in the educated eye these circumstances are suggestive of one another.[1] . . . "Thus as we approach the object, or as it is brought nearer to us, the magnitude of the picture on the retina increases; the inclination of the optic axes required to cause the pictures to fall on corresponding places of the retina becomes greater." . . . Accordingly, Mr. Wheatstone has devised an instrument, being a modification of his reflecting stereoscope, whereby he can expose pictures to the two eyes in such a manner that the distance can be changed while the convergence of the two eyes remains the same, or the convergence be altered while the distance remains the same; thus disassociating two facts that constantly go together in ordinary vision. The result of the experiments showed the influence of both circumstances,—namely, the convergence of the eyes and the size of the picture on the retina (which is greater as the object is nearer) in determining our judgment of distances. He finds that the distance of the object remaining the same, the greater convergence of the two eyes makes the object seem smaller, this increased convergence being required in ordinary vision when a thing is brought nearer. It appears, therefore, that while the retinal magnitude is unaltered, greater convergence gives a perception of smaller size. On the other hand, leaving the inclination of the axes unchanged, and bringing the pictures nearer, thereby increasing the picture on the retina, there is a perception of increased size in the object. . . . Now, according to Mr. Wheatstone, the inclination of the axes, in company with a given retinal picture, suggests the magnitude first, and from the true magnitude thus known and the retinal magnitude we infer the distance.'[2]

Perhaps some intractable adversary of metaphysics will reproach Mr. Bain with having gone away from experimental analysis to ask *how* we perceive the exterior world? and *why* we believe in it? We shall reply that he submits a few remarks.

'There is no possible knowledge of the world, except in reference to our minds. Knowledge means a state of mind; the

[1] Wheatstone.

[2] Bain, *Senses and Intellect*, p. 377, 378.

notion of material things is a mental thing. We are incapable of discussing the existence of an independent material world; the very act is a contradiction. We can speak only of a world presented to our own minds. By an illusion of language, we fancy that we are capable of contemplating a world which does not enter into our own mental existence; but the attempt belies itself, for this contemplation is an effort of mind.'[1]

Let us observe, besides, that which we ourselves put into the act of perception. Solidity, extension, and space, which are the fundamental properties of the material world, respond to certain movements of our own bodies, and exist in our minds in the form of sentiments of force, and of visual and tactile impressions. The sense of exteriority is then the consciousness of particular energies and activities proper to us. All the difference between ideal sensation and an actual sensation is, that the latter is entirely at the mercy of our movements. We turn our head to the right, or to the left; we move our body, and our perception varies; thus we arrive at distinguishing things, which our movements cause to change their places, from the ideas or dreams which vary of themselves, when we are in repose. In communicating with other beings, and in knowing that they have the same experiences as ourselves, we form an abstraction of our past experiences, and of those of others, and that is the greatest height we can attain with relation to the material world. 'Nevertheless, a possible world implies a possible mind to perceive it, just as an actual world implies an actual mind.'

The conclusion at which Mr. Bain arrives in these remarks, so far as we can define it, would not displease an idealist, since it would place a portion of the reality of the world in the mind: the *feeling* and the *felt* being for him not two terms, but two complementary parts of the same whole.

He says in a note to his recent edition of James Mill:—

'The contrasted terms "Object" and "Subject" are the least exceptionable for expressing the fundamental antithesis of consciousness and of existence. Matter and Mind, External and Internal, are the popular synonyms, but are less free from mis-

[1] Bain, *Senses and Intellect*, p. 370.

leading suggestions. Extension is the object fact by pre-eminence; Pleasure and Pain are the most marked phases of pure subjectivity. Between the consciousness of extension and the consciousness of a pleasure there is the broadest line that can be drawn within the human experience; the broadest distinction in the whole universe of being. These then are the Object and Subject extremes, and, in the final analysis, the Object extreme appears to be grounded on the feeling of expended muscular energy.'[1]

IV.

A second method of association is founded upon resemblance. The law which regulates it is thus enunciated: 'Actions, sensations, thoughts, or emotions which are present, tend to revive those which resemble them among anterior impressions or states.'

Association by contiguity serves above all to acquire, association by resemblance serves above all to discover: it plays a preponderant part in reason, and in the various scientific processes. At one time we grasp the resemblances between continued co-existent aggregates; for example, we forget the differences which separate a horse, a fall of water, a steam-engine, in order to see in them nothing but a motive power. At another time we grasp resemblances in successions. Thus, in studies of embryology, the same being is recognised through all the different phases of its evolution. In the comparative study of social and political constitutions, understood in the manner of Aristotle, Vico, Montesquieu, Condorcet, Hume, De Tocqueville, we must have 'a penetrating mind; in other words, a strong identifying faculty, which can unite and extract obscure resemblances from differences.'[2]

The progress of a classification consists of associating in the same groups beings more and more similar; in passing from superficial identities to fundamental identities, from the Aristotelian division of animals into terrestrial, marine, and aërial, to Cuvier's division, founded upon true nature, and not upon accidental resemblances.

---

[1] Mill's *Analysis*, note 1, p. 5, line 20.

[2] Vol. i. p. 519.

In the mineral kingdom we naturally group the metals together. A greater progress consists in discerning, as Davy has done, that there is a metallic substance in soda and potash, by building upon purely intellectual resemblances.

In the vegetable kingdom, division into trees and shrubs preceded that of Linnæus. At a later date Goethe grasped an analogy between the flower and the entire plant. Oken recognised the plant in the leaf.

In the animal kingdom comparison between the different part which compose each individual leads to the discovery of *Homologies*. Oken, walking one day in a forest, came upon the bare and whitened skull of a wild beast. He took it up, examined it, and discovered that the skull consists of four vertebræ, that it is only a continuation of the vertebral column.

The modes of reasoning and scientific processes founded upon an association by resemblance are arranged by Mr. Bain under these four titles :—

1st, Classification, abstraction, generalization of notions, general names, definitions: the classification consisting in grouping objects according to resemblance, whence results a generalization, or abstract idea which represents what there is in common in the group; and a definition which expresses the common characteristics of the class.

2d, Induction, indirect generalization, conjoint properties, affirmations, propositions, judgments, laws of nature. Here we obtain no longer ideas, as in the first case, but judgments.

3d, Inference, deduction, reasoning, syllogism, extension of inductions. Mr. Bain adopts, without restriction, the doctrine of Stuart Mill, that all reasoning goes from the particular to the particular. The syllogism is only a precaution against error, or, as Mr. Herbert Spencer says, a verification.

4th, Analogy. Here is less than identity; hence those false comparisons which have given rise to false conclusions, such as the assimilation of society to the family, which would tend to make of a sovereign a guardian or a despot.

V.

It remains to us to consider the cases in which a plurality of rings or links concur in reviving some anterior thought or mental condition. Associations individually too weak to revive a past idea may succeed in doing so when they act together. The general law of this mode of association is thus established. 'Past actions, sensations, thoughts, and emotions are more easily recalled when they are associated by contiguity or resemblance with more than one impression, or with a present object.'

Compound associations result from single contiguities, from single resemblances, or from united contiguities and resemblances.

Here are some examples of the first case:—We feel the odour of a liquid; this sensation alone does not suffice to recall its name; but we afterwards taste it, and remembrance is effected by these united sensations. Complex objects, and *concrete wholes*, which we see in nature, such as a tree, an orange, a locality, or a person, are aggregates of ideas, and of contiguous sensations.

A person who has previously read the two Œdipes of Sophocles will recollect them in reading 'King Lear;' because a composition of resemblances naturally leads to comparison.

Finally, if, in describing a tempest, you say, 'the strife of the elements,' you associate by resemblance, because there is strife and combat in a tempest; and by contiguity, because this metaphor is so generally used that the two ideas are connected. Whence the defects of the *banal* style, and of frequently used expressions.

It may be asked, why the author has not recognised a particular mode of association by contrast? It is because he sees therein not so much a form of the fundamental law of intelligence, as the condition inherent to every act of knowledge, and without which it is not possible.

'Contrast is the reproductive phase of the first law of mind, relativity, or discrimination: everything known to us is known in connexion with something else, the opposite or negation of itself; light implies darkness; heat supposes cold. Knowledge, like consciousness, in the last resort is a transition from one state to another, and both states are included in the act of knowing either.[1]'

The necessity inherent in every idea of completing itself by its contrary, produces the love of contradiction in discussions. Among the Greeks it gave rise to the doctrine of the Nemesis.

VI.

Hitherto we have only had in sight the resurrection, the literal awakening of sensations, images, emotions, consequences of anterior thoughts.

But there are other modes of association, known under the names of imagination and creation. Here we unite new forms, we construct images, pictures, conceptions, mechanisms, differing from all which experience has previously given. The painter, the poet, the musician, the inventor in the arts and sciences, furnish us with examples. This is the law :—

'By means of association the mind has the power of forming combinations or aggregates, differing from everything which has been presented in the course of experience.'

The essay upon *constructive association*, or the theory of imagination, is equal to the best analyses of the work, for its order, its clearness, its fulness, the exactitude of its details, and the interest of the questions which it raises.

Constructiveness permits us by associations of sensations to imagine new sensations. You hear a passage read, you have already heard Rachel or Macready, and you say : 'Imagine Macready or Rachel delivering that passage.' You wish to remodel the plan of your garden, it is by a constructive association that you can imagine the effect which will be produced when the new plan shall be realized.

So it is with the emotions. The sentiments of men who differ altogether from us in their position, their character, their occupations, can only be conceived by a constructive proceeding. Every one has experienced fear, anger, love, etc., these are the elementary facts which serve for our constructions; but it is

[1] Bain, *The Senses and the Intellect*, p. 579.

impossible to comprehend a sentiment of which one has not in one's-self the source : this it is which renders religious or artistic forms, different from those to which they are accustomed, unintelligible to so many people. Many historians have made this remark—Mr. Grote for example :—'We cannot comprehend,' he says, 'the terror of the Athenians on learning the mutilation of the Hermes, except by remembering that, in their eyes, it was a pledge of security that the gods should dwell upon their soil.'

Constructive association in the fine arts, or imagination properly so called, presents a peculiarity: it is the presence of an emotional element in the combinations. It is the artist's ambition to give pleasure to human nature, 'to increase the sum of its happiness.' The first aim of the artist must be to satisfy taste. 'I cannot, then,' says Mr. Bain, 'accept the current doctrine which would make of nature his criterion, and of reality his end. The criterion of the artist is sentiment, his end is a delicate pleasure.'

Here we perceive the æsthetics of the author. We shall find them amply explained under the title of the *emotions*.

CHAPTER III.

THE EMOTIONS.

The Feelings.—1. Judgment of Mr. Herbert Spencer—2. Classification of the emotions—3. Æsthetic feeling : of laughter—4. Moral feelings.

I.

WE are now about to consider the weakest portion of the great work which occupies us,[1] and its objects are the emotions. Although the author announces in his preface that he wishes to proceed as a naturalist, and to continue in the affective region what he has done for intelligence, appetites, and sensations, we do not find such certainty of method as satisfies the mind, more than it is satisfied by analyses and discoveries. The

---

[1] Such also is Mr. Mill's opinion in the article previously quoted.

method of the naturalist, in fact, comprehends two essential operations—classification and description. The descriptive portion is excellent, and we could not desire it to be more complete. Each species of emotion is carefully characterized, considered in its effects, in its modifications, its influence, and its transformations. The author never fails to study it under its double aspect, *physical* and *mental*, thus attaching the psychology of the passions to the physiology of the passions; and thereby exhibiting, as he remarks, the relation of the physical to the moral. This explanation, made in detail, and by fragments, under the special title of each emotion, gains in precision by this method, in which we find all the ability of his preceding essays.

The defect of the work appears to us to exist in its classification of the affective phenomena. And here we will allow a better judge than ourselves to speak. Mr. Herbert Spencer, in an article published in 1860 by the *Medico-Chirurgical Review*, and since reproduced in his essays (volume i., 1868), has given a detailed criticism of Mr. Bain's book upon the emotions, of which we reproduce the substance.

Notwithstanding its merits, Mr. Bain's work is provisional—it is a transitional study. His declared intention is to follow a natural method, and he does it in many respects. But his classifications are not founded on this method, for this reason: A natural classification supposes two things—a comparison of phenomena, and a close analysis, which, without stopping at its accidental characteristics, penetrates to all that is fundamental. This double labour is missing here; description replaces analysis too far. Mr. Bain acknowledges that he has adopted as the the basis of classification the most manifest characters of the emotions, such as they are given to us, subjectively and objectively. From the objective point of view he refers to the natural language of the emotions, and the social phenomena which result from them. From the subjective point of view, he holds as primitive, and not to be decomposed, the emotions, given as such by the analysis of consciousness. Nevertheless, psychologists know well that there are intellectual acts which consciousness gives as simple, and not to be decomposed, and which analysis perfectly resolves. It ought to be the same in the case of the emotions as in that of intellectual acts. Just as the conception of space resolves itself into experiences altogether different from that conception; so it is probable that the sentiment of affection or of respect is composed of elements each acting differently from the whole which they compose.

How is it that Mr. Bain has not seen that to keep to the *manifest* characteristics is to follow the method of the ancient naturalists, who, in virtue of exterior and superficial resemblances, place cetacea among fish and zoophytes among seaweeds? Every classification which is not founded upon real relations may contain many truths; it is useful at the commencement of a science, but it can only be provisional.

Mr. Herbert Spencer then asks how the strict analysis which ought to precede classification should have been set about. It is assuredly more easy, he says, to compare animals and organs than emotions; there is the first difficulty. A second, which is more grave, is that of a good psychological classification, supposing that a certain number of biological questions had been resolved, which in the actual state of science are not so. We may then aspire to progress, not to a definite result; and the following are the conditions of that progress:—

1. We must study the ascending evolution of the emotions through the animal kingdom; seeking out those which appear first, and which co-exist with the lowest forms of organization and intelligence.

2. We must note the emotional differences which exist between the lower and higher human races; those which are common to all may be considered as primitive and simple, and those which are proper to the civilized races as ulterior and compound.

3. We must observe the order of evolution, and of the development of the emotions, from earliest infancy to mature age.

The comparison of this triple study of emotion in the animal kingdom, the progress of civilisation and of individual development, will render a truly scientific analysis of the affective phenomena more easy. The order of the evolution of the emotions would give the order of their mutual dependence. We should see, for example, that the lowest savage races ignore justice and pity; that they hardly know certain æsthetic emotions, like those of music; that the love of property is produced late, and is consequently an ulterior and derived sentiment.

Finally, Mr. Bain has taken no account of hereditary transmission, which, nevertheless, creates such great differences between savage and civilized races.[1]

To these criticisms we venture to add a final one: Mr. Bain considers the number of simple emotions to be nine. Must we believe that they are absolutely irreducible? Is there not some fundamental inclination which is their source, and which explains them? Cannot all the affective phenomena be reduced to a final law, as the intellectual phenomena may be reduced to a particular mode of association? Spinoza, as we know, explained all our passions by desire, joy, and pain, which he referred to the fundamental inclination of every being 'to be and to persevere in his being.' Jouffroy arrived at the same conclusion in another form, and in another manner. All the simple or compound emotions had the love of self for their first source. The positivists divided them into two sections—egotistical affections, affections for others. It seems to us regrettable that Mr. Bain should not have also tried a reduction, or at least that he should not have given us his mind upon the current doctrines.

II.

'Feeling,' he says, 'comprehends all our pleasures and pains, and certain modes of excitement of a neutral character, which shall be defined later.' Feeling comprehends at once diverse *sensations* previously examined, and the *emotions*.[2] The former

[1] Mr. Bain has replied in a note to the last edition of *The Emotions and the Will*, p. 601. He points out that the point of view of Mr. Spencer, that of the doctrine of evolution, must have brought with it a difference of plan. He believes, in addition, that the disagreements are more apparent than real, and thus concludes the discussion: 'It appears, therefore, that I have given a classification as nearly agreeing with Mr. Spencer's, as two independent minds can be expected to agree in so vast a subject; the scheme whereby he proposes to reorganize, on an advanced idea, the psychology of the feelings, differing from mine only in form and appearance.'—Bain's *Emotions and the Will*, p. 605.

[2] *Emotions and Will*, chap. iv.

are the primitive feelings, the latter the secondary, derivative, complex feelings.

'The most general principle that we are able to lay down respecting the concomitance of mind and body may be called the *law of diffusion*. It is expressed thus: "When an impression is accompanied with feeling, or any kind of consciousness, the aroused currents *diffuse* themselves freely over the brain, leading to a general agitation of the moving organs, as well as affecting the viscera."'[1]

The reflex action, on the contrary, which is not felt, is restrained in its influence to a very narrow nervous circuit.

This law of diffusion causes motions to be transmitted by waves to the heart, stomach, and viscera, and manifests itself by the features of the countenance, etc. 'It constitutes a considerable support to the doctrine of *the unity of consciousness*. Several nervous excitements may co-exist, but they can only affect consciousness successively, each one in its turn.'

It is upon these exterior manifestations of the emotions, upon their results, and their subjective characteristics, that their classification is founded. The author acknowledges the eleven following classes:—

1. We will begin with the LAW OF HARMONY and CONFLICT. The principle that HARMONY is connected with PLEASURE, and CONFLICT with PAIN, is probably an offshoot of the LAW OF SELF-CONSERVATION.

2. There are certain emotions essentially depending on the LAW OF RELATIVITY. Such are NOVELTY, WONDER, and the FEELING OF LIBERTY. These are all purely relative to certain other states that go before; NOVELTY and WONDER presuppose the ordinary or the common; LIBERTY implies foregone restraint. The emotion of POWER also subsists upon comparison with some allied state of impotence.

3. The emotion of TERROR is a wide-spread influence in human life. The revulsion from suffering implied in our volitional nature, instead of producing always the simple effect of inspiring actions for relieving the pain, not unfrequently excites a convul-

[1] Bain, *ibid.* p. 3.

sive trepidation of the whole system, accompanied with a new state of suffering, and with other important consequences. This special outgoing belongs to certain modes of pain rather than to others; and all sentient beings are subject to the condition, although in very unequal degrees. As a general rule, the susceptibility to terror is a weakness and an evil, and the consideration of the means of avoiding or subduing it is of great practical moment.

4. The extensive group of feelings implied under the title of the TENDER AFFECTIONS constitutes a well-marked order or genus of emotion. Being principally manifested towards living beings, their first development in the child comes with the recognition of personality. When they are once made to flow freely, human attachments begin to be formed; and a considerable portion of the pleasure of life springs from this fountain-head. If it were permitted to writers on the human mind to advert specifically to the feelings of the sexual relations, these would find an appropriate place anterior to the present division.

5. When a human being recognises or imagines in himself the qualities that draw forth admiration, love, reverence, esteem, when seen in others, he is affected by a peculiar kind of emotion, which passes current under such names as SELF-COMPLACENCY, SELF-GRATULATION, SELF-ESTEEM. I am disposed to think that there is here only a special offshoot or diversion of the tender sensibility. [A still further emotional effect is produced by being the subject of the admiration or esteem of our fellows, which is commonly denominated APPROBATION, PRAISE, GLORY, REPUTATION, and the like.]

6. The elation of superior POWER is a very marked and widely ramifying sentiment of our constitution: implying, as its correlative, the depression of IMPOTENCE, inferiority, and insignificance.

7. The IRASCIBLE EMOTION is a notable attribute of our humanity, the peculiar characteristic of which is the pleasure arising from *malevolent* action and sentiment.

8. Under ACTION there are certain distinct modes of feeling to be mentioned, as contributing largely to the interest of life. Besides the pleasures and pains of exercise, and the gratification of succeeding in an end, with the opposite mortification of miss-

ing what is laboured for, there is in the attitude of pursuit a peculiar state of mind, so far agreeable in itself that factitious occupations are instituted to bring it into play. When I use the term PLOT-INTEREST, the character of the situation alluded to will be suggested with tolerable distinctness.

9. The exercise of the INTELLECT gives birth to certain species of emotions which it is interesting to study. The routine operations sustained by mere contiguity evolve no feeling; the more perfect the intellectual habits, the less consciousness is associated with them. A practised accountant approaches to a calculating machine. But in the operation of the Law of *Similarity*, where new identifications are struck out, there is an emotion of agreeable surprise accompanying the flash. Hence, although routine is unconscious, originality is intensely stimulating. Part of the pleasure of works of genius proceeds from this effect, and we shall see in it one of the rewards of intellectual pursuit. [Under the same head is to be reckoned the very characteristic pain produced by *Inconsistency*, in the susceptibility to which temperaments differ greatly. The genuine love of Truth is greatly fostered by the desire of escaping from contradictions.[1]]

While the sentiments ranged under the nine preceding titles are simple and irreducible, the æsthetic and the *moral* emotions which form the two last groups are compound. The author has studied them in detail, and we must now pause to consider them.

III.

Two entire chapters (the thirteenth and fourteenth) on sympathy, imitation, and ideal emotion, that is to say, the emotion which is caused by pure ideas, and not by realities, precede the æsthetic explanation.

'We understand by sympathy and imitation, the tendency of an individual to agree with the active or emotional conditions of others; these conditions being revealed by certain means of expression.' Sympathy and imitation have an identical foundation; but the one expression is used for feelings, and the other for action. Two laws regulate sympathy. The first is the tendency

[1] Bain, *Emotions and the Will*, 2d edition, 1865, p. 36.

to take a condition, attitude, or *corporeal* movement, when we see another person producing it. The second is the tendency to take a *state of consciousness* by means of the corporeal conditions which accompany it. These two laws explain contagious emotions,—the propagation of yawning or laughing. A grea. nervous weakness predisposes to sensations of sympathy, and to the strange facts produced by magnetic sleep.

It would be inexact to say that Mr. Bain has given us in his work a system of æsthetics, or of morals; we do, however, find them sketched there. His experimental method, which is very good when applied to simple psychical phenomena, does not appear to us so happy, when it consists less of facts than of an ideal, —less of what *is*, than of what *ought to be.* The relation between the good and the beautiful is so intimate that some, for instance Goethe, have thought that morals are only æsthetics applied to life,—an idea to which Plato was not a stranger. Virtue then appears like another form of beauty. And no doubt, when we think of it, we must consider these researches, whose object is to fix the essence of the beautiful and the good, as somewhat vain. Here precision is only awkwardness and want of skill; these things are so delicate, that all scholastic stiffness endangers or breaks them. We must renounce the idea of grasping the unfathomable, and of translating the ideal by the imperfect formulæ of science, whose apparent exactitude is on the surface only.

Only one single truly serious method is to be found in æsthetics, one method which can not lead to illusion, while we believe that it tends to truth. It is that which proceeds subjectively, which does not seek out the beautiful, which does not try to add a new definition, equally, though otherwise insufficient, to those already given, which limits itself to the study of internal phenomena; that is to say, the effects which the beautiful produces upon us. There are a certain number of sentiments or emotions which we call æsthetic; what is their nature, what are their characteristics? Thus the whole task of æsthetics is to state phenomena, to analyse them, and to describe them. Jouffroy has given an example in his *Cours d'esthétique*, unhappily unfinished. Æsthetics, thus understood, is a necessary accompaniment of psychology; it forms a chapter of it, which can hardly be detached, and it seems that at least it cannot be otherwise understood in any analytical treatise upon the phenomena of consciousness.

All our senses, says Mr. Bain, are not capable of furnishing us with æsthetic emotions; because we must exclude from this category the purely sensual pleasures: in the first place, because, being indispensable to our existence, they have not a disinterested character; secondly, because they are sometimes united to certain repugnant facts; finally, because they are egotistical or individual; two men may enjoy the same picture, they cannot enjoy the same piece of food. In order that sensations may have an æsthetic character, they must cease to be a simple property of the individual; thus it is that the eye and the ear are especially æsthetic senses.

'Ever since the dawn of philosophical speculation, the nature of the Beautiful has been a matter of discussion. In the conversations of Socrates, in the dialogues of Plato, this inquiry had a place side by side with others conducted in a kindred spirit, as into the Good, the Just, the Fit. Most of the inquirers laboured under a fallacy or misapprehension, rendering the discussion futile as regarded analytic results; they proceeded on the supposition, that some single thing could be found, entering as a common ingredient into the whole class of things named beautiful.'[1]

But that is not the case; were it so, two thousand years ago this beautiful type would have been discovered. Besides, we moderns, habituated to the doctrine of the plurality of causes, have no repugnance in admitting not only the beautiful in itself, but many things which are beautiful. The whole meaning of this æsthetic exposition is, that harmony is the soul of art. The sublime is a sentiment explained by sympathy.

'The objects of the sublime have, in fact, a certain community of character, such as belongs only to very small portions of the wide field of the beautiful. They are principally the objects, aspects, and appearances that betoken great might, energy, or force, and which are capable of dilating the mind with a borrowed sentiment of power. . . . So enjoyable is the sense of power, that

[1] Bain, *Emotions and Will*, p. 249.

we welcome every mode of making it present. When we have it not in actual, though unmanifested, energy of our own, we seek for it in the ideal by witnessing the energy displayed around us.'[1]

'Human power is the true and literal sublime, and it is the starting-point for the sublimity of power in everything else. Nature, by a bold extension of analogy, is assimilated to humanity, and invested with mental attributes.'

An interesting question, but little studied hitherto, terminates this sketch of æsthetics: it is that of laughter. Mr. Bain merely touches upon it. Mr. Herbert Spencer has published a brief but substantial essay upon the same subject. We shall unite them here.[2]

The causes of laughter, says Mr. Bain, are sometimes *physical*, for instance cold, tickling, certain acute pains, and hysteria; sometimes *mental*, for instance, gaiety: the laughter of the gods, in Homer, is the exuberance of their celestial joy, after their daily banquet. It seems that everything which produces an augmentation of gaiety, by setting us free from constraint, or by increasing the consciousness of our energy, produces an agreeable emotion which manifests itself by laughter. A tender feeling, on the contrary, would give rise to a manifestation of a less distinct character, the smile; if indeed it be correct to define the smile as a species of laughter.

It is commonly said that the *laughable* is caused by an incongruity; that in order to produce it there must be at least two things or qualities naturally opposed to each other. But there are incongruities which cause anything but laughter; an old man bending under a heavy burthen, snow in May, a wolf in a sheepfold, and twenty other facts of this kind, excite pity, astonishment, fear, but not laughter. Hobbes defines laughter as 'a sudden feeling of exultation springing from the sudden idea of some superiority proper to us, in comparison with the inferiority of

[1] Bain, *Emotions and Will*, p. 273.

[2] *Physiology of Laughter*, in *Macmillan's Magazine*, March 1860, reprinted in the *Essays*, vol. i., on *Laughter*; see Lévêque, *Revue des Deux Mondes*, 1st September 1863, and Léon Dumont, *Des Causes du Rire.*

others, or with our own previous inferiority.' This purely egotistical application of laughter explains neither that which is caused by sympathy nor that which is induced by comic literature.

Mr. Bain seems to trace the cause of laughter to a feeling of power or of superiority, and in liberation from constraint. A serious, grave, dignified, solemn demeanour obliges us to be constrained; as soon as we can throw it off we feel free. Seriousness demands toil and effort; abandonment, liberty, *laisser-aller*, are produced of themselves, and have an air of gaiety which arises from the absence of all constraint.

We must now let Mr. Herbert Spencer speak. His short article upon the physiology of laughter seems to us one of the best of his *Essays*. We perceive by the title that he is less occupied with the psychological side of the question than Mr. Bain; perhaps he is the more successful in consequence. Nowhere has he leaned more firmly upon his great doctrine of the continuity of natural phenomena, in virtue of which there are no creations but only transformations of motions. Consequently he has not studied laughter separately in itself; he has attached it to its causes, to its conditions, and considered it as the moment of a whole, from which it cannot be separated.

When we ask, Whence comes laughter? the ordinary answer is, From an incongruity. In allowing that this reply does not admit of an objection, we must also admit that it hardly affects the problem, since the real difficulty is this:—Why, when we experience a keen pleasure, when we are struck by an unexpected contrast between ideas, is a particular contraction of the muscles of the face and of certain muscles of the chest and the abdomen produced? Physiology only can answer that question.

It teaches us that it is of the nature of nervous force to expend itself, to discharge itself in one of the following ways:—

1. Nervous excitement always *tends* to produce muscular motion, and always *produces* it when it attains a certain intensity. Hence gestures, the expression of the physiognomy, in short all those states of the muscles which allow us to read the feelings of others. The nervous discharge can even produce extraordinary effects, for instance, in the case of paralytics who have momentarily recovered the use of their limbs, in consequence of some

violent emotion. The emotions and the feelings tend then to produce bodily movements in proportion to their intensity.

2. But this is not the only direction which nervous action can take in order to expend itself. The viscera as well as the muscles can receive the discharge. Hence the influence of the emotions upon the heart and the digestive organs.

3. Finally, the nervous discharge may be effected in another direction, which it usually takes when the excitement is not great. It consists in causing the excitement to pass into some other part of the nervous system. This is produced when our thoughts and feelings are calm, and thence result the successive conditions which constitute consciousness. Sensations excite ideas and emotions; the latter, in their turn, awaken other ideas and emotions, and so on; that is to say, the tension which exists in certain nerves or clusters of nerves, when they procure sensations, ideas, or emotions for us, engender an equivalent tension in other nerves with which they are connected.

It is a necessity that nervous force, existing in every instant, and producing in an inexplicable manner what we call feeling, should follow one of these three directions; to excite new feelings, to act upon the viscera, to produce motion. Well-known facts attest this. Great griefs are silent. Why? Because in their case the nervous excitement awakens melancholy ideas instead of producing exterior manifestations. Those persons who conceal their anger are always the most vindictive. Why? Because emotion increases by accumulation. Bodily activity, on the contrary, the necessity for a life of effort, weakens the emotions, because the nervous excitement expends itself materially.

All this explains the question of laughter. Nervous excitement must follow that one of the three channels which shall open itself most readily: in the case of laughter the discharge acts upon the muscles. Take the laughter which results from a *physical* cause (cold, tickling, etc.); the discharge will act first upon the muscles which are the most habitually moved, that is to say, upon those of the mouth and of the organs of the voice; if it be very strong, it will act upon the other parts of the body, as in violent laughter. Now take the laughter which arises from an incongruity. You are at the theatre, an interesting drama is being played, and the actors have reached the chief scene, the reconciliation of the hero and the heroine, after a long and grievous estrangement. But, of a sudden, a goat makes its appearance from behind the scenes, and after surveying the audience with amazement, goes ba-a-ing towards the lovers. You laugh. Why? Because you were under the influence of a strong emotion, or, to put it physiologically, your nervous system was in a state of tension. A sudden interruption takes place, the sight of the goat cannot cause you an emotion equal to that caused by the reconciliation of the two lovers; there is then a surplus of emotion which must run over; it discharges itself through the channel which it finds open, and produces laughter.

If we examine, in the sense of a counter proof, the incongruities which do not produce laughter—such as an old man carrying a heavy burthen—we shall see that here the two states of consciousness, though opposed, are of the same bulk, and therefore there is no discharge to be expended. The orator who, in Parliament, incessantly takes out and replaces his eyeglass, the schoolboy who, while reciting his lesson, constantly twists something between his fingers, the automatic actions of certain advocates and other persons while speaking in public, are so many examples of the manner in which the surplusage of the emotions expends itself, and consequently escapes from paralysing intelligence.

IV.

The preceding study is another proof of how systematic is Mr. Spencer's analysis; so that we would not neglect this important psychological monograph. Let us return to Mr. Bain and his analysis of the moral emotions. Very clear in detail, it is more difficult to grasp and exhibit in its entirety. It seems that his chief care has been to give a purely human character to morality. The conception of a higher law appears to be repugnant to him, because it presents itself as a super-sensible fact, in disagreement with his empirical habits. If the language of German philosophy should not seem out of place here, we would say in one word that Mr. Bain's theory of morals is *immanent*, and opposed to all *transcendence*. He has aimed above all at founding it, not upon an abstraction, but upon a fact, and a human fact.

In their proper sense, says Mr. Bain, I consider the words, morality, duty, obligation, right, as belonging to the class of actions, which is supported and reinforced by the sanction of a *punishment*. We may disapprove a mode of conduct, but so long as we do not proceed against it, we do not regard it as obligatory.

'The powers that impose the obligatory sanction are Law and Society, or the community acting through the Government by public judicial acts, and apart from the Government by the unofficial expressions of disapprobation and the exclusion from social good offices. The murderer and the thief are punished by the law; the coward, the adulterer, the heretic, the eccentric person are punished by the community acting as private individuals, and agreeing by consent to censure and excommunicate the offender. A third power concerned in obligation is conscience, which is an ideal reflection of public authority growing up in the individual mind, and making to the same end.'[1]

The various moral systems founded upon positive law, the divine will, strict reason, moral sense, personal interest, and general interest, are successively examined and rejected by the author. He very clearly shows the insufficiency of egotistical and utilitarian doctrines. It is not true that all our acts reduce themselves to the love of ourselves, 'because sympathy is a fact of human nature whose influence makes itself readily felt at a distance, and constantly modifies and contradicts purely egotistical impulses.' And in the same way utility does not always explain all our actions, since it is not rare to see a man refuse to embrace a lucrative profession, which would appear to him to be dishonourable to the traditions of his family pride, and to choose instead a life of privations and poverty.

The doctrine of an independent moral law which serves as a criterion and regulator, is not more acceptable, because it attributes to this criterion an independent existence relating to nothing,—in fact, hardly conceivable. We have for our weights and measures an independent standard, by which we can compare them; for the regulation of our watches we have our astronomi-

[1] Bain, *Emotions and Will*, p. 286.

cal observations, and we have the Observatory at Greenwich, which is our regulator; but in morals there is no criterion of this kind. It is doing violence to language to maintain the existence of an abstract truth; it is the same with moral ideas. They must be sought in the human mind, and not in anything exterior to the human mind. If mechanical and metaphysical laws are true, it is not in virtue of a certain abstract truth from which they are derived, but *because the perceptions of men in this region of phenomena are uniform when they are compared.* When this uniformity does not exist in our perceptions (those of taste, for example), then the criterion fails. 'There is no more universal consciousness than universal reason; consciousness, like reason, is always individual.' Only men agree in their moral approbation and disapprobation, as they agree in their judgment upon truth. To suppose a true or a good independent of individual judgments is to resemble a man who, hearing a choir sing, should suppose an abstract universal voice, distinct and independent of particular voices.

We may translate this doctrine into the language of Kant, by saying, scientific and moral truths are subjective; all their reality is in us, and not out of us. The true and the good are only realized abstractions: they result from our judgments, instead of being the cause of them; so far from being anterior to them, they are produced after and by them. The fundamental fact is then that of moral approbation and disapprobation. Are all men agreed to approve and disapprove the same things? In order to answer this question it would be necessary to have a complete collection of all the codes which have ever existed. In the absence of them, we may say that the supposed uniformity of moral decisions resolves itself into the two following elements:—

The duties which tend to preserve public security, which includes individual security. Consequently respect for protective authority, distinction between the *meum* and the *tuum*, the union of the sexes, the care of the mother for the child. Every society which does not fulfil these conditions, disappears, being destroyed by a vice inherent in its own nature.

The duties of *pure feeling*, imposing prescriptions not essential to the maintenance of society; duties which are variable according to time and peoples: such as drinking wine in honour of Bacchus, going out veiled like the Mussulmans, abstaining from animal food like the Brahmins, etc.

Finally, we must conclude '*that the moral laws which prevail in almost all societies, if not in all, are partly founded upon utility, and partly upon feeling.*' And to this question, What is the moral criterion? we must reply:—'*The laws promulgated by existing society, which were derived from a man who was invested in his time with the authority of a moral legislator.*' In support of this doctrine we may invoke the mode of promulgation of moral laws: they are imposed by a real power, and by an individual whose power is sometimes dictatorial. Such were Mahomet, Confucius, Buddha, Solon, and the 'traditional' Lycurgus. We may also invoke their mode of abrogation, of which the Reformation and the French Revolution have given us examples.

As to individual consciousness, the author declares himself in complete disagreement with those who consider it to be primitive and independent. 'I maintain, on the contrary,' he says, 'that consciousness is an imitation, from within ourselves, of the government which is without. It is formed and developed by education.'[1]

The object of my work being to explain, not to criticise, I shall not stop here to discuss this doctrine, however open to objection it may appear to me in many respects. Still I cannot refrain from making a few short remarks upon it.

Nothing appears more contrary to facts than to place the rule of morals in a promulgated legislation, and to regard it as the type upon which the individual conscience fashions itself. In the first place one objection naturally presents itself. How can it be then that the individual conscience frequently makes for itself an individual law in disagreement with the general laws, or at least outside of them? The author has stated this difficulty, which he considers 'formidable in appearance,' but I venture to think that he has not in any degree resolved it. Besides, how can we fail to

[1] Page 283.

see that these promulgated laws are the result of individual consciences, of a dull latent labour which has lasted sometimes for centuries? History teaches us that all new or good legislation is in agreement with the desires and the tendencies of particular consciences, and that it is accepted by the majority, and imposes itself by degrees upon its opponents, or else it is the work of a caprice, and then it has neither duration nor stability. Promulgated laws are then the result of individual consciences, instead of being their cause. The legislations of Buddha, of Solon, of Lycurgus, of Confucius, of Mahomet, are not pure creations of their brain. Confucius declares that he follows the tradition of his ancestors, who were so powerful in China. Mahomet states himself to be a restorer. Buddhism is born of an effusion of hearts towards charity, tenderness and the doctrine of inaction. Solon and Lycurgus give a body to ancient Ionic or Doric institutions. All these men have only told the secret of all the world.

Is it not also to be regretted that the study of moral sentiments should say nothing of their development? How can their nature be shown, if their evolutions be not described? Undoubtedly, we cannot accept either the doctrine which maintains the absolute immutability of morals, to which facts give the most utter denial, or the doctrine of its absolute mobility, which is not less forcibly contradicted by experience. But how does the development take place, and in what measure? How, by the composition of simple elements, have new moral emotions been able to produce themselves for man? The reply to these questions is missing.[1]

[1] On the moral theory of Bain see Janet, Revue des Deux Mondes, Oct. 15, 1868.

CHAPTER IV.

THE WILL.

Will.—1. Division of the subject—2. Of the germ of the will—3. Growth of the voluntary power—4. Motives and resolution—5. Free will—6. Conclusion.

I.

THE idea of progress, evolution, and development, which we regret is wanting in the study of Mr. Bain upon the emotions, appears in the half volume devoted to the Will. In that he follows through all its phases the growth of voluntary power, from the moment when it was scarcely an obscure germ, an almost physiological instinct, to its final period of completion, when in the name of liberty it supposes intelligence and founds morality. In the place of an artificial and abstract method, which, taking the will as completely constituted in its adult age, can only half explain it, we have here a natural and concrete method which completes the static study by a dynamic explanation. It is remarkable that in France the plan followed in the study of the will has almost always issued in metamorphosing it into an abstraction. The fact of determining its conditions and its results, that which precedes and that which follows it, has been so exclusively isolated, that it has been reduced to a mathematical point, to an almost imperceptible moment, which has no more reality. The current theories, in short, when reduced to what they have essentially in common, distinguish three moments in a voluntary act; the production of motives and their conflict, the resolution and the action which interpret it. They are not occupied with the first or with the third, because they belong either to intelligence or to physiology; they intrench themselves in the second exclusively, in order to work out the *whole* of the will. Hence these factitious questions and strange assertions; for example, that the will 'is equal in all men,' it is in complete disagreement with the facts, but in complete agreement with the abstraction which has been substituted for reality. Here, as everywhere, the important matter was to state the question clearly, but the method of the faculties has not a little contributed to separate that which ought not to be disunited, and thus to produce a false interpretation of the facts. To follow them in their development, is not only to be more complete, but also to be more exact; it is to rectify an error; because to give only a portion of the truth is error.

The table of the genesis of our volitions, as drawn up by Mr. Bain, may be reduced to the following points:—

1. Examination of the instinctive germ of the will.
2. First essays of voluntary power.
3. Motives, their conflict, resolution, and effort.
4. Finally, the so often discussed question of liberty.

II.

The instinctive germs, the primitive elements, of will are two in number: the existence of a spontaneous activity and the link which exists between our feelings and the actions which interpret them.

We have already seen (ch. i.) that there exists in us a spontaneous activity which displays itself without an exterior exciting cause, and which can only be explained by a superabundance, an excess, and an effusion of power; that it especially exhibits itself in the restless activity of childhood and youth; that it acts upon our locomotive members, and that often faint cries and emissions of the voice are due to a surplus of central energy.

There is one condition indispensable to the commencement of voluntary power: it is that the organs which afterwards we shall command separately or individually, should be, in the first instance, susceptible of being isolated. For example, we can make the forefinger produce an independent movement, while with the third finger this is impossible; the external ear is motionless in man, but moveable in other animals; with the foot the toes go together, although they may sometimes be isolated, as we see in persons who write or work with their feet. It is necessary for this that the nervous current should be capable of isolation and rendered independent. In short, every movement produced voluntarily must be preceded by a spontaneous movement.

What are the conditions of this spontaneous discharge? The most general are: the natural vigour of the constitution, and the unaccustomed afflux of central nervous energy, due to physical exciting causes, such as food or drink, and intellectual excitements, such as pleasure and pain.

The second germ of the will is found in the natural tie uniting sentiments and action (ch. i. sec. 3). The law of self-preservation, we have seen, unites pleasure to an increase of activity, and pain to a diminution of vitality. But the movements caused by the emotions are very different from those caused by the will: the former act upon the often exerted muscles, like those of the face and of the voice, the latter act especially upon those which can increase pleasure or diminish pain. Our spontaneous movements naturally give birth to pleasure or to pain. Is pleasure produced? Then there is an increase of vital energy, which produces a new increase of movement, and consequently of pleasure. Is pain produced? Pain diminishes the vital energy, the movements which have caused the pain diminish also, and this diminution will be the remedy. Now let the fortuitous concurrence of a pleasure and of a certain movement be produced several times, and soon, under the influence of the law of retentiveness, these things will be so intimately united that pleasure, or even the simple idea of pleasure, will evoke an appropriate movement.

In short, spontaneity or chance always produces, in the first place, actions united to our sensations and feelings; conscious and intelligent activity produces them afterwards.

III.

The bases of voluntary power are then spontaneity, self-preservation, and retentiveness. Let us now enter into the history of its development; let us see by what processes determinate actions unite themselves to determinate feelings, so that afterwards the one may command the other.

'The will is a machinery of detail: the learning of a foreign tongue is not more a matter of multiplied and separate acquisitions. The fancied unity of the voluntary power suggested by the appearance assumed by it in mature life, when we seem able to set agoing any action on the slightest wish, is the culmination of a vast range of detailed associations, whose history has been lost sight of or forgotten.'[1]

Let us examine how the edifice of our will is constructed, piece by piece, by passing in review the different sorts of sensations and feelings.[2] The exercise of our muscular sense, of the organism of taste, smell, hearing, touch, and sight, cannot become voluntary, except after numerous efforts, and sometimes unfruitful attempts. We cannot follow Mr. Bain in his details; a few examples will suffice.

In organic life, there is not at the commencement any connexion between physical suffering, and the actions calculated to relieve it. There is a general tendency to diminish vitality; that is all. 'It is impossible to say how many fortuitous conjunctions are required to produce an adhesion sufficiently strong to raise us above the indecisions of a spontaneous commencement.' Few of our necessities are so pressing as thirst; nevertheless, an animal does not distinguish at first that the water in the pond can appease it: maternal milk, the moisture of the food, suffice in the beginning; it is only later in his wanderings that he comes to apply his tongue to the surface of the water, and to feel the relief which it affords, and thus to learn what he ought to will. An act so simple in appearance as that of spitting, demands so many efforts that a child can only accomplish it at the end of his second year. We only arrive at smelling an object when we know how to shut our mouth and respire. It is by tactile sensations that animals are trained; pain is inflicted upon them to lead them to the desired end. The animal produces movements, and sees that one of these is not followed by blows; these two facts, a movement produced, and the absence of the blow, unite themselves in his mind,—thus the first step of his education is made. One established connexion serves to establish others: the beginning only is difficult.

We may also regulate and control our sentiments. This is too common a fact to be doubted. If a feeling, such as anger, de-

---

[1] Bain, *The Emotions and the Will*, p. 343.

[2] Chap. ii. and iii.

termines violent movements of the muscles, a counter current may act upon the same muscles.

IV.

It may be said that the proper function of our active faculties is to divert pain, to preserve and reproduce pleasure.[1] Thither tend the different motives which cause us to act, and which may be classed under the following heads :—

All the *phenomena of pleasure and of pain* derived from the muscular system, from the organic sensations, from the five senses properly speaking, from the various emotions; these motives can determine us, either by their *actual*, real, present existence, or else by an *ideal* action, by an influence of pure provision. Precautions against the causes of illness, against attacks on our property, on our reputation, etc., are of the second kind. Retentiveness and repetition tend to strengthen those motives which have not for their aim an actual object.

Aggregate or grouped ends, such as money, health, education, social position, professional success, all those things which suppose the addition of several special ends.

Derived or intermediate ends, which consist in seeking and loving for itself that which was at first only a means. Such is the love of forms, and of money as money.

Passionate and exaggerated ends; discordant with reason, such as fascination, intoxication, a fixed idea, these are to be seen in the eccentric facts of the magnetic sleep and of table-turning.

Such are the motives between which conflict takes place; now the strife is waged between two *actual* motives, again between an actual motive and an *idea*, and the latter will carry the day, if remembrance be sufficiently keen to enable the ideal to vanquish the real, as in the case of persons much preoccupied about their health. Impetuous and passionate motives do not admit rival considerations, they can be neutralized only by a motive of their own nature.

Deliberation is voluntary action producing itself under a con-

[1] Chaps. v. and vi.

currence or complication of motives.[1] A well-disciplined will is one which acts neither too soon nor too late; but various causes, such as youth and a vigorous temperament, do not admit of delay. In order to remedy the dangers of hasty decision, Franklin invented his *Moral Algebra.* You are hesitating, he says, on a course to be taken. Reflect three or four days, rule a sheet of paper in two columns, one to note the *pros*, the other the *cons*; enter each of your provisional conclusions; then, when that time shall have elapsed, compare the two columns, strike the balance, wait for three days longer, and then act. He frequently resorted to this method, upon which he congratulated himself.

The term of deliberation is *resolution.* The nature of the will is to pass on immediately to the act. When there is a suspension, that results from a new influence, which arrests the ordinary and regular course of the will. You are in a shop, several objects solicit your preference; one of them obtains it; you have taken your resolution.

It is followed by a feeling of a special kind which we call *effort.* 'This word signifies in reality the muscular consciousness which accompanies voluntary activity, and the more specially when it is painful.' Great importance is attached to the feeling of effort; it has been supposed that there is in it a mechanical power whose source is a purely mental activity.

'The doctrine, so long predominant, which represents volition as the source of all motive power, is regarded as receiving its strongest confirmation from the effort which accompanies the production of muscular energy.' Let us see what we are to believe. According to Mr. Bain, the source of effort ought to be looked for in organism; consciousness asserts effort and does not constitute it; it is only the accidental portion of it. On this important point we shall let him explain himself.

A labourer prepares himself, in the morning, to work in a field: that is his will. And in that volition there is a certain consciousness, but it is not that consciousness which, in itself, put him into the condition to labour.

'A large expenditure of muscular and nervous energy, derived

[1] Chap. vii.

in the final resort from his well-digested meals and healthy respirations, is the true source, the veritable antecedent of all that muscular power. It is now-a-days a truism to compare a living animal with a steam-engine as regards the source of the moving power. What the coal by its combustion is to the engine, the food and inspired air are to the living system; the concurring consciousness of expended power is no more the cause of that power than the illumination cast by the engine furnace is the source of the movements generated.' [1]

Is it not strange to think that consciousness of effort is the cause of the voluntary motion, when we see that if power be as great as possible, effort is *nil*, and if effort be as great as possible, power is *nil?* [2]

'The pleasure or pain, that is, the mental antecedent of a voluntary act, is embodied in the nervous and other organs, and rises and falls with their physical condition. When a feeling of either sort prompts the voluntary executive, a new kind of consciousness arises, that belonging to the expenditure of motive power; but in a way, if possible, still more decided, does this consciousness repose upon material processes. The nervous centres are drained of their energy, the muscles part with theirs, and in a very short time the whole system is run down like a steam-engine with its fire burnt out. . . . On a close examination it turns out that the animal system puts forth active energy without as well as with consciousness; but in no case without the expenditure of nutritive material. . . . . .

. . . .

Voluntary actions are distinguished from reflex and spontaneous activity by the directive intervention of a feeling in their production; and the phenomenon is altogether a remarkable one. . . . If it so please us, we are at liberty to say mind is a source of

---

[1] Bain, *Emotions and Will*, p. 475.

[2] We must not forget that Mr. Bain, arguing upon the tendency of idea to pass into action, never separates resolution from action. The latter mode is part of the voluntary development, and crowns it. To him, resolution not followed by action is a demi-volition, a sort of psychological abortion. 'The form of volition in which there is a motive, without the ability to accomplish it, is *Desire*.'—Chap. viii.

power; but we must then mean by mind the consciousness in conjunction with the whole body; and we must also be prepared to admit, that the physical energy is the indispensable condition, and the consciousness the casual.' [1]

V.

'All that has hitherto been explained in relation to the voluntary actions of living beings, implies the predominance of a uniformity, or of a law in that class of phenomena, by granting a complication of numerous antecedents which are not always perfectly known.' The practice of life is generally in accordance with this theory; we predict the future conduct of each person according to his past; we call a just man, Aristides; a moral hero, Socrates: a monster of cruelty, Nero. Why? Because we take for granted a certain persistence and regularity in the influence of motives almost as much as when we affirm that bread nourishes, that smoke rises, or any other such attribute of material bodies. The question of *liberty*, 'that hampered lock of metaphysics,' that 'paradox of the first degree,' 'that inextricable knot,' belongs to the category of artificial problems, like the famous arguments of Zeno, on the race between Achilles and the tortoise, and the difficulties raised by Berkeley against the differential calculus.

The notion of human free-will appeared for the first time among the Stoics, and later in the writings of Philo the Jew; by a metaphor the virtuous man was called free, and the vicious man was called a slave. The metaphysical elaboration of the doctrine of free-will and necessity is especially due to Saint Augustine, in his controversy with Pelagius, and to the strife between the Arminians and the Calvinists. 'A fitting answer to the advocates of free-will is the utter unfitness of the word or the idea to express the phenomenon in question.' We may produce an entire mystery, an entire extricable difficulty, by persisting in preserving a phraseology which does not adopt itself to the facts. The Newtonian theory of gravitation explains natural phenomena in a complete and scientific manner, but substitute another idea

[1] Bain, *Emotions and Will*, p. 475-6.

for *gravity*, that of a *polarity*, for example, such as exists in a loadstone, make of it the type and the foundation of all the groundwork of all the forces of nature, and see how everything becomes entangled, how you substitute an unintelligible mystery for a simple explanation. In the same way, to ask whether or not our volitions are free, is to confuse everything, it is to add artificial difficulties to a problem not of itself insoluble, it is to resemble the personage whom Carlyle makes to ask, 'Is virtue a gas?' A motive, hunger, impels me: I take the food which is before me: I go to an eating-house, where I fulfil some other preliminary condition: here is a plain and simple sequence; make the idea of liberty enter into it, and it becomes a chaos. The term *ability* is inoffensive and intelligible, but the term *liberty* has been forcibly dragged into a phenomenon with which it has nothing in common. A metaphor relative to virtue having given rise to this question, we might as well have asked ourselves whether the will is rich or poor, noble or ignoble, sovereign or subject, since all that has been said about virtue!

The word *necessity* is also an improper expression, which ought indeed to be banished from all the sciences, physical or moral. At present it is only troublesome, and the words which we are tending to substitute, such as *uniform*, *conditional*, *unconditional*, *sequence*, *antecedent*, *consequent*, have a precise meaning, and do not admit of confused associations.

By *liberty of choice*, we mean one thing only, the denial of all foreign intervention. It is no more than this: if, a person intervening, I am led by that person to act in a certain manner, as a child who is taken into a shop to purchase an article of clothing, but who is not suffered to choose for himself. But, applied to the various motions of my own mind, the word 'liberty of choice' has no meaning. Various motives concur in pushing me into action; the result of the conflict shows that one group is stronger than another, and the whole case lies in that. The question of liberty of choice consists, then, in knowing whether the action is my own, or whether another person has used me as an instrument; and it cannot be too much deplored that psychology should have been pulled up for so long in the front of an entirely gratuitous difficulty.

Now, what is to be understood by spontaneity, by *self-determination?* Must we look for something more in it than the operation of sensible motives, added to the central spontaneity of the system? Is some *unknown*, mysterious power hidden behind the scenes? Is there, between the feelings, the will, and the intelligence, *a fourth* unexplored region—that of the *Ego?*

'The proper meaning of self can be nothing more than my corporeal existence, coupled with my sensations, thoughts, emotions, and volitions, supposing the classification exhaustive, and the sum of these in the past, present, and future. . . . I am not able to concede the existence of an inscrutable entity in the depths of one's being, to which the name *I* is to be distinctively applied, and not consisting of any bodily organ or function, or of any one mental phenomenon that can be specified.'[1]

As to the appeal which has been made to consciousness, as testifying in an indisputable manner to our freedom of will, we must think of that as follows:—Consciousness has been said to be our ultimate and infallible criterion of truth; to affirm that it deceives itself is to destroy the mere possibility of every certain science. In the first place, let us remark that consciousness is to internal phenomena what observation is to external facts. The generality of people know that they think and feel, without exactly knowing the laws of thought, of mental co-existences and sequences, in the same way as their senses reveal rivers, mountains, cities, etc., to them, but without giving them an exact and precise knowledge of these things. Nothing is more common than disagreement in human appreciations of size, forces, weight, forms, colours, etc. If this be so in the case of the objects of our external senses, what reason have we for believing that the internal sense is more exact? Are not metaphysical disputes in themselves a proof of the contrary? Besides, if we grant to consciousness the privilege of infallibility, it can last for only a short moment; and that does not constitute a science. Consciousness being strictly applicable to any individual person, and for one instant only, it contains the minimum of information.

[1] Bain, *Emotions and Will*, p. 554.

This is the atom of knowledge. If we wish to go beyond this short moment, we must have recourse to memory, and we know that memory is fallible. Thus, while the infallibility lasts, there is no science, and when the science begins, there is no infallibility. Now, the notion of free-will is in nowise an intuition; there is in it a collection of anterior volitions, and a comparison established between them and a certain condition of sentient beings, the condition of being free from constraint, like that of a dog untied, or a prisoner set at large; and comparison is not an infallible operation.

VI.

Here we come to the end without lingering over some chapters in which the author completes his moral theory, but which do not add anything essential to it. Let us summarize the merits and defects of this important *Treatise on Psychology*. It will please those who love facts, who think that facts are the very substance of an experimental science, that it only lives by them; that every generalization is empty and vain, without an ample collection of phenomena which serves it as a starting-point, and as a verification. It is, to my knowledge, the most complete repertory in existence of exact and positive psychology, placed *au courant* of recent discoveries: we in France have nothing to approach it. Garnier's *Traité des Facultés*, founded, as its title indicates, upon a method which subordinates phenomena to causes, facts to faculties, embarrassed too by metaphysical discussions, cannot be compared in any way to Mr. Bain's work. Let us add, that, according to the customs of the Eclectic School, this treatise has given so ample a space to the history of theories that the dogmatic part is singularly limited. In its mode of explanation, its method, and the general impression it produces upon the reader, Mr. Bain's work can only be compared to a physiology. Examined in detail, the composition of the book is not quite irreproachable; its order is sometimes more apparent than real; the author takes up the same questions several times, and discusses them over and over again. But, perhaps, this is an inherent defect in works of this nature, in which the number and variety of observations are such that one can hardly avoid losing one's-self in the crowd.

I regret, for my part, that the author should have dealt so briefly with the phenomena which mark the transition from normal psychology to morbid psychology (dreams, magnetic sleep, etc.), and which he seemed in such favourable conditions for studying. But the want of comparative method is one of the defects of the book. Let us add to this the too frequent absence of the idea of progress, and the consequent neglect of the dynamic study of phenomena.

'The work of Mr. Alexander Bain gives us, in orderly arrangement, the facts brought to light by anatomists and physiologists during the last fifty years. It is not in itself a system of mental philosophy, properly so called, but a classified collection of materials for such a system, presented with that method and insight which scientific discipline generates, and accompanied with occasional passages of an analytical character. It is indeed that which it in the main it professes to be—a natural history of the mind. Were we to say that the researches of the naturalist who collects, and dissects, and describes species, bear the same relation to the researches of the comparative anatomist tracing out the laws of organization, which Mr. Bain's labours bear to the labours of the abstract psychologist, we should be going somewhat too far, for Mr. Bain's work is not wholly descriptive. Still, however, such an analogy conveys the best general conception of what he has done; and serves most clearly to indicate its needfulness. . . . Until recently mental science has been pursued much as physical science was pursued by the ancients: not by drawing conclusions from observations and experiments, but by drawing them from arbitrary *a priori* assumptions. This course, long since abandoned in the one case with immense advantage, is gradually being abandoned in the other; and the treatment of psychology as a division of natural history shows that the abandonment will soon be complete. Estimated as a means to higher results, Mr. Bain's work is of great value. . . . We repeat, that as a natural history of the mind, we believe it to be the best yet produced. It is a most valuable collection of carefully elaborated materials. Perhaps we cannot better express our sense of its worth than by saying that to those who hereafter give to this branch of psychology a thoroughly scientific organization, Mr. Bain's book will be indispensable.'[1]

In addition to the great works which have served as a foundation for the preceding essay, Mr. Bain has published a book *On the Study of Character, including an estimate of Phrenology* (1861), with the object of reviving analytical studies upon human character, 'which seemed to have followed the decline of phrenology.'

After having passed in review the very few works devoted to the science of character before Gall (Theophrastus, La Bruyère, and Fourier), and after having devoted half the work to a detailed and impartial criticism of phrenological classifications, Mr. Bain explains his own ideas.

His method is identical with that indicated by Mr. Stuart Mill (*vide* page 103.) It consists in founding ethology upon psychology, in coming down from the general laws of human nature to individual varieties. He then proposes, as the basis of the study of character, the triple division of the mind into will, emotion, and intelligence.

1st, The source of volition, as we have seen, is in that spontaneous energy which has its physical seat in the muscles, but which depends still more upon the brain than the muscular system, and gives birth, when it is in its maximum to the character or energetic temperament.

2d, The emotional character is distinguished by the predominance of the affections, and of their external manifestations. We may cite as examples the Celtic races, and amongst individuals, Fox, Mirabeau, Alfieri, etc.

3d, A third type is that in which intelligence predominates.

We shall not follow Mr. Bain into his examination of the very numerous varieties of this and of the preceding types; seeing that his work is rather a sketch than a definitive exposition of ethology.

---

[1] Spencer's *Essays,* edition 1863, vol. i. p. 121, 122 (Lewes).

MR. GEORGE H. LEWES.

MR. LEWES is a physiologist. But as all reflective spirits who please themselves with conceptions of entirety, find philosophy at the end of every science, so Mr. Lewes has found it there. He embarked early in search of it. It is twenty-four years since (in 1845) he addressed 'to the public rather than to the learned,' a *Biographical History of Philosophy*, with the avowed intention of disgusting them with metaphysical speculations. Twice revised, and partly re-written, this book has become a history of philosophy from Thales to Auguste Comte: an original work, especially dogmatic and critical, as we shall see. Mr. Lewes, a man of refined and elegant mind, who does not disdain anecdote and satire, lends variety and interest to every subject of which he treats. Although well acquainted with the philosophical and scientific literature of the Continent, and of France in particular, he plainly prefers the researches of the naturalist to those of the scholar.[1]

In philosophy, he declares himself a positivist. While Mr. Herbert Spencer and Mr. Mill are at variance with this school upon several important points, notably upon the classification of the sciences and method of psychology; while Mr. Bain has not made any avowal upon the subject,—the adhesion of Mr. Lewes is full and entire, not to be shaken, even enthusiastic, as we shall see.

'I adhered to the Positive philosophy in 1845, and I adhere to it still,' says he, in a preface dated May 1867. 'What I have

---

[1] Besides his *History of Philosophy* and his *Physiology of Common Life*, which we are about to mention, his works are:—*Studies of Animal Life; Studies on the Sea-shore; Aristotle—A Chapter from the History of Science; The Life of Goethe.*

attempted is not such a detailed exposition as would flatter the incurious indolence of men who love to talk confidently upon second-hand knowledge, but such general indications of the Positive philosophy as will enable the student to appreciate its drift and importance, and will guide him in the understanding of Comte's writings. I am often asked to recommend some "brief account of the system," by those who wish to profit by Comte's labours (or perhaps only to talk knowingly of them), yet shirk the labour of reading the works which they profess to consider of importance. My answer is, study the *Philosophie Positive* for yourself, study it patiently, give it the time and thought you would not grudge to a new science or a new language, and then, whether you accept or reject the system, you will find your mental horizon irrevocably enlarged. "But six stout volumes!" exclaims the hesitating aspirant. Well, yes, six volumes, requiring to be meditated as well as read: I admit that they "give pause" in this busy, bustling world of ours; but if you reflect how willingly six separate volumes of philosophy would be read in the course of the year, the undertaking seems less formidable. . . . And no one who considers the immense importance of a doctrine which will give unity to his life, would hesitate to pay a higher price than that of a year's study.'[1]

This admiration is nowhere weakened, and the book finishes by a triumphal act of faith in the future. I do not know to what point this positivism is rigorously orthodox. When we see with what eagerness Mr. Lewes draws into his camp several contemporaries who are frequently at variance with the school, we may believe that he is very lenient on many points, and his positivism appears to me to be, above all, *independent*. This, however, it is not our place to decide.

As the psychological doctrines of Mr. Lewes, with which only we are now occupied, are not reduced to a system, we cannot pursue so methodical an exposition of them as in preceding instances. It appears to us that to reduce detached views to a rigorous order and a systematic connexion, would be to force the thought of the author, and to incur the risk of inexactness.

---

[1] Lewes's *History of Philosophy*, Preface.

We borrow our materials from the *History of Philosophy* (2 vols.) and from the *Physiology of Common Life* (2 vols.).

CHAPTER I.

THE HISTORY OF PHILOSOPHY.

The History of Philosophy.—1. Characteristics of his *History*—2. His philosophy—3. The Ancients: the Sophists, Plato, the Academicians; of exterior perception—4. The Moderns: Descartes, Hobbes, Berkeley (Idealism and Realism), Cabanis, Gall; French Eclecticism.

I.

History may be written in many ways. The best, the only true way, consists in the minute examination of documents and of facts, and in a complete and conscientious exposition of them. The historian forgets himself in the presence of his work, and has no care except for truth. He imposes nothing, he proposes; and although it is impossible that the long sojourn in the midst of doctrines, and of the strife of systems, should have left his thoughts indifferent, he would aim at the appearance of impassiveness, in consequence of the impartiality of his judgment, and the sincerity of his studies. Ritter is amongst this number; his history of philosophy, scrupulous, loyal, to which polemics are unknown, is a safe guide in study.

Another manner, entirely opposed to the preceding one, consists in making history a pretext for conflict. The author is less occupied with the exposition of facts than he is with his method of warfare; he thinks less of being exact than of being clever. Books of this kind, which are interesting, and often valuable, are evidently not histories.

In short, we seek for instruction, for lessons, from the history of philosophy; we derive morality from it; it is like a verification on a large scale in support of a thesis. Mr. Lewes's work appears to us to belong to this category. He has evidently no taste, or if we prefer so to put it, he has not the virtue necessary to face these formidable folios, these undigested texts of scholastic learning which the historian of philosophy ought to penetrate, however repulsive to his positive and lucid mind. 'More than once,' he tells us, *à propos* of Albertus Magnus, 'I have opened his ponderous folios, with the determination to master at least some portion of their contents; but I shut them again with an alacrity of impatience, which will be best comprehended by any one who makes a similar attempt.'[1]

What an immense task must be a history composed at first hand; obscure texts and strange theories in antiquity; empty dissertations in the middle ages; complicated doctrines and a superabundance of documents in modern times; here is work for any historian. The life of a man would not suffice for it; especially if to this list we were to add the materials supplied by the East.

Mr. Lewes lacks the vocation of the scholar, which indeed is generally wanting in original minds. His history resembles rather that of Hegel, than that of Ritter. His review of the labours of philosophers is rather occupied with that which they have thought, than with their comparative importance. He judges rather than expounds: his history is fastidious and critical. It is the work of a clear, precise, and elegant mind, always that of a writer, often witty, measured, possessing no taste for declamation, avoiding exclusive solutions; and making its interest profitable to the reader whom he forces to think. There are many ideas in this book. Besides an important introduction consisting of 120 pages, the author frequently expresses his own opinions, in appreciating those of others: an almost entire system of philosophy may be extracted from them. This gives him a right to figure in our work; we should have had nothing to ask for in an ordinary history; in this instance so much has been given us that we are obliged to make a choice.

What is the thesis of Mr. Lewes? It is the radical weakness of all metaphysics, demonstrated by history. In his first edition (1845), he proposed to himself as his object to turn men's minds away from this study by demonstrating the successive failures of successive schools: at present he declares that his adhesion to positivism is firm and complete. This avowal is more loyal

[1] *History of Philosophy*, vol. ii. p. 74.

than reassuring: no doubt it appears strange and interesting to see the history of philosophy reconstructed by a positivist; but has he nothing to dread from inquiry? I acknowledge that I expected it. Nothing of the sort has taken place. Pythagoras and Parmenides, Plato and Plotinus, Spinoza and Berkeley are treated as masters of human thought, and with sincere admiration. No indifferent person has written these lines upon Pythagoras: 'He who could transcend all earthly struggles, and the great ambition of the greatest of men, to live only for the sake of wisdom, was he not of a higher stamp than ordinary mortals? Well might later historians picture him as clothed in robes of white, his head crowned with gold, his aspect grave, majestical, and calm; above the manifestation of any human joy, of any human sorrow; enwrapt in contemplation of the deeper mysteries of existence; listening to music and the hymns of Homer, Hesiod, and Thales, or listening to the harmony of the spheres. And to a lively, talkative, quibbling, active, versatile people like the Greeks, what a grand phenomenon must this solemn, earnest, silent, meditative man have appeared!'[1] And afterwards, comparing Homer and Xenophanes, both of them rhapsodists: what a fate is that of the philosopher! his mutilated work is visited only by some rare scholar, or by some *dilettanti* spiders; the other, the poet's, lives in the memory of all mankind. Joy and universal life are echoed by Homer; in Xenophanes, distress, convulsive agitation, infinite doubt, infinite sadness.[2]

More than once we shall find this melancholy strain of the historian, upon the vain effort of human thought which seeks without finding, and aspires without attaining.

II.

An ample, but entirely dogmatic, Preface first calls for our attention.[3] 'Theology, philosophy, and science,' says Mr. Lewes, 'constitute our spiritual triumvirate.' 'Its [theology's] main province is the province of Feeling; its office is the *systematization of*

[1] Lewes, *History of Philosophy*, vol. i. p. 23. [2] *Ibid.* p. 43.

[3] These prolegomena comprise the following questions:—What is philosophy? Objective and subjective method. Criterion of truth. Some infirmities of thought. Necessary truths.

our religious conceptions. The office of Science is distinct. It may be defined as the *systematization of the order of phenomena considered as phenomena.* The office of Philosophy is again distinct from these. It is *the systematization of the conceptions furnished by Theology and Science.* It is ἐπιστήμη ἐπιστημῶν.' [1]

Psychology is to the other sciences what geography is to topography. Its history is the story of its emancipation with regard to theology, its transformation into science.

Understood in the sense of metaphysics, philosophy is completely vain; because it seeks for noumena which will always be out of its reach. And the objection is founded less upon the objects of its research, God, liberty, causality, etc., than upon its method, which, being separated from verification, is therefore outside of science.

'The History of Philosophy presents the spectacle of thousands of intellects—some the greatest that have made our race illustrious—steadily concentrated on problems believed to be of vital importance, yet producing no other result than a conviction of the extreme facility of error, and the remoteness of any probability that truth can be reached. The only conquest has been *critical,* that is to say, psychological.' [2]

'There are many who deplore the encroachment of Science, fondly imagining that Metaphysical Philosophy would respond better to the higher wants of man. This regret is partly unreasoning sentiment, partly ignorance of the limitations of human faculty. Even among those who admit that Ontology is an impossible attempt, there are many who think it should be persevered in, because of the "lofty views" it is supposed to open to us. This is as if a man desirous of going to America should insist on walking there, because journeys on foot are more poetical than journeys by steam; in vain is he shown the impossibility of crossing the Atlantic on foot; he admits that grovelling fact, but his lofty soul has visions of some mysterious overland route by which he hopes to pass. He dies without reaching America, but to the last gasp he maintains that he has discovered the route on which others may reach it.' [3]

[1] Lewes, *Prolegomena,* p. xvii. [2] *Ibid.* xxvii. [3] *Ibid.* p. xxviii.

Science seeks truth; but what is truth? 'Truth is the correspondence between the order of ideas and the order of phenomena, so that the one is the reflection of the other—the movement of Thought following the movement of Things.'[1]

Let us remark these terms, 'the order of ideas,' 'the movement of thought,' substituted for the ordinary formula—*conformity of the idea with the object.* If we accept the latter, truth is a chimera, and idealism is irresistible. The utmost end of knowledge is adaptation, and we call truth precise adaptation. What the body and the fall of bodies are in themselves matters not to us. If the movement of our thought is controlled by the movements of things, there is truth: if our ideas are arranged in an order which does not correspond with the order of phenomena, there is error.

To attain this correspondence between an internal and external order is what we seek, and for this we employ two methods:—

'*α*. The Objective Method, which moulds its conceptions on realities by closely following the movements of the objects as they severally present themselves to Sense, so that the movements of Thought may synchronize with the movements of Things.

'*β*. The Subjective Method, which moulds realities on its conceptions, endeavouring to discern the order of Things, not by step by step adjustments of the order of ideas to it, but by the anticipatory rush of Thought, the direction of which is *determined* by Thoughts and not *controlled* by Objects.'

Every research contains an observation, a conjecture, and a verification. The subjective method stops at the second term: its function is hypothesis. The objective method embraces three terms: its function is verification. It absorbs whatever there is of good in the subjective method, adding to it control. The subjective method seeks for truth in the relations of ideas, the objective method seeks for truth in the relations of objects.

An exact reasoning is the ideal union of objects in their true relations of co-existence and succession: it is to see with the eye of the mind. A chain of reasoning is an ideal representation of details, actually non-apparent to the senses. This may make us

[1] *Prolegomena*, p. xxxi.

[2] *Ibid.* p. xxxiii.

understand what exact sense we ought to give to the word *fact*. Generally, it is considered as a final verity. This we say is a fact, not a theory; that is to say, an indisputable fact, not a disputable view of truth. But a fact is in reality a bundle of inferences; a fact so simple as that of seeing an apple upon a table, supposes, in addition to the simple sensation of colour, the recall of the ideas of roundness, savour, odour, etc. If facts are inextricably mingled with inferences, and if reasoning is a mental vision which establishes details that are not present, thenceforth how can we sustain the opposition of fact and of theory? They are both fallible, and radical opposition exists between verified inferences and non-verified inferences.

The weakness of the subjective method consists in the impossibility of verification. The objective method simply co-ordains materials furnished by experience, without introducing any which are new. The subjective method commits the fault of drawing *matter* from the subject, instead of simply drawing *form*. The fundamental distinction between metaphysics and science is then in their method, and not in the nature of their object. Add a verifiable method to a metaphysical theory, and you make of it a scientific theory; subtract from a scientific theory the verifiable element, and you make of it a metaphysical theory. Remove from the law of gravitation the verifiable formula 'the direct relation of masses in their inverse relation to the square of the distances,' and there only remains an occult attraction: this is metaphysics.

Two travellers come from a country where clocks are not known, even by hearsay. The one has metaphysical, the other has scientific tendencies. They both stand before this new object. The metaphysician will say: This explains itself by a vital principle: the beating of the pendulum resembles that of the heart, the hands travel like antennæ, the striking of the hour resembles a cry of anger or of pain; and he will exhaust himself in ingenious explanations of this kind. Here you have the subjective method, which deduces instead of verifying. The other man will say to him: I have grave doubts of your conjectures. I have belonging to me a powerful instrument called analysis. I am going to make use of it. I take away the face of this object and all the exterior: nothing is changed; I stop the pendulum, and everything stops. I put it in motion, and everything goes on again. I pull a weight forcibly, I see that the hands move very swiftly, and the sounds are quickened. I repeat the experiments, and I conclude from it that this is a mechanism. I have already seen others which are very different, but I recognise their essential characteristics. Here we see the objective method, which verifies instead of conjecturing.

The metaphysician is a merchant who speculates boldly, but without convertible capital to enable him to keep his engagements. He gives bills, but he has neither money nor goods to represent them. The first obstinate creditor who insisted upon being paid would make him bankrupt. The man of science is also daring, but he always keeps by him a solid capital, which may be produced upon occasion to honour his bills; and he knows that if he exceeds it bankruptcy awaits him. A verification is then necessary. But on what does it rest? What is our criterion of truth?

Consciousness being unable to come out of its proper sphere, it is to it that we must have recourse as a last appeal: in this sense we may say that every criterion is subjective; we can never know objects in themselves, but only by states of consciousness. But as truth is simply a *correspondence* between the internal order and the external order, we assure ourselves of its exactitude by the certainty of its adjustment. The touchstone of knowledge is *prevision.*

'The subjective test of a Truth is the unthinkableness of its negative, in other words the reduction to A is A. . . . Consciousness is only infallible in verdicts limited to identical propositions. Here and only here there is no fallibility.'[1]

As there is always room for error wherever the proposition is not identical, and as a probability variable in degrees is all that we can obtain in the greater part of our conclusions, it is easy to extend the logical principle which determines infallibility to the variable degrees of probability, and consequently to render error impossible. What is the logical justification that A is A?

[1] *Prolegomena*, pp. lxvi., lxii.

The *incomprehensibility* of the negative. What would be the logical justification of a proposition composed of complex and distant inferences, and as such having more or less probability? The difficulty of admitting its negative.

To sum up, 'I have shown that a proposition is *absolutely true* only when its terms are equivalent, and that, as this rests upon the impossibility of our thinking a negative of the proposition, the varying degrees of *probability* will depend on the possibility of admitting a negative.' [1]

I pass over the reflections of the author upon some infirmities of thought, such as belief in final causes, in the distinction between power and act, in the vital principle, etc. This would lead us too far, and a fitter place would be found for it elsewhere. But the great question of necessary truths is within our reach, and merits close examination.

Let us at once give the opinion of Mr. Lewes upon this point. What is experience? It is the sum of the action of objects upon consciousness. This sum comprises two elements: the materials which the senses bring to consciousness; the transformations, combinations, and modifications which consciousness causes them to undergo. Thus there are two factors, sensation and the laws of consciousness; matter and form, as Kant would say. But what are the laws of consciousness? They are the result of the experience of the *individual*, and of the experience of the *race*.

To maintain that experience itself,—which is the product of sensation and of the laws of consciousness,—produces these laws, seems at first an absurdity; but the contradiction is only verbal. In order to dissipate it, we need to distinguish experience from experiences. All particular modification of consciousness is a particular experience. Every modification paves the way for the following ones, and influences them. The laws of consciousness issue by development from these successive modifications, and experience is the general term which expresses the sum of these modifications.

The school of sensation has largely obscured the question by its anti-scientific conception of the *tabula rasa:* the mind is not

[1] Lewes, *Prolegomena*, p. lxxvii.

a mirror which passively reflects objects. The *a priori* school commits a contrary error by regarding consciousness as a pure spontaneity, bearing in itself, and in advance, organized laws which are derived from a supersensible source.

This is not all: we must also take account of inheritance. Biology teaches us that the sensible organism inherits certain dispositions from its parents, as it inherits their structure, so that we may say that the individual summarizes the experience of the race. Faculties increase with the development of race. The forms of thought which are essential portions of the mechanism of experience, are developed like the forms of other vital functions. In fact, as the function is only the form of activity of an organ, it is clear that if the organ is developed, the function develops itself, and with it the laws of its action.

For the mind, as for the body, there is no pre-formation or pre-existence, but evolution and epigenesis. The error of Kant, and of those who proceeded like him, is to confuse anatomy with morphology, and logic with psychology. Taking the adult human mind, they have considered its *constitutive forms* as *initial conditions*. They say: These forms are implied in particular experiences. Granted; because if they were not implied, we could not draw them out. This process is perfect in logic, which has to show the forms of thought, and not their origin. But the question of experience is a question of origin, and psychology reveals to us that experience is the tissue of thought spontaneously woven, of which each thread is an experience. People who reason *a priori*, consider the vertebrate type as the necessary form which renders vertebration possible. Anatomically this is acceptable. But what says morphology? It shows that typical forms come out of successive phases of the development of the animal. Evidently the idea of pre-existence is a fiction—it is simply a ὕστερον προτέρον.

In order to understand the thoughts of the author better, let us see in detail how he estimates Condillac and Kant, the one recognising only pure sensation, the other placing the *forms* of thought as necessary, and *a priori*.

'He [Condillac] was unable to pursue the investigation, not having a right method. Instead of biological, he pursued verbal analysis. A verbal analysis of the phenomena was approximately made, and this was accepted as a substitute for the analysis of organ and function. . . . Thus, while he pretends to evolve all knowledge and all the faculties out of sensation and the transformations of sensation (which is to be his advance on Locke), we cannot but observe that in his evolution the presence is tacitly admitted of those very faculties which are said to be evolved. In fact, he confounds the faculties with the operations of the faculties. Nor was there any alternative for him. In the absence of the faculties which elaborate sensations into perceptions, judgments, reasonings, the senses would never have raised man above the condition of idiocy. A man reduced to mere sensations would be like the pigeon, whose cerebrum is removed, sensitive indeed, but incapable of memory, judgment, thought. . . . The second objection is, that if the mind is a *tabula rasa* as to knowledge, and is not even pre-existent as faculty (according to the metaphysicians), or as organism (according to the biologists); if, in a word, sensations and combinations of sensations create both knowledge and the knowing faculties, how can we explain the phenomena of idiocy? How is it that brutes with senses resembling our own have minds so markedly distinguished from our own? The sensations of the idiot are as vivid and varied as those of a rational man; the differences arise in the *cerebrations* of the two. . . . Finally, if Sensation is the origin and end of all mental faculty, how is it that men of vivid sensuous activity are not also the men of powerful intellect, which they notoriously are not; how can such a case as that of Laura Bridgman be explained? —a girl born deaf, dumb, and blind, yet manifesting unusual and varied and intellectual activity. The biologist sees no difficulty here; nor does the ordinary psychologist. The one sees a cerebral organism with its inherited aptitudes ready for its work; the other sees a Mind with its constituent faculties. But the sensationalist has no such refuge.'[1]

Condillac has confounded under the name of sensation two things, which are in reality different: sensation properly so called, and idealism (or the faculty of having ideas). These are

[1] Lewes, *History of Philosophy*, vol. ii. pp. 333, 334.

two distinct functions, having two distinct organs. Sensation comprehends all that belongs to the organs of sense, and that which is so often neglected, the action of the viscera and the muscles. Ideation is another thing: we can no more separate it from sensation than we can separate the movement of a muscle from the sensation which causes it. But it is the action of a special organ; it is subject to special laws, and that suffices to distinguish it from the activity of the senses. The common opinion that ideas are only weakened impressions, and copies of sensations, has contributed to lead Condillac into error. It is not the case. 'So little is idea a weakened sensation, that it is not a sensation at all, it is totally different from sensation.' And this is not surprising; sensation is the product of a distinct part of the nervous system, the brain. The rigorous distinction between sensation on the one side, and ideation on the other side, is found in no treatise on psychology, even of a spiritualistic kind. Nevertheless comparative anatomy has shown the independence of the organs of sense, and of the brain, although it has not yet discovered the relations connecting them. We know that the brain is an *addition* to the organs of sense, just as these organs are an addition to the nervous system of the lower animals. As we descend to the lowest degree of the animal scale, we shall not find any trace of the nervous system; as we ascend it, we find a simple ganglion with its prolongations; higher still, several ganglions and rudimentary senses; higher still, organs, more complex senses, and a rudimentary brain: in man, complex organs, and a complete brain. Consequently sensation and ideation are as independent of each other as the organs of which they are the function; and though ideation be organically united with sensation, it is only so much united as movement is united with sensation.

Each sense has its special centre or *sensorium*, and each is perfectly independent of the brain, can act without it, and even in its absence. A bird deprived of brains is sensible to light, sound, etc. But in their normal condition, these centres are intimately connected with the brain, and affect it. This explains how we may experience sensations without being conscious of them (for instance, receiving a wound in the heat of battle); we can think without experiencing any special sensation, except those of organic life; as for instance, when we are reflecting in our bed in the midst of the silence of night.

Thus the independence of ideation and of sensation is proved psychologically and anatomically, and uproots the doctrine of Condillac.

Let us now see that of Kant.[1] Mr. Lewes ardently admires this philosopher, whom he calls 'the greatest of modern meta physicians.' He is above all thankful to him for having laid bare the nothingness of ontology, of having shown with more clearness and precision than any one prior to himself, that human knowledge is *relative;* but upon the point which occupies us on the nature of the laws or forms of thought, Mr. Lewes dissents from him. 'The forms of thought like the forms of life are evolutions, not preformations.' Kant did not see that. His method was incomplete. He has employed only the metaphysical method of subjective analysis, when he should also have employed the biological method of objective analysis. Transporting into psychology the old Aristotelian error of matter and of form considered as really separable (while they are only separated by abstraction), he regarded the forms of thought as ready-made factors, anterior to and independent of experience. Now these formulæ ought to be sought, either physiologically, that is to say, in organic conditions; or psychologically, that is to say, in the evolution of thought. Such is the nature of our mind, that we think as successive that which is in its nature simultaneous; the condition of thought is *change.* To think is to exercise judgment, that is, to unite a predicate to a subject. But these forms or conditions of thought are a result of a development, not of pre-existing elements. Kant has done the same thing as if he had said that the form of the oak pre-exists in the acorn, because the form of the oak comes out of the acorn. But scientific botany would not accept this solution, and scientific psychology refuses even to accept as '*a priori* conditions of experience that which is the result of volition and of experience.

Besides this the forms enumerated by Kant are not sufficiently

[1] *History of Philosophy*, vol. ii. p. 474.

numerous to express the subjective conditions. He puts forward for example pleasure and pain, which are inseparable elements of all sensation and which determine every action. He says nothing of the various senses and of their conditions; nevertheless it is the organization of the retina and of the skin which makes vibration upon the one produce the sensation of light, and upon the other the sensation of heat. Sight, heat, and sound are forms of sensibility which serve to clothe the thing in itself (*Ding an sich*), just like time and space, which it gives singly.

The distinction between the subjective element and the objective element of thought is rightly regarded as the principal achievement of critical philosophy. Nevertheless it hides a fundamental error because it endeavours to isolate the elements of an indissoluble act.

'It was one thing to assume that there are necessarily two co-efficients in the function; another thing to assume that these could be isolated and studied apart. It was one thing to say, Here is an organism with its inherited structure, and aptitudes dependent on that structure, which must be considered as necessarily determining the forms in which it will be affected by external agencies, so that all experience will be a compound of subjective and objective conditions; another thing to say, Here is the pure *a priori* element in every experience, the form which the mind impresses on the matter given externally. The first was almost an inevitable conclusion, the second was a fiction. Psychology, if it can show us anything, can show the absolute impossibility of our discriminating the objective from the subjective elements. In the first place the attempt would only be possible on the ground that we could, at any time and in any way, disengage thought from its content; separate in Feeling the object, as it is, out of all relation to Sensibility, or the subject as pure subject. If we could do this in one instance we should have a basis for the investigation. The chemist who has learned to detect the existence of an acid, by its reactions in one case, can by its reactions determine it in other cases. Having experience of an acid and an alkali, each apart from the other, he can separate them when finding them combined in a salt, or he can combine them when he finds them separate. His analysis and synthesis are possible, because he has elsewhere learned the nature of each element separately. But such analysis or synthesis is impossible with the objective and subjective elements of thought. Neither element is ever given alone. Pure thought and pure matter are unknown quantities, to be reached by no equation.'[1]

Thought is necessarily and universally a subject-object; matter is necessarily and universally an object-subject. The subject and the object are combined in knowledge as the acid and the basis are combined in salt.[2]

III.

Let us now pass on to the history properly so called. As it is, above all, dogmatic and critical, and as it has frequently given the author an opportunity for airing his own ideas, we might easily collect these fragments of a scattered doctrine and construct a whole out of them. We have, however, preferred to respect the order followed by the author. We are now going to pass rapidly through the history, rejecting the learning in favour of the ideas, especially those which belong to the domain of psychology.

In his history of ancient philosophy Mr. Lewes appears to attach himself principally to two points; the examination of theories upon knowledge and the bringing out of the negative side of doctrines. Perhaps some philosophers of the adverse schools will consider that he reads a little too favourably for his own view those old texts whose elasticity renders them easily manageable. Thus, he finds in Xenophanes at least the germs of scepticism;[3] his disciple Parmenides 'had not a mere vague and general notion of the uncertainty of human knowledge. He maintained that thought was delusive, because dependent upon organization,'[4] which at least touches upon materialism. Heraclitus sees in everything only *a becoming;* Empedocles laments upon the uncertainty of knowledge and the frailty of human life.

Anaxagoras, 'on the great subject of the origin and certainty of our knowledge, differed from Xenophanes and Heraclitus.

[1] Lewes, *History of Philosophy*, vol. ii. p. 483.
[2] *Ibid.* vol. ii. p. 484.
[3] *Ibid.* vol. i. p. 49.
[4] *Ibid.* p. 53.

He thought, with the former, that all sense-knowledge is delusive; and with the latter, that all knowledge comes through the senses. Here is a double scepticism brought into play. It has usually been held that these two opinions contradict each other; that he could not have maintained both. Yet both opinions are tenable. His reason for denying certainty to the senses was the incapacity of distinguishing all the real objective elements of which things are composed. Thus the eye discerns a complex mass which we call a flower; but discerns nothing of that *of which* the flower is composed. In other words, the senses perceive *phenomena*, but do not and cannot observe *noumena*,—an anticipation of the greatest discovery of psychology, though seen dimly and confusedly by Anaxagoras.'[1]

Mr. Lewes holds that he has made the same discovery in Democritus (p. 97, vol. i.) Whatever we may think of these interpretations, they at least prove that the author takes more seriously than we should have been inclined to think he would these first essays of philosophical thought. His heart is with the men of these ancient days, he admires them, and he cannot think without emotion of this flight of daring human indefatigable curiosity set free for the first time.

The question of the Sophists has been much discussed in our days. After Hegel, who rehabilitates Protagoras, Mr. Grote takes them in hand.[2] Justice is due to every one, even to the sophists; they will not obtain it without difficulty. It is, nevertheless, clear that they were condemned upon the deposition of bitter enemies; that to judge Protagoras or Callicles according to Plato is to judge Socrates according to the *Nubes*. Mr. Lewes, agreeing with his compatriot, shows how far this question has been obscured and misunderstood. He does not wish to glorify the Sophists or to absolve them from all reproach, he merely asks that those who judge them should place themselves in imagination in their time :—

'The Sophists were wealthy; the Sophists were powerful; the

[1] Lewes, *History of Philosophy*, vol. i. p. 75.

[2] In his work on *Plato and the Socratics*, and in his *History of Greece*, vol. viii.

Sophists were dazzling, rhetorical, and not profound. Interrogate human nature—above all the nature of philosophers—and ask what will be the sentiment entertained respecting these Sophists by their rivals. Ask the solitary thinker what is his opinion of the showy, powerful, but shallow rhetorician, who usurps the attention of the world. The man of conviction has at all times a superb contempt for the man of mere oratorical or dialectical display. The thinker knows that the world is ruled by Thought, yet he sees Expression gaining the world's attention. He knows, perhaps, that he has within him thoughts pregnant with human welfare; yet he sees the giddy multitude intoxicated with the enthusiasm excited by some plausible fallacy, clothed in persuasive language. He sees through the fallacy, but cannot make others as clear-sighted. His warning is unheeded; his wisdom is spurned; his ambition is frustrated; the popular idol is carried onward in triumph. The neglected thinker would not be human if he bore this with equanimity. He does not. He is loud and angry in lamenting the fate of a world that can be so led; loud and angry in his contempt of one who could so lead it. Should he become the critic or the historian of his age, what exactness ought we to expect in his account of the popular idol?'

The immorality imputed to them, says Mr. Lewes, is not sustained by examination. Athens was not peopled only by architects, sculptors, poets, and philosophers; there were true citizens, human beings having human passions. How can we suppose that they have suffered it to be proclaimed and repeated that all morality is a farce and all law a quibble? That they would have permitted open blasphemy against all justice, against the basis of every social contract? Such charlatans would have inspired only ridicule or horror. And nevertheless the sophists were rich, admired, intrusted with delicate missions, sent on embassies, surrounded by rich and noble young men; they were the intellectual leaders of their age, and 'if they had been what their adversaries describe them, Greece could only have been an earthly Pandemonium, where Belial was King.' [2]

Lewes, *History of Philosophy*, p. 106.   [2] Vol. i. p. 110.

There was no sophistic *doctrine*, but a sophistic *art*. This art might have grave consequences, as Aristotle and Plato saw, but the Sophists did not profess them ; and we can quite understand that Gorgias, after having read the dialogue which bears his name, should have said, 'I do not recognise myself; but the young man has a great talent for satire.'

'The Sophists were the natural production of the opinions of the epoch. In them we see the first energetic protest against the possibility of metaphysical science. This protest, however, must not be confounded with the protest of Bacon—must not be mistaken for the germ of positive philosophy. It was the protest of baffled minds. The philosophy of the day led to scepticism; but with scepticism no energetic man could remain contented.'[1] Then Socrates appeared.

The principal merit of Socrates is his negative method ; up to his time dogmatism had had it all its own way; he applied himself to examination. His process of truly contradictory discussion and cross-questioning is a first attempt at verification ; unhappily it is entirely subjective. Further, it was at this epoch that the human mind, for the first time, showed a clear consciousness of the notions of kinds, species, individuals, general terms, and general ideas. The philosopher, according to the showing of Plato, is 'he who sees the one in the many, and the many in the one;' but this had a dangerous tendency. It was imagined that to these general ideas an objective reality corresponded ; it was pretended that the lyre, the horse, the young girl, and the generous action had something in common—*beauty ;* where it ought to have been said, it is because men are capable of an agreeable emotion excited by these various objects, that they are united under the general term 'beautiful.'

Sextus Empirius[2] has told us that the ancients were divided upon the point whether Plato was dogmatic or sceptical.

One can understand this difficulty, and for my part, says Mr. Lewes, 'after having read every one of Plato's Dialogues (an excessively wearisome labour), and done my best to arrive at a distinct understanding of their purpose, I come to the conclusion

[1] Lewes, *Philosophy*, vol. i. p. 124.

[2] *Hypot. Pyrrh.* i. 44.

that he never systematized his thoughts, but allowed free play to scepticism, taking opposite sides in every debate because he had no steady conviction to guide him; unsaying to-day what he had said yesterday, satisfied to show the weakness of an opponent.'[1]

He does not believe, any more than Mr. Grote, in the system of interpretation which consists in saying that one dialogue resolves the difficulties proposed by another. That which we take for a game of dialectics is really the 'groping' of Plato himself. He had not a philosophy; he had philosophies; he was above all great as a promoter; his doctrine, which is valuable '*ad edocendum parum, ad impellendum satis*, remains still, and always will remain, a source of power.'[2]

Mr. Lewes, as we have already stated, has devoted a special essay to Aristotle; in him he praises the founder of the experimental school; he criticises the author of the Metaphysics. He may be rightly called the father of the inductive philosophy, because he was the first to lay down its principles with an exactness and precision which Bacon himself has not surpassed. 'Anticipating modern Psychology, he taught, confusedly indeed, that intelligence is a late development; that the understanding is built up from sensuous materials,'[3] that memory produces experience, and that experience renders induction possible. But still his method is not that of positive science—verification is missing. That which removes all scientific value from it is his theory of the *Four Causes*—an entirely subjective conception, founded upon pure ideas, and consequently hypothetical, and not verifiable.

The semi-scepticism of the new academy furnishes to Mr. Lewes the materials for an essay on perception. We know that Arcesilaus and Carneades disputed with the Stoics, the dogmatists of that time, upon the legitimacy of the criterion, and in particular upon this question: Does every modification of the mind correspond exactly to the external object which causes it? Sensation, says Mr. Lewes, corresponds in nothing with its object, unless in the relation of effect to cause. At first this will surprise any one who has not reflected upon the point. Ask such a person if he con-

[1] Lewes, *Hist. of Philosophy*, p. 218.
[2] Vol. i. p. 221.
[3] *Ibid.* p. 288.
[4] *Ibid.* pp. 367-372.

siders his perceptions as *copies* of particular objects, if he thinks that the flower which is before him can exist independently of him, or of all human beings, and if it can exist with the same attributes of form, taste, smell, etc.? His answer will be in the affirmative. He will regard you as a mad man if you doubt it. Nevertheless, a modification cannot be in any way a *copy* of the object which modifies. The pain caused by a burn is not the copy of the fire. Does it resemble the fire in any way? It simply expresses the relation between us and the fire, an effect which fire may produce upon us. We hear thunder; our sensation is not a copy of the phenomenon; it simply expresses an effect produced upon us by a certain vibration of the air. It is the same with regard to sensations of sight, although the prejudice to the contrary is very difficult to uproot. There are many persons who will agree that the pain caused by fire is not a copy of the fire, but who will maintain that the appearance produced upon our eyes by fire is the real appearance of the fire, independently of human vision. 'Yet if all sentient beings were at once swept from the face of the earth, the fire would have no attribute at all resembling pain; because pain is a modification, not of fire, but of a sentient being. In like manner, if all sentient beings were at once swept from the face of the earth, the fire would have no attributes at all resembling light and colour; because light and colour are modifications of the sentient being, caused by *something* external, but no more resembling its cause than the pain inflicted by an instrument resembles that instrument.'[1]

The radical error of those who think that we perceive things *as they are*, consists in adopting a metaphor as a fact, and believing that perception resembles a mirror, in which certain objects reflect themselves. Perception is no more than a condition of the subject perceiving, that is to say, a state of consciousness which may be *caused* by external objects, but which it does not in any way *resemble*. Then all that we can do is to endeavour to identify certain external appearances with certain internal changes, to *identify* the phenomenon which we call fire with certain sensations which are produced when we approach it. The world

[1] Lewes, *History of Philosophy*, vol. i. p. 368.

considered independently of consciousness, the world *in itself*, is in all probability very different from the world as we know it. 'Light, colour, sound, taste, smell, are all states of consciousness; what they are beyond consciousness, as existences *per se*, we cannot know, we cannot imagine, because we can only conceive them as we know them. Light, with its myriad forms and colours—Sound, with its thousand-fold life—are the investitures with which we clothe the world. Nature, in her insentient solitude, is an eternal darkness—an eternal silence.' [1]

Perception is then an effect, and its truth is a truth not of resemblance, but of relation. It cannot make us know what things are, but what they are in relation to us.

VI.

'Although the Middle Ages extend over nearly a thousand years, we must, as Hegel says, put on seven-league boots to traverse them.' [2] Thus says Mr. Lewes, and he keeps his word. We shall be perhaps astonished to find that St. Thomas Aquinas, Duns Scotus, Telesio, and Vanini are not named; but if we remember that the aim of the author is, above all, critical and dogmatic, we shall be less surprised at it. He is in haste to reach the moderns.

Of the two founders of modern philosophy, Descartes is the best handled. Bacon [3] was above all an initiator, and he had the merit of crying aloud, of being the herald of a new era, of giving to scientific research the dignity and the hope of a brilliant future. But while insisting upon the importance of the experimental method, he has totally deceived himself upon the process to be followed, and Harvey was not altogether unjust when he said of him, 'he talks of science like a Lord Chancellor.'

Dugald Stewart was right in saying that Descartes is the father of experimental psychology; and Condorcet in maintaining that he has done more than Galileo or Bacon for the experimental method, exaggerated a little, but not without foundation.

[1] Vol. i. p. 371.
[2] Vol. ii. p. 2.
[3] Vol. ii. pp. 119, 120, 126.
[4] *Ibid.* p. 145.

Cartesianism is summed up in two things: consciousness is the sole foundation of certitude; mathematics is the sole method of certitude. Bacon had said nothing of the deductive method: Descartes supplies this deficiency. But the deductive method, excellent in itself, must proceed objectively, and in that Descartes is often wanting. Whilst his reaction against the scholastic philosophy leads him to the objective point of view in cosmology, his psychological studies bring him back to the subjective point of view; he believes that reason can solve theological and metaphysical problems. To found the deductive method upon the basis of consciousness—such was his object. No thinker save Spinoza has so clearly established his criterion. But this criterion is deceptive. Consciousness is the last foundation of certitude: yes, *for me*. But what certitude does it give me for *all which is not me*. Consciousness is restricted, confined to self and to what passes in self; all the ideas which we have upon the non-ego can be founded only upon inferences. I burn myself. I have consciousness of a sensation, I have a certain and immediate knowledge of it. But when from the change produced I infer the existence of something which is not me, consciousness itself guarantees me nothing, and my whole knowledge of the object is mediate and uncertain. Consequently, as soon as we abandon consciousness for inference doubt becomes possible.[1]

We must resolutely but regretfully sacrifice everything in the history of modern philosophy which is apart from our subject, and only show how Mr. Lewes traces and comprehends the process of psychology.[2]

It is Hobbes, he says,[3] and not Locke, who is the precursor of that psychology of the eighteenth century which resulted in the celebrated formula, 'to think is to feel.' We must also

---

[1] Vol. ii. p. 155.

[2] The author is familiar with the most recent works published in France upon the History of Philosophy, whether general histories or monographs. He treats Spinoza at length: it is to be regretted that the essay on Leibnitz is so brief, and that there is nothing about Malebranche.

[3] P. 229.

reproach him with materialism.[1] But the aid he has lent to psychologists is considerable. In the first place, he has proclaimed it a science of observation; he discovered that our sensations do not correspond with external qualities, that they are only a modification of the sentient subject, a discovery which Descartes has adopted or made for himself in his *Meditations;* finally, he wrote a 'masterly' chapter on the association of ideas, 'though he evidently was quite unaware of its extensive application.'

Locke is the founder of modern psychology; he understood the necessity of a critical determination of the limits of the human mind. He commenced the history of the development of our thoughts, others having been content to take ideas as they found them; Locke carefully sought for the origin of all our ideas. In order to complete his psychology he ought to have searched for the origin of our faculties. M. Victor Cousin, who, 'as a rhetorician,'[2] opposes Locke, complains of his speaking of savages, of children, of travellers' tales, and he does not see that Locke was trying the comparative method. When John Hunter sought for the elucidation of several anatomical problems in comparative anatomy, he was laughed at; and now every one knows that comparative physiology and embryology are the surest guides in all biological questions: because simple organisms are more easy to study than complex organisms. Locke also foresaw, but confusedly, the possibility of this comparative study in psychology.

Psychology owes only one thing to Leibnitz, but which is of immense value: the distinction between perception and apperception.[3]

'There are few men of whom England has better reason to be proud than of George Berkeley, Bishop of Cloyne.'[4] He has not been spared raillery or attack, but most frequently his critics have not understood him.

'When Berkeley denied the existence of matter, he meant by "matter" that unknown *substratum*, the existence of which Locke had declared to be a necessary *inference* from our knowledge of qualities, but the nature of which must ever be altogether hidden

[1] Vol. ii. p. 226. [2] P. 246. [3] P. 280. [4] P. 281.

from us. Philosophers had assumed the existence of Substance, *i.e.* of a *noumenon* lying underneath all *phenomena*—a substratum supporting all qualities—a *something* in which all accidents *inhere*. This unknown Substance Berkeley rejects.'[1]

This is why he says that he believes as fully in matter as any one; but that in his belief he separates himself from the philosopher, and agrees with the *vulgar*. He denies matter, then, not in the *vulgar* sense, but in the *philosophical* sense of the word. We must acknowledge, however, that his language is ambiguous, and tends to mistakes.[2]

When philosophy examines the notions of common sense, relative to the exterior world, it meets with this problem. Our senses inform us of certain sensible qualities,—extent, colour, etc. But our reason tells us that these qualities must be the qualities of something. What is that something? It is the unknown substance which serves for support to the qualities. So that in the ultimate analysis our only reason for inferring the existence of matter is *the necessity of a synthesis of attributes*. What says Berkeley to this? He boldly resolves the problem by saying that the synthesis is *a mental synthesis*. He first causes us to remark that the objects of our knowledge are *ideas*, an indisputable assertion, rigidly founded upon the facts of consciousness, and which can appear paradoxical only to those who are unused to questions of this kind. 'When,' he says, 'we do everything in our power to conceive the existence of external bodies, we are all the time doing nothing but contemplating our own ideas.' These objects and ideas are the same thing, then; nothing exists, then, but what is perceived. Can we maintain that in addition to ideas, there are things of which ideas are copies? As an idea can only resemble an idea, of two things one must be true: either the object of which we speak is an idea, and then idealism triumphs; or we maintain that a colour resembles something invisible, the rough object an intangible thing.

Realism, says Mr. Lewes, has not the shadow of an answer to

---

1 Lewes, *History of Philosophy*, vol. ii. p. 283.

2 In support of his interpretation Mr. Lewes quotes several passages from Berkeley. See *Principles of Human Knowledge*, § 35 *et seq.*

make. Applied to the facts of the *adult* consciousness, the analysis of Berkeley is unimpeachable;[1] unless we should deny that consciousness is immediately affected by sensations, and affirm that it is immediately affected by external objects; which no metaphysician would do, because this would lead him to maintain that consciousness is nothing but sensations produced in the organism by external influences, and so cause the substratum mind to disappear altogether.

The question of knowing whether consciousness is something superior to its acts (if it is, to use the language of French psychologists, a distinct faculty) may be considered to have been established since Brown. Nevertheless, we still find the old notion of a duplication of consciousness, of a consciousness which is a feeling of feeling, that will remain until the notion of mind as an entity shall have been banished from psychology.

Are there two distinct existences, matter and spirit?—is there only one? And which? Such is, when we reflect upon it, the point in debate in the question which occupies us.

The idealist says, There is only one existence, the mind. Analyse the conception of matter, and you will discover that it is only a mental synthesis of qualities.

The realist will say, There is only one existence, matter. Analyse your conception of mind, and you will discover that it is only a synthesis of qualities (states of consciousness), which are the activities of the organism. The synthesis is the organism.

The sceptic, in agreement with both, and in disagreement with both, says: Your matter is only a floating succession of phenomena; your mind a floating succession of ideas.

The dualist says, There is spirit, and there is matter; each is essentially distinct; they have nothing in common. Nevertheless, they can act one upon the other. How? That is a mystery.

No doubt; but as philosophy cannot be contented with phrases, it remarks that where realism and idealism admit only one factor, dualism introduces two; consequently it rejects it in virtue of the rule, *Entia non sunt multiplicanda præter necessitatem.*[2]

Must we now, taking the side of idealism, conclude with

[1] Vol. ii. p. 295. [2] *Ibid.* p. 296.

Berkeley, that as we only know ideas, objects must be identified with ideas, and that the *esse* of objects for us is *percipi*? There is an ambiguity in that. No doubt we cannot think of an object without making it subject to the laws of nature, under the conditions of our thought; but it is quite different to say, 'I cannot conceive things otherwise, therefore they cannot exist otherwise.' Idealism here assumes that human knowledge is absolute, not relative; that man is the measure of everything.

'Perception is the *identity* of the ego and the non-ego—the relation of two terms, the *tertium quid* of two united forces; as water is the identity of oxygen and hydrogen. The ego can never have any knowledge of the non-ego in which it (the ego) is not indissolubly bound up; as oxygen can never unite with hydrogen to form water without merging itself and the hydrogen in a *tertium quid.* Let us suppose the oxygen to be a process of consciousness, *i.e.* a feeling of changes. It would attribute the change *not* to hydrogen, which is necessarily hidden from it, *but to water*, the only form under which hydrogen is known to it. In its consciousness it would find the state named water, which would be very unlike its previous state; and it would suppose that this state, so unlike the previous one, was a representation of that which caused it. We say then that, although the hydrogen can only exist for the oxygen (in the above case) in the identity of both as water, this is no proof that hydrogen does not exist under some other relations to *other* gases. In like manner, although the non-ego cannot exist in relation to mind otherwise than in the identity of the two (perception), this is no sort of proof that it does not exist in relation to other beings under quite different conditions.'[1]

We admit then, with the idealists, that our knowledge is subjective; but we believe in the existence of an external world, altogether independent of the perceiving subject. The argumentation by which idealism seeks to disturb this belief is vitiated by the assumption that our knowledge is the criterion of existence; this is conferring upon it an absolute value that it does not possess.

[1] *History of Philosophy*, vol. ii. p. 302.

Hume follows up Berkeley. He suppresses the mind as an entity, and reduces it to a series of impressions, or, as modern psychologists would say, to a series of states of consciousness. But how then is continuity of consciousness to be explained, since between two states there is necessarily an interval? Does consciousness vanish during this interval, to re-appear with the after state? Hume does not solve this question ; he does not even put it.

The metaphysician replies, Yes : the mind continues and unites all its manifestations in one synthesis.

The biologist replies, Consciousness being a vital process, not an entity, has its synthesis in the continuity of the vital conditions. The nervous mechanism, of which consciousness is a function, continues to exist in the interval between two acts of consciousness.

If the metaphysician objects that the reality of the mind is proved by consciousness, and by the fact that I say, *My* body; the biologist will reply, that the testimony of consciousness needs sifting by analysis; and that if I say, My body, I also say, *My* mind. Its personality is a notion whose genesis has not been yet clearly traced by any psychologist.[1]

After Hume, psychology is represented by Hartley, Darwin, and the Scotch school.

Hartley is the first who has attempted to explain the physiological mechanism of psychological phenomena.[2] He explains sensations by vibratory movements; a hypothesis which adds nothing to our knowledge of psychical processes. To speak of vibrations and vibratiuncles does not at all enlarge our horizon. Although since Hartley the progress of science has given a high degree of probability to the general doctrine of vibrations, nevertheless, even now, our knowledge of sensations is much more certain than that of the vibrations involved. The doctrine of vibrations would be useful, if from the known laws of vibratory bodies we could deduce and explain the still unexplained mental phenomena; but nothing of the kind has been done as yet, and the theory of Hartley is much too vague to aid us.[3]

---

[1] *History of Philosophy*, vol. ii. p. 316. [2] *Ibid.* p. 349. [3] *Ibid.* p. 353.

Darwin (Erasmus) professes the same theory, substituting for the word 'vibration' the expression 'sensorial movements.' Although his system is full of 'absurd hypotheses,' he has the merit of seeing that psychology is subordinate to the laws of life, and of cutting short ill-put questions and factitious problems. Why with two eyes do we see objects single? Why, the images being reversed upon the retina, do we see objects straight? These questions and those of the same kind are psychological, and cannot be resolved either by optics or anatomy. We might as well deduce the assimilation of sugar from the angles of its crystals, as deduce the perception of an object from the laws of optics; sugar must be dissolved before being assimilated, and so the retinal images must be transformed by the sensational centre, before affecting the brain.[1] And this is not a gratuitous hypothesis, it is sustained by facts. It can be demonstrated. We see objects single with our two eyes, but we also hear sounds as single with our two ears; our two nostrils give us a single scent; our five fingers give us objects as single. These facts have a bearing upon one another, and they demand reflection. Their explanation ought to be psychological, and I think, says Mr. Lewes, that it is very simple. Here it is:—

'I believe the explanation to be very simple. *We cannot have two precisely similar sensations at precisely the same instant; the simultaneousness of the two sensations renders them indistinguishable.* Two sounds of precisely the same pitch and intensity, succeeding each other by an *appreciable* interval, will be heard as two sounds; but if they succeed each other so rapidly that the interval is inappreciable, no distinction will be felt, and the two will be heard as one, because heard simultaneously. . . . The various Sensational Centres are *variously* affected by the *same* stimuli: electricity giving to the gustatory nerve the stimulus of savorous bodies, to the auditory nerve the stimulus of sonorous vibrations, to the optic nerve the stimulus of luminous bodies, to the tactile nerves the stimulus of touch. . . . Nor is this all: narcotics introduced into the blood excite in each Sensational Centre the

[1] *Ibid.* vol. ii. p. 358.

specific sensation normally excited by its external stimuli. . . . From these indubitable facts it is not difficult to elicit a conclusion, namely, that sensation depends on the Sensational Centre, and not on the external stimulus, . . . and there the *impression* first becomes a *sensation*. . . . When therefore it is asked,—Why do we see objects *erect*, when they throw *inverted* images on the retina? the answer is,—Because we do not see the retinal image at all; we see, or are affected by, the object; and our perception of the erectness of that object does not depend on vision, but on our conceptions of space and the relations of space, which are not given in the visual sensation.'[1]

The Scotch school is summarily treated;[2] although its psychology contains much available matter for students, it is entirely dead as a doctrine. It is dead, and it deserved to die, because it had no object and no true method. It has added verbal analysis to verbal analysis, metaphysical explanation to metaphysical explanation; whilst physiologists and some psychologists were going to the bottom of things.

Those to whom this allusion is made appear to be Cabanis and Gall.

The mention of the name of Cabanis immediately recalls the famous 'secretion of thought.' By an unhappy phrase, says Mr. Lewes,[3] Cabanis has given the advantage to his adversaries, and has prevented the progress of his own doctrines.[4] He has been understood to have said that the brain secretes thought as the liver secretes bile. He never said anything of the sort. It is true that by a deplorable ambiguity of language he may lead us to interpret him as holding that thought is a secretion, while in reality he meant to say that it is a function. 'Certainly, if he did regard thought as a secretion, the error was monstrous, and the outcry against him was justifiable.'[5] But the truth is, that he, like many biologists and psychologists, had very obscure

[1] Lewes, *History of Philosophy*, vol. ii. p. 359-361.

[2] *Ibid.* p. 393.

[3] *Ibid.* p. 375.

[4] For the text of the phrase, see Cabanis, *Rapports du Physique et du Moral*, ed. Peisse, p. 138, with a note by the editor, who does not take it seriously.

[5] *History of Philosophy*, vol. ii. p. 376.

ideas upon function.[1] His great merit has been clear perception of the relations of psychology to the science of life, and the recognition of a great truth, already clearly seen by Aristotle, and thus expressed by St. Thomas Aquinas : 'Impossibile est in uno homine esse plures animas per essentiam differentes, sed una tantum est anima intellectiva quæ vegetativo et sensitivo et intellectivo officiis fungitur.'

Gall is treated with fulness and favour in pages 394 to 435 ; Mr. Lewes attributes to him one merit, that of having rendered service to physiology and to psychology even by the daring of his hypotheses ; and two defects, that of completely neglecting subjective analysis in psychology, and of having founded a phrenology or cranioscopy belied by facts and the progress of science.

If Gall has been accused of materialism, it has been wrongfully, because he has several times declared that he 'confines himself to phenomena,' and that he has never comprised in his researches anything relating to the essence of the body, or of the soul. 'I do not understand,' he says, 'that our faculties are a *product* of organization, because this would be to confound the conditions with the efficient causes.' It may be said that Gall has put a definite end to the dispute between the partisans of innate ideas, and the doctrine of sensation, by showing that there are innate tendencies, as much affective as intellectual, which belong to the organic structure of man. Two psychological facts, already vaguely perceived, have been brought out by him :—

I. The fundamental tendencies are innate, and cannot be created by education.

II. The various faculties are essentially distinct and independent, though intimately united among themselves.

He has also clearly seen and clearly expressed that the greatest obstacle to the progress of psychological researches is to isolate man from the animal series, and to consider him as governed by totally special organic laws.

He has understood that psychology, being a branch of biology,

---

[1] Mr. Lewes, quoting in p. 648 an analogous expression of Vogt's, manifests his distaste to phrases made for effect, aiming at terrifying, and which he calls 'pistol-shots.'

and consequently subject to all the biological laws, must be studied according to biological methods. Zoological, anatomical, philosophical, and pathological observations, all these are necessary as a basis: and certainly Gall has amassed more facts of this sort than any of his predecessors; he has exhibited the patience and the skill of an investigator, although he may have drawn from all his collection of materials false interpretations and unverified conclusions. But there is another very important instrument of research, which Gall has omitted; this is *subjective analysis;* an instrument so necessary that several psychologists, neglecting the importance of biological researches, maintain that psychology ought to be erected into a distinct science, and founded upon that analysis. Hence the weakness of the psychological classifications of Gall, Spurzheim, and George Combe has rendered them rather more acceptable, but no one has had the faintest conception of what psychological analysis ought to be, of its means, of its conditions, and of the problems which it has to solve. How are we to determine whether a mental manifestation is the direct product of a faculty, or the indirect product of two or more faculties? How are we to distinguish between faculties and modes, between elementary actions and associated actions, between energies and synergies? These are very important questions, which no one has tried to solve. Gall attributes to us twenty-seven faculties, among which are those of veneration, of individuality, of colour, of eventuality, and many others which evidently are not at all original faculties. His doctrine is thus very weak on this point. Nevertheless, the great principle of Kant, that we must seek in the laws of thought a solution of philosophical problems, Gall has had the merit of approaching on the biological side.

'We ought to seek our ideas and our knowledge partly in the phenomena of the exterior world, and in their rational employment, and partly in the innate laws of the moral and intellectual faculties.'[1]

Physiologically he takes his revenge. His novelty consists in his precision. The relations between the physical and the moral

[1] Gall, *Functions of the Brain*, i. 84.

nature had been vaguely recognised; also general relations of the nervous system and the mental functions; but none had ever attempted a precise demonstration of them. Many facts were known, such as the following: the toothache, which disappears when we reach the dentist's door; taking water, fancying that it is an emetic, and vomiting in consequence. These facts were explained by attributing them to the imagination. That is well; but by what material conditions did imagination act upon the viscera or upon the tooth? These simple-minded explanations supposed a sort of autocratic imagination, without feeling any necessity of discovering a particular mechanism for the production of the results. Gall has not succeeded in discovering one, but at least he has seen that it was necessary to substitute precise ideas for the vague generalities then current. Phrenology or cranioscopy had this aim; it assigned each part of the cerebral mass as the seat of one particular faculty. But this hypothesis had to be confronted with facts, and it was found to be false. The most eminent neurologists declared against it, so that now phrenology finds itself in the rear of the discoveries of physiology, without having ever succeeded in constituting its psychology.

We have not to follow Mr. Lewes in his explanation of German philosophy, nor in his criticism on Auguste Comte. Here, however, there is one point which we must notice. We know that Stuart Mill has keenly criticised the omission of psychology in the classification of the sciences, such as is admitted by the positive school.[1] Mr. Lewes replies to this criticism by the following distinction: If it is a question of recognising that psychology is a possible science, and of great value, that subjective analysis has been misunderstood by Comte, and that he has done wrong in regarding internal observation as an illusory process, I agree with Mr. Mill. But if it is a question of recognising in psychology an independent science, separate from biology, and to assign it a place of its own in the hierarchy of abstract sciences, then I am with M. Comte. Psychology may be a concrete

[1] On this point see Littré, *Auguste Comte et Stuart Mill*, and two articles in the *Revue des Deux Mondes*, on *La Philosophie positive*, September and November 1867.

science, like physiology and botany, but it must be derived from abstract science of biology.[1]

The conclusion of the work is a rapid review of the present philosophical situation of Europe. The author thinks that, in spite of appearances, the future belongs to positivism, and he carefully notices all the symptoms of it. If, as we sometimes say, the judgment of foreigners is for us a contemporary posterity, perhaps it will not be without interest to know what Mr. Lewes thinks of French philosophy.

It began, he says, by a movement of reaction against the doctrines of the eighteenth century—a vigorous reaction, because the excesses of the Revolution and the saturnalia of the Terror were associated in people's minds with the philosophical opinions of Condillac, Diderot, and Cabanis. Men were afraid of the consequences, and rejected these doctrines *en masse* without troubling themselves to know what good they may have contained.

'Men may, unhappily, be frightened from the truth, and cajoled into error, and in France the cajolery has been openly avowed, Victor Cousin frankly appealing to the "patriotism" of his audience in favour of "*nos belles doctrines.*" . . . The history of the reaction in France is very instructive, but it would require more space than can here be given adequately to narrate the story. Four streams of influence converged into one, all starting from the same source, namely, horror at the Revolutionary excesses. The Catholics, with the great Joseph de Maistre and M. de Bonald at their head, appealed to the religious sentiments; the Royalists, with Chateaubriand and Madame de Staël, appealed to the monarchical and literary sentiments; the metaphysicians, with Laromiguière and Maine de Biran; and the moralists, with Royer-Collard,—one and all attacked the weak points of Sensationalism, and prepared the way for the enthusiastic reception of the Scotch and German philosophies. A glance at almost any of these writers will suffice to convince the student that their main purpose is to defend morality and order, which they believe to be necessarily imperilled by the philosophy they attack. The

[1] P. 624.

appeals to the prejudices and sentiments are incessant. Eloquence is made to supply the deficiencies of argument; emotion takes the place of demonstration. . . . One doctrine, and one alone, emerged from these attempts, and held for some time the position of a School. . . . Eclecticism is dead, but it produced some good results, if only by the impetus it gave to historical research, and by the confirmation it gave, in its very weakness, to the conclusion that an *à priori* solution of transcendental problems is impossible. . . .

'Victor Cousin and Theodore Jouffroy are the chiefs of this School; one a brilliant rhetorician utterly destitute of originality, the other a sincere thinker, whose merits have been thrown into the shade by his brilliant colleague. As a man of letters, M. Cousin deserves the respect which attends his name, if we except the more than questionable use which he has made of the labours of pupils and assistants without acknowledgment. . . . But Victor Cousin's restless activity led him to the study of Kant:—and certain doctrines of the "Königsberg sage" were preached by him with the same ardour as that which he had formerly devoted to the Scotch. As soon as the Parisians began to know something of Kant, M. Cousin started off to Alexandria for a doctrine; he found one in Proclus. He edited Proclus; lectured on him; borrowed some of his ideas, and would have set him on the throne of philosophy had the public been willing. A trip to Germany in 1824 made him acquainted with the modern Proclus—Hegel. On his return to Paris he presented the public with as much of Hegel's doctrines as he could understand. His celebrated Eclecticism is nothing but a misconception of Hegel's *History of Philosophy*, fenced round with several plausible arguments.

'Gifted with great oratorical power, flattering the prejudices and passions of the majority, tempted as most orators are to sacrifice everything to effect, and incapable, from native incapacity or from defective training, of gaining any clear insight, Victor Cousin by his qualities and defects rose to an eminence which was regrettable, because it overshadowed the efforts of nobler minds. He was the source of philosophical patronage, and he filled the chairs of France with professors who were his adherents, or who dared not openly expose his weakness. The consequence was that, being crassly ignorant of Science, he kept Philosophy aloof from all scientific influences. The progress of centuries was ignored, and the methods of Scholasticism were once more brought into vogue. A painful cant of "question-begging" eloquence supplied the place of research. The clear, precise genius of France was for a time ashamed of its clearness, and in sheer terror of being thought superficial and immoral rejected the aid of Science, and went maundering on about *le Moi, l'œil interne, l'Infini, le Vrai, le Beau, et le Bien* [1] in a pitiable manner.'

This judgment is severe, at least in form, but we have contented ourselves with merely translating it.

Is this, of which the foregoing pages are an exposition, an ordinary history of philosophy? Evidently not; it is the work of an original mind which has a great deal to say, and yields voluntarily to the pleasure of saying it, a mind which handles texts like a thinker, not like a scholar. Assuredly we must not search Mr. Lewes's pages for enlightenment upon obscure points and upon controverted passages; but in this long journey from Thales to Comte, the author has taken amazing pains, and has put forth enough teaching to content some, to leave others discontented, and to make every one reflect. We know our philosopher already, although we have only examined the historian in him. Let us now approach the psychologist.

---

[1] These words are in French in the text.

[2] Lewes, *Philosophy*, vol. ii. pp. 645-6.

CHAPTER II.

PSYCHOLOGY.

Psychology.—1. Psychology of common life—2. Organism and mechanism—3. Consciousness : its various forms—4. Discussion of the current doctrine of reflex actions—5. Of sleep and heredity.

I.

WE are destined never to come face to face with Mr. Lewes, we can only take him obliquely. Just now he was an historian, at present he is a psychologist. But while he protests that he will not come out of 'his science,' and that he renounces penetration of the mysteries of psychology, it may be said that he is always coquetting with that science,—that he frequently yields to the temptation of speaking of it, and that it occupies a great part of his work, although he does not treat of it explicitly. The *Physiology of Common Life*, as its title expresses, proceeds to exhibit under a simple form the mechanism of the vital functions, and to give a notion of the principal laws of physiology sufficient to serve as a guide in practice.[1] It differs however from books of popular science, in that the author, instead of being a simple intermediary between the public and the *savant*, brings forward the result of his personal researches, which differ upon more than one point from received opinions.

'FEELING and THINKING are of too profound an interest, and too closely allied with all vital phenomena, not to find a large place in the *Physiology of Common Life.* But what place must we give them? How must these difficult subjects be treated? Their very depth and extent of interest oblige us to select only those aspects which fall strictly within the scope of this work. They have psychological aspects and physiological aspects, both of great importance; but as our business here is not to discuss any but physiological problems, we confine ourselves to what are strictly the physiological aspects of thought and sensation.

[1] *Physiology of Common Life*, vol. ii. p. 453.

'Psychology is the science of Mind. This science may seek—and I follow those who think it *ought* to seek—important means of investigation in the laws of physiology; just as Physiology itself must seek important aids in Chemistry and Physics. But as an independent branch of inquiry, its results cannot be amenable to physiological canons; their validity cannot be decided by agreement or disagreement with physiological laws. To cite an example: Psychology announces that the mind has different faculties. That fact seems established on ample evidence, and is valid in Psychology, although hitherto no *corresponding* fact in Physiology has been discovered.'[1]

Mr. Lewes concedes independence to the two sciences, although he maintains their relations.

This book then being not a treatise on psychology, although containing much of it, we shall proceed, as we did with the preceding one,—that is to say, gleaning from it; and we shall endeavour to embody the doctrines of the author under the following titles :—

1. Of the nature of life, and of the vital principle.
2. Of consciousness and its forms.
3. Of sleep.
4. Of heredity from a psychological point of view.

II.

We must count in the number of infirmities of thought, says Mr. Lewes,[2] the tendency of the human mind to realize abstractions, and to give to them an objective and independent existence. A good example of this tendency is the formerly popular doctrine of a vital principle, which is now by degrees disappearing.

Life is the connexus of organic activities; it is a collection of various particular facts, abstracted from these facts, erected into objective reality, each organ is composed of constituent tissues, each tissue has its constitutive elements, each element,

[1] *Physiology of Common Life*, pp. 2, 3.
[2] *History of Philosophy*, Proleg. § 45-49.

each tissue, has its specific properties, the activity of each organ is the sum of these properties, organism is the connexus of the totality. Life is then only a conception drawn from particular facts. But we have forgotten it, and we have realized this abstraction; we have declared that this *resultant* is a necessary *antecedent.* We have spoken of a vital principle anterior to all organic activities, and independent of them. Although this hypothesis has at the present day eminent partisans, it suffices, to dissipate the illusion, that we should resolve the abstract into the concrete forms from which it is drawn.

A shred of muscle detached from the organism will manifest all its vital properties so long as its specific constitution of muscle shall subsist, so long as it shall resist disintegration; it will absorb oxygen, exhale carbonic acid, it will contract itself under an appropriate stimulus. A gland separated from the body continues to be a small laboratory of chemical changes, secreting as it secreted in the organism. A nerve detached from the body continues to manifest its specific property of neurility. These phenomena prove that what each part does *in* the organism each part does *out of* the organism. In other words, the life of the animal is the sum of particular vital activities; it is not the *source* of the phenomena, but their personification.[1] The action of life is similar to that of mechanism, and differs from it only by the greater complication of its parts and of its effects.

Many persons, however, object to such a conception. Life seems to them the antithesis of mechanical action. This repugnance will be diminished if they could get well into their minds that between a mechanism and an organism there is *resemblance,* but not *identity;* that organism is a mechanism, but a *vital* mechanism, vitality being the source of profound differences. Attention has in general been fixed upon mechanical adjustment, and the *sensations which guide it* have been forgotten. No doubt animal mechanism, when it is put in action, acts like the mechan-

1 'The life of the individual is the sum of a multitude of lives, each belonging of right to one of the elements of the organism.'—Milne-Edwards's *Rapports sur les progrès des sciences zoolog.*, pp. 50 and 59.

ism of a watch, but in order to put it in action and to maintain it in action the constant pressure of sensation is necessary. Sensation is an indispensable portion of mechanism, it is the main-spring of the watch, it is the fuel of the steam-engine. In short, organism is a mechanism, and it acts mechanically, in so far as its actions are necessarily determined by the adjustment of its organs, but organism differs from mechanism in that it has sensibility for mainspring, and that its so-called automatic actions are all determined by the movement of directing sensations.[1]

The hypothesis of a vital principle, which was held for several centuries, and which is now rejected by every one except by a few metaphysicians and metaphysiologists, was only a verbal explanation; it substituted words for ideas; almost the same might be said of the modern doctrine of vital force or vital forces: this is only a realized abstraction,[2] a term which serves to veil our ignorance.

The only three arguments given in favour of a vital principle which deserve consideration are the following:—1st, Life governs chemical affinities; 2d, Life *precedes* organization, and consequently cannot be the *result* of it; 3d, Life is a directing unity.

Does life govern chemical affinities? There is nothing more striking at first than this fact,—a living body preserves its form, and does not seem to yield to the destructive action of chemical agents; whereas, as soon as life is extinct, the molecules yield to the action of chemical affinities. But on looking closer we see that instead of saying that the chemical affinities are controlled by vitality, we ought to say that there is no vital action possible without the incessant and complicated action of chemical affinities; nutrition, secretion, movement, all depend on chemical actions.

Does life precede organization? The word organization includes an ambiguity; but if we remark that by this word we understand the *totality of the necessary conditions*, not less than the organic constitution, we easily understand that *life is proportional to the organization*. The life of a simple cellule is the totality of the activities of that cellule. The life of an animal of higher

[1] *Physiology of Common Life*, vol. ii. chap. ix. [2] *Ibid.* chap. xiii.

organization is the sum of the activities of all the forces in motion, and its complexity is in proportion to the complexity of the organization. Life being then a result, and varying according to the degrees of organism, we cannot say that it precedes organization.

Is it a directing principle? A superior unity? We say the body is one, all its parts are subordinate, assembled together to form a superior unity: our consciousness assures us that life is a unity. This argument is founded upon an important fact, but one which is misinterpreted. Yes, there is a unity, there is a consensus in the organism; but we must not attribute it to a vital principle independent of the organism. It is due to the subordination of the organs; all the parts have relations, all act together by means of the nervous system. Where there is not that connexion between the parts, there cannot be this connexion between the organs. If we cut a polype or a worm into several pieces, each piece will continue to live and develop itself; nevertheless we cannot suppose that in such a case we have cut the vital principle into several principles. It is that there is a life in each part, and a life of the entire organism; each microscopic cellule has its independent existence, furnishes its career from birth to death, and the *totality of these lives* forms what we call the life of the animal; unity is an aggregate of forces, and not a superior force.

'It is surely more philosophical to consider life as an ultimate fact; one of the great revelations of the unknowable; one of the many mysteries surrounding us. . . . We no longer set up fictions of our imagination in the place of a reverent observation. There are minds, indeed, which feel distrust at such resignation; they seem to dread lest life should be robbed of its solemn significance, in the attempt to associate it, even remotely, with inorganic phenomena. But this fear arises from narrow views of nature. It is because reverence for nature has not been duly cultivated, because familiarity with inorganic phenomena has blunted our sense of their unspeakable mystery. Men who are thrilled at the tokens of the past life of man, when they see, or read of, buried cities, Palmyra, Nineveh, or Yucatan, tremble with no delicious awe at the tokens of the past life of this earth, when they stand in a quarry, or ramble through a geological museum. Yet surely the crystal is not less mysterious than the plant, the ebb and the flow of the tides not less solemn than the beating of the human heart? And if patient observation and induction have enabled us to trace something of the order of nature in crystallization and the tides, without aid from the metaphysician, they may also enable us to understand something of the laws of life.'[1]

III.

The theory of consciousness which we are about to study is original in several respects. The author, placing himself especially in a psychological point of view, examines the question of *latent* or *insensible perceptions*, so much disputed since Leibnitz, but which appears in these last days to be almost universally accepted. These *infinitely littles* of perception may play in psychological life a part as important as microscopic organisms in the material world, and one may be more than once surprised at the disproportion which exists between infinitesimal causes and the consequences which they engender. Mr. Lewes accepts them; he even distinguishes varieties, as we are about to see, and builds up, as it were, a hierarchy of consciousnesses.

One of the points which our author is most anxious to establish is, that the *sensorium*, that is to say, the seat of sensation and of consciousness, is not limited to the brain, that sensibility being the fundamental property of the ganglionary tissue inherent in this tissue, we ought to consider the sensorium as having the same extension as the nervous centres. He then defines the *common sensorium* 'the sum of all the nervous centres, each centre being itself a small sensorium.' Sensibility is a *histologic* property, and not a *morphologic* one, the disposition of the organ is then secondary.

'The current view is this: sensibility belongs only to the

---

[1] *Physiology of Common Life*, vol. ii. pp. 22, 23. *Ibid.* p. 43.

centres within the skull; all other centres have only the property of *reflecting* impressions. By this reflection of impressions is meant that when an impression is made on a sensory nerve, and by it carried to the spinal cord, the impression there becomes *reflected* into a motion; the motor-nerve carries the impulse to a muscle, and thus an action results, unprompted or unaccompanied by any sensation whatever. In direct opposition to this, I maintain that unless an impression on the sensory nerve excites a sensation in the centre, *no* motion whatever takes place.' [1]

According to the ordinary doctrine, consciousness being held to have its seat in the brain, we naturally admit that the impression, so long as it is not upon the brain, produces no sensation, and if an animal deprived of the brain gives signs of sensation, physiologists maintain that it has no real sensation, but *sensitive impressions* which produce reflex actions without consciousness on the part of the animal.

The word consciousness has a very vague meaning. Its most general meaning is sensation. It is indisputable that we have a sensitive organism which is necessarily excited by internal and external stimulus, that each of these excitements is a sensation, and that all these sensations must be elements of consciousness. We also admit that amongst these excitements those only which are of sufficient account to predominate over the myriads of vague excitements of organism are properly called sensations. We say that we have consciousness of them—the rest is considered as non-existent;—these are the unconscious impressions which lead to actions, but they are not consciousness.

The apparently contradictory expression, 'unconscious consciousness,' 'unfelt sensations,' often employed in such cases, would not be embarrassing if the difference between *sensation* and *perception* had been clearly distinguished.[2] 'Sensation is simply an active state of sensibility which is the property of

[1] *Physiology of Common Life*, vol. ii.

[2] The distinction drawn by Mr. Lewes between sensation and perception, may be likened to that drawn by Leibnitz between perception and apperception.

the ganglionary tissue.' Sensation being thus defined, can there be sensation without perception?

It is quite certain that we have many sensations that are not at all perceived, and of which we are, as we say, 'totally unconscious.' They are either so weak or so familiar, or so lost in strong sensations, or so incapable of exciting 'associations' of ideas, that we are not 'conscious' of them in the present, and that we cannot recall them afterwards. This happens when we sleep during a sermon or a lecture; we have the sensation of sounds emitted by some one who speaks; we have no perception of them. This cannot be doubted, because, on the one hand, we do not know what has been read or said; on the other hand, if the sermon or lecture cease suddenly, we awake, which shows that we had the sensation of sounds. Mr. Lewes relates that having gone into an eating-house and found a waiter fast asleep, in the midst of the noise he vainly called him by his name, and by his Christian name, but as soon as he had pronounced the word 'waiter,' the sleeper awoke. Admiral Codrington, when a midshipman, could not be raised out of a sound sleep except by the word 'signal.' These facts, which have many fellows, show that there may be sensation without perception and sensation accompanied by perception.

'It would be an unfortunate mistake in language which should make it absurd to speak of non-perceived sensations. Perception has been so often confounded with sensation, because they have been constantly mixed up together, that we are astonished when it is said that one can be produced without the other. In spite of verbal difficulties we must get well into our minds that every excitement of a nervous centre produces a sensation, and that the totality of these excitements form general consciousness, or the sense of existence.

'We do not see the stars at noon-day, yet they shine. We do not see the sunbeams playing among the leaves, on a cloudy day, yet it is by these beams that the leaves and all other objects are visible. There is a general illumination from the sun and stars, but of this we are seldom aware, because our attention falls upon the illumined objects, brighter or darker than this general tone. There is a sort of analogy to this in the general consciousness which is composed of the sum of sensations excited by the incessant simultaneous action of internal and external stimuli. This forms, as it were, the daylight of our existence. We do not habitually attend to it, because attention falls on those particular sensations of pleasure or of pain, of greater or of less intensity, which usurp a prominence among the objects of the sensitive panorama.

'The amount of light received from the stars may be small, but it is present. The greater glory of the sunlight may render the starlight inappreciable, but it does not render it inoperative. In like manner the amount of sensation received from some of the smaller ganglia may be inappreciable in the presence of more massive influences from other centres, but though inappreciable it cannot be inoperative—it must form an integer in the sum.' [1]

We can now close this discussion by rejecting the current hypothesis which will have it that a sensation does not exist except it is perceived, without which it is a *pure impression.* Mr. Lewes points out that in distinguishing sensation from perception he does not make a purely verbal distinction, which would consist in calling that 'sensation' that others call 'impression.' By no means; by sensation he understands the sensibility proper to each centre. The naturalist, he says, knows that there is an enormous difference between the monkey and the oyster, but he also knows that notwithstanding their differences all animals obey the same biological laws. I should like to see the same reform introduced into our physiology of the nervous system. I should wish to see it recognised, that notwithstanding diversities, *all* nervous centres, in so far as they are centres, have properties and laws in common.

Consciousness, in its general sense, being the sum of all our sensibilities, the overflow of several currents of sensations, it results from this, that in the lower animals endowed with a simple nerv-

---

[1] *Physiology of Common Life*, vol. ii. p. 65.

ous system, the sensitive phenomena are simple, and that by degrees as organization increases in complexity the sensible phenomena become necessarily more complex, and the elements of general consciousness become more numerous. This leads to the examination of the question of the various forms of consciousness.

The unity of the nervous system throughout the whole animal kingdom has been generally recognised, but it is strange that unity of consciousness has not been deduced from it.

'The various forms of consciousness or sensibility may be properly grouped under these three titles:—First, systemic consciousness; second, sense-consciousness; thirdly, thought-consciousness.'[1]

Systemic consciousness, which gives us the principal elements of the sense of existence, includes all the sensations springing from the system of the organic functions in general and in particular. Short of adopting the hypothesis of Descartes upon animal machines, we must admit that the humblest animals have this form of consciousness. Those who reject this conclusion are the dupes of equivocal language, which leads them to suppose that there is some element of *thought* included in consciousness, and even in sensation. But though every animal must *feel*, it does not follow that it must think. Let us remark besides the absurdity of the consequences. If a mollusc has no sensation, it would be the same as to the crustacea. If the crab is a machine, the bee, the beaver, the elephant, the dog, and the monkey, are also machines. 'Short of throwing science to the winds, we must admit that all animals have sensations, although they have not each the same form of consciousness.'

Sense-consciousness includes all those sensations derived from the organs of the five senses.

Thought-consciousness includes all those phenomena of thought and emotion with which the psychologist is particularly concerned; all that the physiologist can do is to indicate the relations of this form of consciousness with the lower animals, and

[1] *Physiology of Common Life*, vol. ii. p. 74.

the portions of the nervous system which serve them as organs. As for thought we do not know, and perhaps we never shall know, what it is ; nor do we know what life is. But we can learn what are the *laws* of life and the *laws* of thought. To the physiologist belongs the former task, to the psychologist the latter.

The insufficiency of the preceding theory may be explained by remembering that Mr. Lewes only intends to place himself in a physiological point of view. Mr. Herbert Spencer and Mr. Bain have made us penetrate much more deeply into the mechanism of human consciousness by showing us this double current of integration and of disintegration which constitute it, the condition of time which imposes itself upon it and gives to it the form of a succession. But Mr. Lewes introduces us into another world, and this example appears to us to show, what we have endeavoured to establish in the introduction, namely, that in psychology the subjective method and the objective method are both equally necessary.

IV.

The theory of reflex actions attaches itself strongly to the preceding considerations upon unconscious sensations. It is striking and instructive to remark how little French psychology has occupied itself with this matter. Restricted to the facts of consciousness, it has avoided everything which has a physiological appearance. And whilst the invading spirit of physiology led it constantly to extend its domain, and even to come out of it on all sides, psychology, confined within strict limits, allowed many a portion of its territory to escape, and asked nothing. The discussions upon the boundary line of the two sciences, which filled the first half of the nineteenth century, sought to define frontiers which have no existence.

Between psychology and physiology there are no natural boundaries. No doubt a purely physiological act, such as circulation, differs entirely from a purely psychological act, such as deductive reasoning ; but there is an entire order of facts, insensible perceptions, reflex actions, instincts, etc., by means of which the two lives mingle and are confounded. This subject might have been less discussed if it had been better understood that our divisions are to a great extent arbitrary in consequence of the continuity of phenomena: that man distinguishes that which nature mixes, and that, if science is an analysis, the world is a synthesis.

The study of reflex actions is the continuation of that of consciousness. In fact, whilst according to the current theory the sensorium is restricted to the brain, the action which has its centre in the spinal marrow is called reflex, and is considered to be of a totally different nature; the theory of Mr. Lewes, which extends the sensorium to all the nervous centres, only admits that there is a difference of degree between the action of the brain and that of the spinal marrow. To establish that the *spinal cord is a sentient centre* is his aim, building upon his own experience, upon that of others, and upon the deduction which he draws from them. He wishes to 'give the final blow'[1] to the theory of reflex action, upon which he even casts ridicule.

The doctrine of the schools, he says, is this:—

'Mental nervous actions (*acts of volition and sensation*) *cannot take place without a brain.* . . . If you pinch a dog's tail, he cries out. His cry is supposed to indicate a sensation of pain. But the physiologist who would reprove you for having hurt his yelping puppy would quietly assure you that this puppy's cries were no evidence of pain or sensation after its brain had been removed. "Merely reflex, my dear sir," and he would smile at your supposition that an animal without a brain could feel any sensation.'[2]

In support of this doctrine he quotes facts and experiments. 'The researches of Flourens had their time. They were truly striking; the conclusions which he drew from them were commenced in that systematic, derisive, absolute style which characterizes French writers;' hence their European popularity, in spite of the reservations of Müller and Cuvier. Flourens maintains that the animal deprived of brain loses all sensation, all perception, all instinct, and all volition. But the contrary experiences of Bouillaud, Longet, and Dalton have weakened his conclusions.

[1] *Physiology of Common Life*, p. 526.

[2] *Ibid.* vol. ii. pp. 84, 85.

'It would be to misunderstand me,' says Mr. Lewes, 'if it were supposed that I do not consider the brain as the principal and dominating organ of all psychical life.

'I have said before that it has the noblest functions, but it does not exclude the other ganglia from their share in the general consciousness. In it all the sensations derived through the senses and viscera are summed up, combined, modified, and in some profoundly mysterious manner elaborated into ideas. It is generalissimo of the whole army, controlling, directing, and inspiring the actions of all subordinate officers. But to suppose that the subordinates have not also their independent functions is a mistake. The generals, colonels, captains, sergeants, corporals, and common soldiers, are individual men, like their commander-in-chief, with inferior power and with different functions, according to their respective positions. But if the commander-in-chief be killed, the army has still its generals. If the generals be killed, the regiments have still their colonels. Nay, even a corporal's company may be kept together by an energetic corporal. And this we shall see to be the case with animals when their brain has been removed; each separate part of the organism has its general, colonel, or corporal.'[1]

Every nervous centre having, then, a sensibility belonging to itself, 'a fundamental point,' says Mr. Lewes, 'which appears to me totally inadmissible, is the hypothesis that reflex mechanism is independent of sensibility, and that reflex actions take place without sensation.'[2]

He cannot 'refrain from expressing his surprise at the weakness of the evidence which serves as a basis for the celebrated theory of reflex actions.'[3] In order to prove that reflex actions are independent of sensation, it is necessary to prove in the first place that the actions of the spinal cord are independent of sensation; this has never been proved, and has even been placed beyond all evidence.[4]

It would be beside our subject, and out of our power, to follow Mr. Lewes in his long essay upon reflex actions; we can

[1] *Physiology of Common Life*, vol. ii. pp. 96, 97.
[2] P. 167.
[3] P. 183.
[4] P. 226.

only summarize its principal points, and briefly state the reasons upon which he founds his belief that the spinal cord is a centre of sensation.

1. *The opinions of previous physiologists.*—The doctrine which recognises sensitive functions in the spinal cord is not new. Robert Whytt held it. Prochaska considered the spinal cord as forming a considerable portion of the *common sensorium*, and he advanced in proof of it the well-known facts of sensibility manifested by headless animals. J. J. Sue, father of the celebrated novelist, saw that the spinal marrow could, to a certain extent, replace the functions of the brain. Legallois, Wilson, Philipi, Lallemand, and Calmeil arrived at analogous conclusions, under different forms. Thus several facts establishing the sensitive functions of the spinal cord were known, and even a vague conception of their real sense was generally spread abroad, up to the time when the *reflex theory* arose to explain these facts as the result of a mechanical adjustment. But this doctrine has found its opponents. J. W. Arnold has refuted it. Carus said ironically that the word *reflex* was a key to open every lock. Schiff maintains that all the *cerebral* actions, as well as the spinal, are reflex, and depend upon a mechanical arrangement.[1]

If we pass from historical considerations to the facts themselves, we may consider the evidence which they furnish under two aspects, deductively and inductively.

2. *Deductive evidence.*—A resemblance of structure implies a resemblance of property, and the ganglionic structure of the spinal cord being of a nature similar to the ganglionic substance of the brain, there must necessarily be a community of property between the two.

'The only ground for denying that the actions of decapitated animals are determined by sensation, is because the brain, or encephalon, is believed to be the sole seat of sensation. To explain the resemblance between the actions of animals with and without their brains, a theory is invented, which says, These actions are reflex. But in the uninjured animal there is reflex action *plus* the transmission of an impression to the brain, and

[1] *Physiology of Common Life*, vol. ii. p. 231.

it is *this* which produces sensation; in the headless animal we see reflex action, *minus* the transmission to the brain.' [1]

A gentleman once maintained that there were no gold mines except in Mexico and Peru. His assertions were met by showing him an ingot just come from California. Without being in the least disconcerted, he replied: 'This metal, I acknowledge, resembles gold closely; you tell me that it passes for such among the essayers and on the market. I do not dispute that; nevertheless this metal is not gold, but auruminium; it cannot be gold, *because* gold only comes from Mexico and Peru.'

The decapitated animal defends itself instinctively from the suffering that it is caused, disentangles itself, accomplishes several of its ordinary actions; but they say that it does all this without that sensibility which would guide it if it were not decapitated. This is a case of gold being not gold but auruminium.

In the Fiji Islands, when a man is about to die, some hours before his death his body is taken out of his house. Some of these persons during that time can eat and speak. But they are reported dead. To eat, to drink, to speak, are involuntary acts of the body, of the empty shell, as the inhabitants of these islands say, but according to them the soul has left it; the theory of reflex action recalls this eccentric belief to Mr. Lewes's memory.[2]

3. *Inductive evidence.—Spontaneity* and choice are two palpable signs by which we recognise the presence of sensation and of will. Let us then see if decapitated animals manifest these palpable signs. In the first place, let us look for spontaneity. We should remark, says Mr. Lewes, that a decapitated animal is deprived of the various stimuli which he may receive through the eyes, the ears, and the smell, which determine his movements; he therefore necessarily remains in repose if he be not excited by visceral sensations. He affirms that an attentive and repeated examination of decapitated animals furnishes an abundant evidence of spontaneous actions.[3] Let us give an example. Mr. Lewes subjects a strong and healthy triton to various experiments. He touches it, pricks it, burns it with acetic acid, etc. . . . He

[1] *Ibid.* p. 234. [2] P. 236. [3] P. 240.

carefully notes the movements of the animal. Next, having decapitated it, he afresh subjects it to the same experiments; the reactions of the animal are precisely similar; it tries to free itself from the pain, to rub off the acid which is burning it. These experiments, to which Mr. Lewes adds a good number of others, lead him to conclude that the evidence of spontaneity and of choice, of sensibility and of volition, does not admit of mistake, and that, consequently, 'the Spinal Cord is a sentient centre.'[1]

4. *Examination of objections.*—After having examined the reasons and the facts in favour of the sensibility of the spinal marrow, we must see what is the value of the evidence set against it. Let us lay aside the first argument, drawn from the universal prejudice that the brain is the only sensorium, because that is simply begging the question. Let us lay aside a second argument, that several actions take place without awaking a consciousness or a distinct attention, such as breathing, digesting, etc. This argument either proves nothing, or it proves too much. An action may be sensational without producing this secondary feeling, generally called consciousness, and in this sense we might even say that thought is unconscious, much more truly than sensations are so. There remains the striking case of maladies or injuries of the spinal marrow, as a result of which nothing is felt below the wounded part. This is the *cheval de bataille* of the reflex theory.

'But,' says Mr. Lewes, 'when a man has a diseased spinal cord, the seat of injury causes for the time at least a division of the cerebro-spinal axis into two independent centrès. For all purposes of sensation and volition it is the same as if he were cut in half; his nervous mechanism *is* cut in half. How then can any cerebral volition be obeyed by his legs? how can any impression on his legs be felt by his cerebrum? As well might we expect the man whose arm has been amputated to feel the incisions of the scalpel when that limb is conveyed to the dissecting-table, as to feel in his brain impressions made upon parts wholly divorced from organic connexion with the brain.

[1] Lewes, *Physiology of Common Life*, vol. ii. pp. 245-258.

'But, it may be objected, this is the very point urged. The man himself does not feel the impressions on his limbs when his spine has been injured; he is as insensible to them as to the dissection of his amputated arm. Very true. *He* does not feel it. But if the amputated arm were to strike the anatomist who began its dissection, if its fingers were to grasp the scalpel and push it away, or with the thumb to rub off the acid irritating one of the fingers, I do not see how we could refuse to admit that the *arm* felt, although the *man* did not. And this is the case with the extremities of a man whose spine is injured. . . .'[1]

'It is true that the man himself, when interrogated, declares that he feels nothing; the cerebral segment has attached to it organs of speech and expressive features, by which *its* sensations can be communicated to others; whereas the spinal segment has *no* such means of communicating *its* sensations, but those which it *has* it *employs*.'

We here terminate this brief explanation of the opinions of our author upon the current doctrine of reflex actions. Perhaps it seems slightly external to our subject. But the new psychology, which we are endeavouring to exhibit here according to its most eminent representatives, embraces a much wider domain in the reign of facts than the ordinary psychology. It believes that these obscure phenomena into which psychical life has hardly begun to penetrate are in many respects the most curious and the most profitable to study. We have already seen that Mr. Herbert Spencer assigns a place to reflex action in the ascendant evolution of mental life, and the identity of the doctrines of Mr. Bain and Mr. Lewes upon the nature and the seat of the common sensorium must also have been remarked by the reader.

V.

The remainder of the work is devoted to the senses and sensations, to sleep and to the phenomena of heredity.

'"How many senses have you?" inquired the traveller from

[1] *Ibid.* pp. 263-264.

Sirius, in Voltaire's exquisite satire; upon which the inhabitant of Saturn replied, "Seventy-two; but every day we live we lament we have so few."

'The European has been taught to be so well satisfied with five senses, that he is apt to regard as an absurdity the attempt to alter or enlarge that sacred number. . . . "The division of our external senses," says Hutcheson, "into five common classes, is ridiculously imperfect."'[1]

Mr. Lewes thinks that this is a very difficult question, and that only a profound anatomist can determine how many distinct organs we have for the senses. He adopts however the following division:—

1. Sensations proceeding from the system, which comprehend, 1st, organic sensations; 2d, surface sensations, given to us by the skin.

2. Sensations proceeding from the senses properly so called, and which comprehend touch, taste, hearing, smell, and sight.

'Finally, I would call attention to the psychological importance of that vast class of sensations which has been termed Systemic consciousness, and which psychologists and physiologists have so strangely neglected. They have given to the Sense-Sensations an almost exclusive part in the formation of our sensational activity, and often spoken of the mind as a mere educt of the Five Senses. The most striking example of this is seen in Condillac's famous statue, which is endowed successively with each of the five senses, and with each endowment develops gradually a complete mind. Monstrous as this hypothetical statue is, it is only a logical development of the conception that mind is the combination of the five senses.

'In these pages an attempt has been made to show that Mind is the psychical aspect of Life—that it is as much the sum-total of the whole sensitive organism as life is the sum-total of the whole vital organism—that various organs may be set apart for the performance of various special functions, mental as well as vital, but that no one exclusive organ of Mind can be said to exist any more than one exclusive organ

[1] Lewes, *Physiology of Common Life*, vol. ii. p. 273.

of Life can be said to exist. The reader may reject this view, which is submitted to him as the result of many years' meditation, and with that hesitation which naturally belongs to an opinion incapable of proof.'[1]

If we now wish to know (2.) under what principal divisions these psychical phenomena may be grouped, we shall find that the popular classification into *feeling* and *thinking*, or mind and heart, indicate roughly the first groups. We can divide them afterwards into 'six centres, three for each division.' In the first group we may place *sensations*, *perceptions*, and *ideas*, which represent intellectual activity. In the second group we may place sensations, instincts or appetites, and emotions which represent moral activity. Thus sensation forms the starting point of each series. But we have already seen that there are different species of sensations, forming two principal groups,—sensations of the senses, and sensations of the system.

The first have been almost always considered as *impersonal*, because they place us in conscious relation with external objects, with the non-ego. The second (sensations of the muscles and of the viscera) are on the contrary extremely *personal*, because they place us in conscious relation only with that which takes place in our body. The emotions are profoundly rooted in our personality.

The exteriority of the sensations of the senses, and the interiority of the sensations of the system, create a wide line of demarcation between the perceptions which are produced from the one, and the appetites or instincts which are supplied from the other; and the latter in their turn give birth to the various forms of sensibility, known under the names of thought and emotion.

It has never been doubted that our perceptions and ideas have their origin in sensation. The old adage *nihil est in intellectu*, etc., may be equivocal, but it shows this incontestable fact, that sensation is at the foundation of every intellectual operation.

'I feel myself justified, therefore, in considering *ideation* as the form of cerebral sensibility which is determined by the

[1] *Ibid.* p. 344.

cerebral connexions with the ganglia of special Sense. In like manner, *emotion* may be considered as the form of cerebral sensibility which is determined by connexions with the ganglia of visceral sensation.'[1]

And thus the popular opinion which places in the 'bowels' the principal source of the emotions would be justified.

Sleep and hereditary transmission have been the object of such important and such numerous studies in France, that we cannot dwell upon them long, our object being above all to make known the *newest results* of English psychology.

Under the title of 'a new theory of dreaming,' Mr. Lewes explains this phenomenon as follows :—

'If we reflect that the nervous centres must be incessantly called into activity, either through the imperfectly closed channels of the Five Senses, or through the Systemic Senses, and that these centres, once excited, must necessarily play on each other, and if we reflect further, that the sensational and ideational activities thus stimulated operate under very different conditions, and in very different conjunctions, during sleep, we shall be at no loss to understand both the incoherence and the coherence of dreams—the perfect congruity of certain trains of thought amid the most absurd incongruities. The coherence of dreams results from the succession of associated ideas; the train of thought follows very much the course it would follow in waking moments, at least when uncontrolled by reference to external things—as in Reverie. The incoherence results from this train being interrupted or diverted from its course by the suggestion of some other train, either arising by the laws of association or from the stimulus of some new sensation. . . . That Law of Sensibility, which has been so fully expounded in previous pages, whereby every sensation discharges itself either in a reflex action or a reflex feeling (or in both together), and whereby every centre once stimulated must inevitably stimulate some other, gives us the explanation why subjective sensations may arise in sleep or waking, and why they must stimulate cerebral action. . . . In our waking condition we are familiar with what has been styled

[1] Lewes, *Physiology of Common Life*, vol. ii. p. 118.

subjective sensations; that is to say, we *see* objects very vividly where no such objects exist; we *hear* sounds of many kinds where none of their external causes exist; we *taste* flavours in an empty mouth; we *smell* odours where no volatile substance is present; and we *feel* prickings or pains in limbs which have been amputated. These are actual, not imaginary sensations. . . . And as it is the inevitable tendency of our nature to connect every sensation with an external cause—to project it outside of us, so to speak,—we should never think of doubting that every one of these subjective sensations had a corresponding object, did not the suggestions of some *other* sense control this idea. A man feels prickings in his amputated fingers, but he sees that the fingers are not there, and consequently he knows that his sensation is deceptive. He smells the horrible stench of a sewer long after he has passed out of the reach of its volatile gases. He tastes the bitter flavour long after the bitter substance has been removed. But the sensations require constant confrontation with the reports of other senses, otherwise they would be credited as sensations, produced by actual objects. . . . If I sit in my study, and my thoughts wander to Bagdad or Bussora, the continual presence of my books, chairs, microscope, engravings, etc., infallibly brings me back again before long, and prevents my believing myself to be in the East. . . . In the state of cerebral excitement named Hallucination this confrontation is *disregarded;* in the state of cerebral isolation named Dreaming this confrontation is *impossible.* The first condition is one in which the cerebral activity completely domineers over the excitations from without; the second condition is one in which the cerebral activity, though feeble, is entirely isolated from external excitations,—thus, in both cases, the cerebral reflexes are undisturbed, uncontrolled by reflexes from Sense.' [1]

This doctrine, which agrees with that of the highest French writers, leads Mr. Lewes to answer the question, 'Do we always dream?' in the affirmative. Since the nervous centres are constantly excited by internal or external stimuli, and since this activity gives birth to a succession of ideas, induction leads us

[1] *Ibid.* pp. 370-372.

to conclude that we always think, though we may lose the remembrance of our thoughts.

The chapter devoted to inheritance may perhaps seem rather meagre. But in a *Physiology of Common Life*, a subject still so full of obscurity and important problems could hardly be touched upon. Mr. Lewes, who is very severe upon the most important work which has appeared upon this question in France, recognises its importance and its difficulties. In our opinion, the studies upon hereditary transmission, considered from a psychological point of view, are destined one day to play a great part, when science shall have completely entered upon that path which it is now only attempting. We have seen that Mr. Herbert Spencer and Mr. Lewes[2] demand from heredity an entirely novel solution of the origin of ideas. But those who may refuse to follow them to that point, and who admit that heredity may decide one of the most important and the most controverted questions of philosophy, even they may be obliged to agree that a large number of psychological facts have their source in hereditary transmission. As I think there is no spiritualist who would deny the influence of the organism upon our tendencies, our passions, our ideas, and our aptitudes, and as organism is inherited, it is a matter of course that the influence of heredity must make itself felt at least mediately upon our psychological constitution. Common experience made this discovery a long time ago; it remains for science to define and explain it. Certain monstrosities in the moral order, certain precocious depravities and extraordinary tastes, appear explicable only by heredity. Thus we, together with Mr. Lewes, may be astonished to find one of the most celebrated philosophical historians of England, Mr. Buckle, maintaining that in the quoted cases there is nothing but empirical coincidences, of which we may make what we can.[3]

---

[1] Prosper Lucas, *Traité physiologique et philosophique de l'hérédité naturelle.* Mr. Lewes calls it 'an extensive but uncritical work.' See also Moreau de Tours, *Psychologie morbide.*

[2] See on this point Moreau de Tours, p. 110 *et seq.*

[3] Buckle, *Civilisation in England*, vol. i. chap. ii.

The opponents of heredity quote facts which appear to them conclusive: the frequent absence of resemblance between parents and children, and the frequent mediocrity of the descendants of men of genius. Pericles produced a Paralus and a Xanthippus. The austere Aristides produced the infamous Lysimachus. The powerful-minded Thucydides was represented by an idiotic Milesias and a stupid Stephanos. Was the great soul of Oliver Cromwell to be found in his son Richard? What were the inheritors of Henry IV. and of Peter the Great? What were the children of Shakespeare and the daughters of Milton? What was the only son of Addison? An idiot.

The supporters of heredity retort upon this argument by saying, What is the meaning of these proverbial phrases, 'the wit of the Mortemarts,' 'the wit of the Sheridans,' if one does not believe in transmission? Torquato Tasso was the son of a celebrated father. We have the two Herschels, the two Colmans, the Kemble family, and the Coleridges. Finally, the most striking example is that of Sebastian Bach, whose musical genius was found, in an inferior degree, among three hundred Bachs, the children of very various mothers.

The question of heredity is still more complicated when we endeavour to find out if it be true, as certain authors have advanced, that the father gives the organs of animal life, and the mother the organs of vegetable life.

Mr. Lewes, who rejects this opinion, maintains the law of heredity, remarking that it is the *rule*, but that we must take account of the disturbing causes which explain the exceptions. Physiology tells us that always and necessarily the race inherits the organization of the parents; and that if the organization be inherited, so are the tendencies and aptitudes. Our experience of heredity is so constant that nothing can seem to us more incredible than that negro parents should give birth to a child with the features of a European, or that two sheep should produce a goat. But while there is a constancy in the transmission of *general* characteristics, there is a considerable variation in the transmission of individual peculiarities.

A child may inherit from both parents, or from one only. We do not expect two scrofulous parents to have healthy children, irascible parents to produce gentle natures, or two idiots to give birth to a man of genius. But if the aptitudes of the parents are different, if the father have a talent for music and the mother have not, and if two children be born of their marriage, it is very possible that one may be musical like the father, the other insensible to music like the mother, or that both may be musicians, or neither. We should not have exaggerated the bearings of the objections, if we had remarked that the influence of one of the two parents may destroy that of the other, and that, consequently, the apparent exceptions to the law of heredity on the contrary confirm that law.

This question leads to many others, says Mr. Lewes, upon which he declines to enter, and he sends us to Mr. Herbert Spencer for everything which concerns the hereditary transmission of intellectual or moral development. It is perhaps appropriate to remark that he brings forward a collection of facts which may serve as proofs in favour of the law of evolution, and of the continuity of natural phenomena.

MR. SAMUEL BAILEY.

MR. SAMUEL BAILEY would merit a separate essay in consequence of the number of his philosophical publications, many of which date very far back,[1] if we had proposed to ourselves anything but a short sketch of English contemporary psychology. It is not possible to classify him. As a declared partisan of experience, he forms a sort of transition between the Scotch school and the psychologists of whom we have just spoken. In his clear, exact, precise, and rather dry manner, he differs totally from the descriptive psychology of which Mr. Bain has offered us the most complete type; he reminds us rather of the eighteenth century, and the somewhat meagre lucidity of Condillac and of Destutt de Tracy. He is, like them, more a logician than a psychologist, and his verbal analysis does not penetrate sufficiently far into a science 'so buried in facts' as psychology. With a mind penetrating rather than extensive, greedy for clearness, he pursues metaphors with intense enmity; he hates all vague phraseology, all rhetorical arguments which usurp the place of science, and explanations which pretend to resolve its difficulties; he demands for psychology a language as precise as possible. He is nevertheless not so devoted to algebra but that he will yield to the attractions of eloquence in its proper place, and he has revindicated the rights of science in language so firm and so lofty that we must quote it:—

'What! shall thousands of scientific men, with triumphant acclaim, employ themselves in almost infinitesimal physical investigations; in searching into the atomic composition and

[1] His principal works are: *Letters on the Philosophy of the Human Mind*, 3 vols. 1855-1863; *The Theory of Reasoning; A Review of Berkeley's Theory of Vision*, etc.

microscopic structure of bodies; in exploring the innumerable forms of animal and vegetable life which are invisible to the unassisted sight; in discovering planets that have for ages rolled unmarked through their obscure orbits; in condensing with telescopic power into suns and systems what was recently regarded (so to speak) as the elemental vapour of stars; in throwing into arithmetical expression inconceivably rapid vibrations, in the apparently steady ray that even the strongest wind cannot shake; thus bringing into view, from the distant and the diminutive, the most recondite parts of the material universe; and shall the exact analysis of the phenomena of consciousness, the discrimination of differences in feeling and intellectual operations, however fine and minute, the vigilant detection, the subtlest concatenations of thought, the firm yet delicate grasp of mental analogies which elude the rough and careless handling of common observation, the nice appreciation of language, and all its changing hues and latent expedients; the decomposition of the processes of reasoning and laying bare the foundations of evidence,—shall these, I say, be stigmatized as an over-exercise of acuteness, a waste of analytic power, a useless splitting of hairs, and a worthless weaving of cobwebs? Amidst the honours lavished on investigations into the most secluded recesses of the material world, are we to be told that the close and minute and discriminating examination of our own mental nature is a vain and superfluous labour, leading to no beneficial or important issue?

'Believe it not: rest assured that here untiring investigation, minute analysis, close scrutiny, careful discrimination of things apt to be confounded, scrupulous accuracy in pursuing processes, and precision in recording results, are as apposite, as fruitful, as important, as indispensable, as dignified if you will, as they are (I say it without disparagement) in tracking invisible stars, calculating the millions of imperceptible undulations in a ray of light, weighing the atoms of chemical elements, peering into the cells of organic structures, studying the anatomy of mites and midges, and even searching into the specific characters and peculiar habits of molluscs and animalcules.'[1]

---

[1] Bailey, *Letters on the Philosophy of the Human Mind*, vol. ii. p. 271.

Mr. Bailey recognises only one method for the facts of consciousness,—that of the sciences of matter.[1] He nevertheless complains in another place[2] of the invasions of physiology; he even maintains that the knowledge of physiological facts does not clear up that of psychological facts; that even if we knew the material conditions of memory and of perception, etc., we should still remain ignorant of what it is. The science of acoustics, he says, is useless in producing good music; in the same way the knowledge of physical or mechanical means which engender or influence psychological phenomena does not enable us to penetrate their nature.

It is not very easy to reconcile these assertions. In all cases the reasoning of the author, incontestable from the point of view of first causes, appears to be deficient in solidity so far as second causes are concerned. Now the proper object of every science which separates itself from metaphysics is the research of these immediate and approximate causes. Let us add that the progress of science seems to contradict the author.

We have seen in the Introduction,[3] with what vivacity he combats the doctrine of faculties; so also he classes facts of conscience only cursorily and without attaching much importance to matter.[4] The following is his classification of the phenomena of consciousness:—

1st Order.—Sensitive affections.
Genus 1. Corporeal sensations.
Genus 2. Mental emotions.

2d Order.—Intellectual operations.
Genus 1. Perceiving.
Genus 2. Conceiving.
Genus 3. Believing (judging).
Genus 4. Reasoning.

3d Order.—Will.
Genus 1. Relative to the body.
Genus 2. Relative to the mind.

We shall not follow him into detail, which indeed is not very

[1] Vol. i. Letter 2. [2] Vol. ii. Letter 16. [3] § 8. [4] Vol. i. Letter 6.

exact, because the author had no intention of producing a complete methodical treatise, but merely meant to indicate the questions upon which he has something to say. We shall limit ourselves to these two points,—exterior perception and will. On the first of these he writes almost like Reid; on the second, he goes beyond his contemporaries.

Let us briefly recall the explanation of external perception given by the Scotch school. Properly speaking, that school does not explain it; it is plain to us that we perceive the external world, because we have the faculty of perceiving it. This is an irreducible fact; more than that, we perceive things as they are. I see a cat, I touch a glass. According to Reid and his disciples, the cat is in itself such as I see it, the glass such as I touch it.

Supposing that neither I nor my fellows were to see the cat or touch the glass, these objects would nevertheless remain such as I saw them, with their proper qualities of form, of resistance, etc. To maintain the contrary is, according to them, to introduce scepticism. According to the contemporary school, perception is the common act of the subject and of the object; my perception is my work; I put into the external world at least as much as I receive from it. There is some external thing which I call a cat or a glass, but nothing proves that they correspond with the idea which I form of them; it is even probable that they differ very much from it. Perception being a relation, there is nothing astonishing in its varying with the two terms, and as they do; this is a quite natural fact, there is no shadow of scepticism in maintaining it.

Mr. Bailey agrees with Reid, or differs from him only by a shade. 'I differ,' he says, 'from the Scotch school, because it admits an irresistible *belief* in an external world, and I admit a *knowledge*.' The criticism which he makes of Berkeley does not appear to me to go to the root of the question; that on Kant is inexact, if we are to believe that he reproaches him with having regarded perception as an analysable fact, in place of seeing in it a fact of indecomposable consciousness;[1] now it is precisely herein that we find progress.

[1] Vol. ii. Letter 2.

The celebrated opinion of the author upon sight hangs upon his doctrine of passive and immediate perception. In England the name of the Berkeleyan theory of vision is given to that which distinguishes the natural perceptions of sight (light, colours, etc.) from the acquired perceptions (distance, movement, etc.), the latter being matter of induction, and not of direct perception. The eye gives us only the apparent figure, position, and size; touch alone gives us the real figure, position, and size. But as the differences in the reality are usually accompanied by differences in appearances, the mind infers the real from the apparent. Mr. Bailey has strongly opposed this theory in order to expressly admit a direct and immediate vision. Although the entirety of his arguments does not appear naturally to produce conviction, we must acknowledge that he has brought forward facts very difficult to explain by an opinion contrary to his own. Among children, he says, sight is developed before touch. He maintains most positively that young animals see *as soon as they are born.* The duckling runs to the water on coming out of its egg, the little crocodile, hatched without being incubated by its parents, also runs to the water, or bites a stick if it be presented to it. In short, he denies that the famous blind man operated upon by Cheselden, who said that every object touched his eyes, furnishes an argument against this doctrine.

Mr. John Stuart Mill, who has discussed this theory,[1] comes to the conclusion that the arguments of Mr. Bailey have thrown no new light whatever upon the question, and have left the theory of Berkeley such as it was before. It seems difficult to be of any other opinion.

We have said that in his essay upon the Will, Mr. Bailey appears no longer as a dissenter from the Scotch school, but as a precursor of his contemporaries.

'If,' he says, 'psychology studied the affections and operations instead of the faculties, and regulated its language in consequence, it seems as if we should be rid of a number of embarrassing

[1] In an article in the *Westminster Review*, reprinted in the *Dissertations and Discussions*, vol. ii. p. 84.

questions, among which we must number the controversy upon the freedom of the will, which is literally the liberty of a non-existence.'[1]

The question, when closely examined, reduces itself, according to the author, to demanding, not if we are free to act in certain cases as we please—for nobody, I think, will dispute that we are—but if there are regular causes which place us in a condition to wish to act as we do act. Now this is a question of fact, and examples abound which show that, in many cases, the circumstances being determined, our acts may be predicted, and that there are regular causes which determine us to will, as there are physical causes which produce the different material facts.

Forty-three years ago (in 1826) Mr. Bailey published a dissertation upon the *Uniformity of Causality*, with the object of bringing voluntary phenomena under the common law. This is the subject of the curious essay which he has reproduced in his *Letters upon the Philosophy of the Human Mind*.[2]

It is surprising that the connexion of motives and actions could have been theoretically regarded as doubtful. Practical life depends entirely upon this principle, which is speculatively rejected. The speeches of an orator, the treatises of an author, the prescriptions of the legislator, the manœuvres of the general, and the decrees of the monarch, all equally resemble it. A general who commands an army and directs a battle counts on the obedience of his officers and of his soldiers; is he less confident in the result of his orders, than when he accomplishes some material act, such as drawing his sword or sealing a despatch?

Commercial transactions of every kind attest the same sort of confidence. A merchant draws upon his banker a bill payable on such a day; the bill circulates, and the drawer does not doubt about the final volition which will cause the banker to pay it.

Political economy offers us still more numerous examples. It is in a great measure an inquiry into the action of motives, and it is founded upon this principle, that human volitions are under the influence of precise and determinable causes—the rise and

[1] *Letters, etc.*, vol. ii. chap. xv. [2] *Ibid.* p. 166.

the fall of stocks, the fluctuations in exchange, the variations between supply and demand, the return of paper to the banker after an excessive issue, the disappearance of specie,—all the facts of this nature result from definite causes which act with regularity.

Thus, when we lay aside vague language upon the liberty of the will—which, as we have said, is the liberty of something which does not exist—the true question presents itself under a form that no longer allows room for divergence of opinion.

But after all, it may be objected, when we thus predict or calculate the voluntary actions of our fellows, we only regard their production as *probable;* there is no necessity in this case, they may produce themselves or not produce themselves; there is a sort of latitude which prevails, and does not permit us to suppose that these actions depend upon regular and invariable causes.

To this Mr. Bailey replies, as may be expected, that it is our ignorance of all the causes in action which render voluntary events only probable to us; if we knew them *all*, there would be a perfect certainty—the variations in probability are entirely due to variations in the state of our own knowledge; and this is equally true as regards physical and moral phenomena.

In short, there are two incontestable facts, says Mr. Bailey, '*1st*, That voluntary actions are not only constantly predicted, but purposely produced by the motives which human beings present to each other; and *2dly*, That in performing such actions we nevertheless do as we please: we act with perfect freedom; an option is presented to us, and we choose to do the actions rather than not to do them. Mankind, however, seem not to understand the relation in which these two facts (both incontrovertibly true) stand to each other. It is generally apprehended that there is some discrepancy, or inconsistency, or incompatibility between them, but for my own part I see none; and if both are real facts, they cannot, I scarcely need say, be discordant or incompatible one with the other.

'Why should there seem to be any incompatibility between your doing as you please, and my predicting what you will do, and even causing you to please to do it?

'My purposely producing in you the state of pleasing to do a thing—which implies, of course, my foreseeing the action—is not compelling you to do it, but the reverse. . . . The same human actions may be willed with perfect freedom by the performer, and predicted with perfect confidence by the looker-on.[1]'

This theory of the Will agrees so perfectly with that of the contemporary school, that Mr. Bain has transcribed several pages of it in his great work on *The Emotions and the Will.* If we add that in his special treatise on *The Theory of Reasoning* (2d edition) Mr. Bailey approaches Mr. John Stuart Mill in several respects, we may conclude that his psychology bears the mark of an epoch of transition, being however nearer to the future than to the past.

[1] Bailey's *Philosophy of the Human Mind*, vol. ii. p. 172.

CONCLUSION.

In perusing the preceding pages the reader must have been struck by two things—the agreement of the philosophers whom we have passed in review, upon the chief questions of psychology, and their disagreement upon certain secondary points. If, then, laying aside personal opinions and disputed solutions, we bring forward the points on which they are agreed, we shall thus procure a summary of the labours and results of the experimental school of psychology. We shall endeavour to reduce them to certain fundamental propositions, and to exhibit them in methodical order.

The object of psychology is the facts of consciousness, their laws, their immediate conditions and causes. Psychology proposes to itself either to analyse complex facts, or simply to show how they are formed by a synthesis of simple facts.

Psychology deals with phenomena only. It does not know what the soul or the mind is. That is a question out of its reach, which it refers to metaphysics. It is neither spiritualist nor materialist: it is experimental.

Its method is double: it studies psychological phenomena, subjectively, by means of consciousness, memory, and reasoning; objectively, by means of the facts, signs, opinions, and actions which interpret them. Psychology does not study the facts of consciousness simply in the adult state; it endeavours to discover and to follow their development. It contains a morphology.

It also has recourse to the comparative method. It does not disdain the humblest manifestations of psychical life, remembering that nothing has been more useful to comparative physiology than the study of minute organisms.

Consciousness is the word which expresses, in the most general way, the various manifestations of psychological life. It consists of a continuous current of sensations, ideas, volitions, feelings, etc.

The first fundamental fact—that which constitutes conscious ness—is the perception of a difference.

The second fundamental fact—that which continues consciousness—is the perception of a resemblance.

The only primitive and irreducible psychological fact is SENSATION.

Our various sensations may be classed in seven principal groups:—1. muscular sensations; they inform us of the nature and the degree of effort of our muscles; these sensations, of a very general character, and which come first in chronological order, form a separate kind; 2. organic sensations, which reveal to us the good or bad state of our internal organs; 3. taste; 4. smell; 5. touch; 6. hearing; 7. sight. The sensations of this last group are the most elevated and the most important; they only, with the sensations of hearing, have an æsthetic character.

The most general law which regulates psychological phenomena is the LAW OF ASSOCIATION. In its comprehensive character it is comparable to the law of attraction in the physical world. Association takes place either between facts of the same nature, association of sensations among themselves, of ideas among themselves, of volitions among themselves, etc., or between facts of a different nature: associations of sentiments with ideas, of sensations with volitions, etc.

The two principal facts which serve as the basis of association are resemblance and contiguity.

Association produces either successions or simultaneities.

The objects which we call external (a man, a house) are aggregates formed by simultaneous association. How do we perceive them?

Perception of the external world is not a purely passive state, in which the mind would resemble a mirror reflecting objects in a dull dead way. It is the common work of the sentient subject and the object felt.

Outside of us, and independently of our perceptions, there exists a material world, which condemns idealism. It is conformable to the data of the sciences to believe that this material world, taken in itself, does not resemble the perceptions of it which we have; this condemns vulgar realism.

Our perceptions are then internal conditions which *correspond* to external existences, but which do not resemble them. When I perceive an oak, my perception corresponds to a particular external object, *but it is not the copy of it.*

Perception is a product which differs from its two factors (subject, object) as water differs from oxygen and hydrogen.

The correlatives 'subject' and 'object' are the two least inexact term by which the fundamental antithesis of knowledge and of existence can be expressed. Matter and Spirit, external and internal, are the popular synonyms for them, but lend themselves more to an equivocal interpretation.

The fundamental irreducible experience which gives the notion of externality is resistance.

The facts of consciousness having the property of lasting, of leaving their trace, and reappearing, thence result memory and imagination. Association is the groundwork of these phenomena, although it does not entirely explain them.

The question of belief or affirmation remains stated, but not solved, by common consent. Some, Mr. James Mill and Mr. Herbert Spencer, explain it by an indissoluble association; others, Mr. A. Bain and Mr. John Stuart Mill, discern in it a form of our active nature, that is to say, of our will.

Reasoning, under its primitive form, goes from the particular to the particular. By the accumulation of particular truths general propositions are formed; and then reasoning is called induction. The general proposition is a simplification, a *memorandum*, a register of notes grouped under a single formula. It serves as a starting-point for deduction.

In short, the process of reasoning, taken in its totality, sets out from the particular and issues in the particular, by traversing the general, which is a collection of particulars.

Syllogism is so little the type of reasoning that it is, properly speaking, only a process of verification.

On the origin of ideas the school with which we are now occupied does not go with the sensualists (Locke, Condillac), nor with the rationalists (Descartes, Leibnitz), nor with the criticists (Kant).

It says to the sensualists: Your hypothesis of *tabula rasa* is false, contrary to facts. It forgets that in the act of knowing the mind gives out at least as much as it receives. Whence comes it that two men, having had the same education, the same impressions, the same surroundings, are sometimes entirely different in everything? This fact alone checkmates your theory.

It says to the rationalists: You have correctly perceived that in the act of knowing there is something which comes from within, but your hypothesis of ideas innate, or virtually so, is untenable. What is an idea in a latent state, an idea which one does not think? Besides, if these ideas are primitive and ready-made in intelligence, why are they produced so late, instead of being the first in chronological order?

It says to the partisans of Kant: Your transcendental doctrine of the *forms* of thought, though sound in logic, is bad in psychology. It is quite true that these forms are at the bottom of our consciousness, since we can draw them from it, but how do they come there? This is a question of genesis which you do not examine, because you always reason upon the hypothesis of an adult and completely constituted mind.

These solutions set aside, the school gives its own. It recognises in mind a proper spontaneity which elaborates and transforms materials which come from without; but this spontaneity has its root in the organism, especially in the constitution of the nervous system. Several peculiarities are explained by the transmission of the hereditary system.

In short, this solution is the physiological transformation of the Kantian doctrine of the forms of thought.

The two most general relations conceived by human intelligence are those of succession and simultaneousness.

The relation of succession is the more simple: it constitutes the fact of primitive consciousness.

The relation of simultaneousness is a duplication of the preceding: it consists in a succession which can be reversed, that is to say, thought indifferently, at first in a certain order, afterwards in the contrary order, so that one goes from A to C and from C to A equally.

An important notion attaches itself to the relation of succession, that of cause, or, as the school has it, of sequence, of which it is only a particular case.

Causality is constant and uniform succession. The invariable antecedent is called cause, the invariable consequent is called effect. The hypothesis of an efficacious power, forming a mysterious link between them, is an imaginary complication, in so far as we hold to phenomenal causes, as the school intends us to do.

The *whole* of the relations of succession is Time.

The *whole* of the relations of simultaneousness is Space.

The character of infinitude proper to these two ideas of time and space, that is to say, the impossibility to our intelligence of conceiving them to have limits, is explained by the law of association. We cannot conceive a moment of time without that idea awakening irresistibly in us the idea of a moment to follow, and then of another. It is the same with space. Association is irresistible, because the experimental data which serve as its basis have always been without exception.

The study of the affective phenomena,—emotions and feelings,—is very incomplete in the English experimental school. The following small number of points are those on which its members are agreed :—

The two fundamental facts are pleasure and pain.

The emotions or passions are of two kinds, simple and compound.

There is no agreement upon either the name or the number of the simple emotions.

All manifestations of æsthetics or moral feeling are unanimously ranged among the compound emotions.

The will has its source in the activity either of the organism or of the instincts, appetites, and passions.

Under its adult form, will is a directing, regulating power. But before it reaches that condition it goes through a period of gropings, of efforts, and of conquest. Voluntary power, though simple in appearance, is a complicated machine, made of self-adjusting pieces.

Voluntary facts are subject to the universal law of causality.

Are they our own work? No doubt, since they are the result of the totality of the states of consciousness which precede the resolution, and that this *whole* of states of consciousness is our *ego*.

Are they free? This question is artificial, unintelligible, consequently insoluble. The word *liberty* must be expunged from psychology, as an inexact term which serves only to create confusion, and the word *aptitude* must be substituted for it.

Psychology thus conceived can and *ought* to be a distinct science. But it neither can nor ought to isolate itself from the kindred sciences, especially physiology, and, strictly speaking, there is no line of demarcation to be traced between them, because certain phenomena are common to both.

If psychology has its basis in physiology, it serves in its turn as a basis for the moral, social, and political sciences.

Therefore it ought to complete itself by a practical study, by ethology, or the science of the formation of characters, whether individual or national.

Such is the summary of the fundamental solutions of associative psychology. Our aim was to explain them: it is fulfilled. We leave the task of estimating their value to those who have something further and better to say.

THE END.

LIST OF AUTHORS AND SUBJECTS OF THEIR BOOKS,

TO BE PUBLISHED IN THE

INTERNATIONAL SCIENTIFIC SERIES.

Rev. M. J. BERKELEY, M. A., F. L. S., and M. COOKE, M. A., LL. D., *Fungi; their Nature, Influences, and Uses.*

Prof. OSCAR SCHMIDT (University of Strasburg), *The Theory of Descent and Darwinism.*

Prof. VOGEL (Polytechnic Academy of Berlin), *The Chemical Effects of Light.*

Prof. W. KINGDON CLIFFORD, M. A., *The First Principles of the Exact Sciences explained to the Non-mathematical.*

Prof. T. H. HUXLEY, LL. D., F. R. S., *Bodily Motion and Consciousness.*

Dr. W. B. CARPENTER, LL. D., F. R. S., *The Physical Geography of the Sea.*

Prof. WILLIAM ODLING, F. R. S., *The Old Chemistry from the New Stand-point.*

Prof. SHELDON AMOS, *The Science of Law.*

W. LAUDER LINDSAY, M. D., F. R. S. E., *Mind in the Lower Animals.*

Sir JOHN LUBBOCK, Bart., F. R. S., *The Antiquity of Man.*

Prof. W. T. THISELTON DYER, B. A., B. S. C., *Form and Habit in Flowering Plants.*

Prof. MICHAEL FOSTER, M. D., *Protoplasm and the Cell Theory.*

Prof. W. STANLEY JEVONS, *The Logic of Statistics.*

Dr. H. CHARLTON BASTIAN, M.D., F.R.S., *The Brain as an Organ of Mind.*

Prof. A. C. RAMSAY, LL. D., F. R. S., *Earth Sculpture; Hills, Valleys, Mountains, Plains, Rivers, Lakes; how they were Produced, and how they have been Destroyed.*

Prof. RUDOLPH VIRCHOW (University of Berlin), *Morbid Physiological Action.*

Prof. CLAUDE BERNARD (College of France), *Physical and Metaphysical Phenomena of Life.*

Prof. A. QUETELET (Brussels Academy of Sciences), *Social Physics.*

Prof. H. SAINTE-CLAIRE DEVILLE, *An Introduction to General Chemistry.*

Prof. WURTZ, *Atoms and the Atomic Theory.*

Prof. DE QUATREFAGES, *The Negro Races.*

Prof. LACAZE-DUTHIERS, *Zoology since Cuvier.*

Prof. BERTHELOT, *Chemical Synthesis.*

Prof. J. ROSENTHAL, *General Physiology of Muscles and Nerves.*

Prof. C. A. YOUNG (Dartmouth College), *The Sun.*

Prof. JAMES D. DANA, M. A., LL. D., *On Cephalization; or, Head-Characters in the Gradation and Progress of Life.*

Prof. S. W. JOHNSON, M. A., *On the Nutrition of Plants.*

Prof. AUSTIN FLINT, Jr., M. D., *The Nervous System and its Relation to the Bodily Functions.*

Prof. W. D. WHITNEY, *Modern Linguistic Science.*

Prof. BERNSTEIN (University of Halle), *Physiology of the Senses.*

Prof. FERDINAND COHN (University of Breslau), *Thallotyphes (Algae Lichens Fungi).*

Prof. HERMANN (University of Zurich), *Respiration.*

Prof. LEUCKART (University of Leipsic), *Outlines of Animal Organization.*

Prof. LIEBREICH (University of Berlin), *Outlines of Toxicology.*

Prof. KUNDT (University of Strasburg), *On Sound.*

Prof. LONMEL (University of Erlangen), *Optics.*

Prof. REES (University of Erlangen), *On Parasitic Plants.*

Prof. STEINTHAL (University of Berlin), *Outlines of the Science of Language.*

Opinions of the Press on the "International Scientific Series."

I.

Tyndall's Forms of Water.

1 vol., 12mo. Cloth. Illustrated. . . . . Price, $1.50.

"In the volume now published, Professor Tyndall has presented a noble illustration of the acuteness and subtlety of his intellectual powers, the scope and insight of his scientific vision, his singular command of the appropriate language of exposition, and the peculiar vivacity and grace with which he unfolds the results of intricate scientific research."—*N. Y. Tribune.*

"The 'Forms of Water,' by Professor Tyndall, is an interesting and instructive little volume, admirably printed and illustrated. Prepared expressly for this series, it is in some measure a guarantee of the excellence of the volumes that will follow, and an indication that the publishers will spare no pains to include in the series the freshest investigations of the best scientific minds."—*Boston Journal.*

"This series is admirably commenced by this little volume from the pen of Prof. Tyndall. A perfect master of his subject, he presents in a style easy and attractive his methods of investigation, and the results obtained, and gives to the reader a clear conception of all the wondrous transformations to which water is subjected."—*Churchman.*

II.

Bagehot's Physics and Politics.

1 vol., 12mo. Price, $1.50.

"If the 'International Scientific Series' proceeds as it has begun, it will more than fulfil the promise given to the reading public in its prospectus. The first volume, by Professor Tyndall, was a model of lucid and attractive scientific exposition; and now we have a second, by Mr. Walter Bagehot, which is not only very lucid and charming, but also original and suggestive in the highest degree. Nowhere since the publication of Sir Henry Maine's 'Ancient Law,' have we seen so many fruitful thoughts suggested in the course of a couple of hundred pages. . . . To do justice to Mr. Bagehot's fertile book, would require a long article. With the best of intentions, we are conscious of having given but a sorry account of it in these brief paragraphs. But we hope we have said enough to commend it to the attention of the thoughtful reader."—Prof. JOHN FISKE, in the *Atlantic Monthly.*

"Mr. Bagehot's style is clear and vigorous. We refrain from giving a fuller account of these suggestive essays, only because we are sure that our readers will find it worth their while to peruse the book for themselves; and we sincerely hope that the forthcoming parts of the 'International Scientific Series' will be as interesting."—*Athenæum.*

"Mr. Bagehot discusses an immense variety of topics connected with the progress of societies and nations, and the development of their distinctive peculiarities; and his book shows an abundance of ingenious and original thought."—ALFRED RUSSELL WALLACE, in *Nature.*

III.

Foods.

By Dr. EDWARD SMITH.

1 vol., 12mo. Cloth. Illustrated. . . . . Price, $1.75.

In making up THE INTERNATIONAL SCIENTIFIC SERIES, Dr. Edward Smith was selected as the ablest man in England to treat the important subject of Foods. His services were secured for the undertaking, and the little treatise he has produced shows that the choice of a writer on this subject was most fortunate, as the book is unquestionably the clearest and best-digested compend of the Science of Foods that has appeared in our language.

"The book contains a series of diagrams, displaying the effects of sleep and meals on pulsation and respiration, and of various kinds of food on respiration, which, as the results of Dr. Smith's own experiments, possess a very high value. We have not far to go in this work for occasions of favorable criticism; they occur throughout, but are perhaps most apparent in those parts of the subject with which Dr. Smith's name is especially linked."—*London Examiner.*

"The union of scientific and popular treatment in the composition of this work will afford an attraction to many readers who would have been indifferent to purely theoretical details. . . . Still his work abounds in information, much of which is of great value, and a part of which could not easily be obtained from other sources. Its interest is decidedly enhanced for students who demand both clearness and exactness of statement, by the profusion of well-executed woodcuts, diagrams, and tables, which accompany the volume. . . . The suggestions of the author on the use of tea and coffee, and of the various forms of alcohol, although perhaps not strictly of a novel character, are highly instructive, and form an interesting portion of the volume."—*N. Y. Tribune.*

IV.

Body and Mind.

THE THEORIES OF THEIR RELATION.

By ALEXANDER BAIN, LL. D.

1 vol., 12mo. Cloth. . . . . Price, $1.50.

PROFESSOR BAIN is the author of two well-known standard works upon the Science of Mind—"The Senses and the Intellect," and "The Emotions and the Will." He is one of the highest living authorities in the school which holds that there can be no sound or valid psychology unless the mind and the body are studied, as they exist, together.

"It contains a forcible statement of the connection between mind and body, studying their subtile interworkings by the light of the most recent physiological investigations. The summary in Chapter V., of the investigations of Dr. Lionel Beale of the embodiment of the intellectual functions in the cerebral system, will be found the freshest and most interesting part of his book. Prof. Bain's own theory of the connection between the mental and the bodily part in man is stated by himself to be as follows: There is 'one substance, with two sets of properties, two sides, the physical and the mental—a *double-faced unity.*' While, in the strongest manner, asserting the union of mind with brain, he yet denies 'the association of union *in place,*' but asserts the union of close succession in time,' holding that 'the same being is, by alternate fits, under extended and under unextended consciousness." '—*Christian Register.*

D. APPLETON & CO., Publishers, 549 & 551 Broadway, N. Y.

V.

The Study of Sociology.

By HERBERT SPENCER.

1 vol., 12mo. Cloth. . . . . Price, $1.50.

"The philosopher whose distinguished name gives weight and influence to this volume, has given in its pages some of the finest specimens of reasoning in all its forms and departments. There is a fascination in his array of facts, incidents, and opinions, which draws on the reader to ascertain his conclusions. The coolness and calmness of his treatment of acknowledged difficulties and grave objections to his theories win for him a close attention and sustained effort, on the part of the reader, to comprehend, follow, grasp, and appropriate his principles. This book, independently of its bearing upon sociology, is valuable as lucidly showing what those essential characteristics are which entitle any arrangement and connection of facts and deductions to be called a *science*."—*Episcopalian.*

"This work compels admiration by the evidence which it gives of immense research, study, and observation, and is, withal, written in a popular and very pleasing style. It is a fascinating work, as well as one of deep practical thought."—*Bost. Post.*

"Herbert Spencer is unquestionably the foremost living thinker in the psychological and sociological fields, and this volume is an important contribution to the science of which it treats. . . . It will prove more popular than any of its author's other creations, for it is more plainly addressed to the people and has a more practical and less speculative cast. It will require thought, but it is well worth thinking about."—*Albany Evening Journal.*

VI.

The New Chemistry.

By JOSIAH P. COOKE, JR.,

Erving Professor of Chemistry and Mineralogy in Harvard University.

1 vol., 12mo. Cloth. . . . . Price, $2.00.

"The book of Prof. Cooke is a model of the modern popular science work. It has just the due proportion of fact, philosophy, and true romance, to make it a fascinating companion, either for the voyage or the study."—*Daily Graphic.*

"This admirable monograph, by the distinguished Erving Professor of Chemistry in Harvard University, is the first American contribution to 'The International Scientific Series,' and a more attractive piece of work in the way of popular exposition upon a difficult subject has not appeared in a long time. It not only well sustains the character of the volumes with which it is associated, but its reproduction in European countries will be an honor to American science."—*New York Tribune.*

"All the chemists in the country will enjoy its perusal, and many will seize upon it as a thing longed for. For, to those advanced students who have kept well abreast of the chemical tide, it offers a calm philosophy. To those others, youngest of the class, who have emerged from the schools since new methods have prevailed, it presents a generalization, drawing to its use all the data, the relations of which the newly-fledged fact-seeker may but dimly perceive without its aid. . . . To the old chemists, Prof. Cooke's treatise is like a message from beyond the mountain. They have heard of changes in the science; the clash of the battle of old and new theories has stirred them from afar. The tidings, too, had come that the old had given way; and little more than this they knew. . . . Prof. Cooke's 'New Chemistry' must do wide service in bringing to close sight the little known and the longed for. . . . As a philosophy it is elementary, but, as a book of science, ordinary readers will find it sufficiently advanced."—*Utica Morning Herald.*

DESCRIPTIVE SOCIOLOGY.

Mr. Herbert Spencer has been for several years engaged, with the aid of three educated gentlemen in his employ, in collecting and organizing the facts concerning all orders of human societies, which must constitute the data of a true Social Science. He tabulates these facts so as conveniently to admit of extensive comparison, and gives the authorities separately. He divides the races of mankind into three great groups: the savage races, the existing civilizations, and the extinct civilizations, and to each he devotes a series of works. The first installment,

THE SOCIOLOGICAL HISTORY OF ENGLAND,

in seven continuous tables, folio, with seventy pages of verifying text, is now ready. This work will be a perfect Cyclopædia of the facts of Social Science, independent of all theories, and will be invaluable to all interested in social problems. Price, five dollars. This great work is spoken of as follows:

From the British Quarterly Review.

"No words are needed to indicate the immense labor here bestowed, or the great sociological benefit which such a mass of tabulated matter done under such competent direction will confer. The work will constitute an epoch in the science of comparative sociology."

From the Saturday Review.

"The plan of the 'Descriptive Sociology' is new, and the task is one eminently fitted to be dealt with by Mr. Herbert Spencer's faculty of scientific organizing. His object is to examine the natural laws which govern the development of societies, as he has examined in former parts of his system those which govern the development of individual life. Now, it is obvious that the development of societies can be studied only in their history, and that general conclusions which shall hold good beyond the limits of particular societies cannot be safely drawn except from a very wide range of facts. Mr. Spencer has therefore conceived the plan of making a preliminary collection, or perhaps we should rather say abstract, of materials which when complete will be a classified epitome of universal history."

From the London Examiner.

"Of the treatment, in the main, we cannot speak too highly; and we must accept it as a wonderfully successful first attempt to furnish the student of social science with data standing toward his conclusions in a relation like that in which accounts of the structures and functions of different types of animals stand to the conclusions of the biologist."

www.ingramcontent.com/pod-product-compliance
Lightning Source LLC
LaVergne TN
LVHW010202110826
845151LV00002B/581

* 9 7 8 1 4 2 5 5 3 5 8 6 5 *